MANY PERSPECTIV

"My Negro Problem—And Ours" by Norman Podhoretz

This provocative, well-known piece about a Brooklyn-born Jew's experiences with blacks first appeared in 1963. Here it is reprinted with new reflections and an evaluation by its author, written specifically for this volume.

"The Other and the Almost the Same" by Paul Berman

A sensation when it was published in *The New Yorker*, Berman's article traces the roots of recent conflicts to the fundamental similarities between blacks and Jews, as well as to some jarring differences.

"Keeping a Legacy of Shared Struggle" by bell hooks

A plea for unity and a reminder of shared history, shared struggle, and shared futures comes from feminist theorist and cultural critic bell hooks, who believes that eradicating anti-Semitism will also help end racism.

"The Battle for Enlightenment at City College" by Jim Sleeper

New York *Daily News* columnist and author Sleeper looks at the controversial Professor Leonard Jeffries and his anti-Semitic lectures at City College—and their long-reaching damage to America's liberal institutions.

"The Lives People Live" by Julius Lester

From the unique perspective of a black Jew, this public figure and University of Massachusetts professor discusses how ethnic identity is becoming a substitute for personal identity—and what needs to be done to bring blacks and Jews together.

BLACKS AND JEWS

ALLIANCES AND ARGUMENTS

Edited
by
Paul Berman

Delta
Trade Paperbacks

A Delta Book
Published by
Dell Publishing
a division of
Bantam Doubleday Dell Publishing Group, Inc.
1540 Broadway
New York, New York 10036

ISBN: 0-385-31473-6

Reprinted by arrangement with Delacorte Press

Manufactured in the United States of America

Published simultaneously in Canada

October 1995

10 9 8 7 6 5 4 3 2 1

BVG

CONTENTS

■

HISTORICAL
AND POLITICAL
REFLECTIONS

■

■

SEVERAL
CONTROVERSIES

■

■

PHILOSOPHICAL
OBSERVATIONS

■

Preface:
On Spiegelman's Valentine
and Having a Headache

■ Tucked into the upper right-hand corner of the cover of this book is an illustration by Art Spiegelman, the creator of *Maus: a Survivor's Tale,* showing a kiss between a man and a woman. The kiss originally ran on the cover of *The New Yorker,* February 15, 1993. It was Spiegelman's Valentine's Day card to the squabbling Jews and blacks of America. And no sooner did those amorous lips meet on the cover of *The New Yorker* than fumes of indignation came pouring forth from people who might have disagreed on every possible issue except that Spiegelman had done a terrible thing.

For Spiegelman's romantic man appears to be a Hasidic Jew, whose austere and elaborate religious obligation ought to forbid him from touching, let alone kissing, a woman who is not his wife. And while the dusky-skinned object of the Hasidic kiss, the woman with the glamorous earrings and necklace, might well be a properly Jewish wife, she does seem more likely to be a gentile, possibly of the very kind whose Caribbean-immigrant brothers or sons might have gone into the streets of Crown Heights, Brooklyn, in 1991 to riot against the Hasidim. What kind of Hasidic kiss could that be, then? Those of the real-life Hasidim of Brooklyn who look at *The New Yorker* took one glance at Spiegelman's cover painting and were not especially pleased, and a good number of other Jews were offended on behalf of the Hasidim.

Nor was the illustration any more acceptable to a good many of the African-American and Caribbean-immigrant residents of Brooklyn. For why, it was asked, would such a woman find herself in the embrace of such a man? Are blacks nothing more than objects of lust and sexual fantasy? So there were blacks, too, who looked, and frowned. Yet it was just a Valentine's Day illustration! What kind of zealous touchiness can sour a valentine's sweetness into a multiethnic offense? Mightn't love be a good thing between the blacks and Jews of Brooklyn, and between blacks and Jews everywhere, and between all peoples? Spiegelman's illustration asks that question. And the more you look at his artfully mischievous kiss, the more your head aches with the thrust and counterthrust of your own answers.

The Jews of America and the African-Americans began to pay special attention to one another at the beginning of the twentieth century. In the decades that followed, a political cooperation between the two groups flourished (though not at every moment) in the trade unions, in the left-wing and liberal organizations, and in the civil rights campaigns, with consequences that have rendered America's claim on democracy vastly more convincing. Even today, if you look at voting patterns in Congress and elsewhere, the collaboration between blacks and the more liberal Jews remains almost miraculously firm. But nobody has failed to notice the tensions as well—the tensions that were illustrated in their most amusing fashion by Spiegelman's *New Yorker* cover but have not lacked for grimmer illustrations in the streets.

The alliance between blacks and liberal Jews reached its high point in the 1960s, and it was in the sixties, too, that tensions between the groups gave rise to a sustained discussion. An intricate conversation—alternately pleasant, firm, angry, and venomous—cropped up among Jewish and black writers, not to mention among writers who were neither Jewish nor black and writers who were both. And after thirty years of back and forth, the pleasant, the firm, the angry, and the venomous can finally be declared to be, in its noisy way, a literature.

The pages that follow offer a sampling from that literature: some immortal essays, some newspaper polemics of the passing moment, some scholarly studies, much disagreement, some agreement. Some of the pieces were written expressly for the book, and others have appeared elsewhere. Two of the selections, the essay by James Baldwin, "Negroes Are Anti-Semitic Because They're Anti-White," from 1967, and the essay by Norman Podhoretz, "My Negro Problem—and Ours," from 1963, mark the beginning of the literature, not because they were the first pieces ever written on the topic of blacks and Jews but because those particular two essays continue to be cited. Podhoretz has taken the occasion of this volume to look back on his own early essay and to offer a new reflection on it.

The essay by Cynthia Ozick, "Literary Blacks and Jews," written in 1972, stands as one of the first important discussions of the black-Jewish theme in the field of literary criticism. This author, too, has agreed to look back on her old essay and to comment on its relevance for the 1990s. The author of the fourth essay in the collection, Joe Wood, comes from a younger generation whose thinking has been shaped not only by the ordinary social reality of black-Jewish relations but by the literature itself. For by now the literature on blacks and Jews has itself become part of the cityscape social reality.

The next section, "Historical and Political Reflections," offers analyses by Clayborne Carson, Cornel West, Andrew Hacker, Julius Lester, and Shelby Steele. The third section, "Several Controversies," gets down to case studies. The essay by Ellen Willis, written in 1979 and updated in her prologue, comments on the controversy surrounding Andrew Young's departure from the Jimmy Carter administration in 1979. Richard Goldstein's essay reflects on the Crown Heights rioting of

1991. The first of the two contributions by Henry Louis Gates, Jr., "The Uses of Anti-Semitism," which originally appeared on the op-ed page of *The New York Times* in 1992, is probably the best known of all the recent discussions of relations between blacks and Jews. Mentions of that single article crop up in several of the essays by other authors—for instance, in the essay by bell hooks. In the second of his contributions, Gates himself comments on the commentary. And there are essays by Jim Sleeper, who discusses the Leonard Jeffries affair at New York's City College, and by Leon Wieseltier and Derrick Bell, who discuss the flap over anti-Semitism within the Nation of Islam.

The final section, "Philosophical Observations," contains an analysis by Michel Feher which originally appeared in the French intellectual monthly *Esprit,* addressed to readers who are not too familiar with the American background; but American readers will find in it a useful examination of the broad American left and of the black and Jewish (as well as feminist) components within it. The last piece is a philosophical analysis by Laurence Thomas, who makes some points that bear on each of the preceding pieces. My own views appear in the introduction. And to anyone who disputes the evenhandedness of my introductory discussion, I say: Read on. Somewhere in the book you may find one writer or another making your very own point. And one writer or another will make you wince.

A sign in the New York subways used to say: "You don't have to be Jewish to love Levy's Real Jewish Rye Bread." No, and you don't have to be Jewish or black to find something provocative in these essays about Jews and blacks. The question of how different groups should live together civilly leaves nobody outside its scope. Some of the arguments that are presented in this book were written just yesterday, and others thirty years ago, but all will end up being invoked in the debates of tomorrow, not just in discussions about the alliances and arguments of the Jews and the blacks.

PAUL BERMAN

BLACKS AND JEWS

ALLIANCES AND ARGUMENTS

Paul Berman

Introduction:
The Other and the
Almost the Same

■ **T**he striking thing is always the intensity. In the Kean College affair, for instance, Khalid Abdul Muhammad, the "Representative" and "National Assistant" of Minister Louis Farrakhan and the Nation of Islam, arrived at Kean,in Union, New Jersey, on November 29, 1993, and rays of zeal and hatred beamed from his mouth. His topic was a book published by the Nation of Islam called *The Secret Relationship Between Blacks and Jews*. He said that the Jews were "impostor Jews"—demonic liars who rejected Jesus. He said to the Jews, "Jesus was right. You're nothing but liars. The Book of Revelation is right. You're from the synagogue of Satan."

The National Assistant outlined a Jewish conspiracy over the millennia. The Jews crucified Jesus. They dispossessed the Palestinians. They exploited the Germans: "Everybody always talk about Hitler exterminating six million Jews. But don't nobody ever ask what did they do to Hitler. . . . They went in there, in Germany, the way they do everywhere they go, and they supplanted, they usurped. . . . They had undermined the very fabric of the society." In the United States, they took control of the Federal Reserve and the White House. And they persecuted the blacks. They dominated the slave trade. They conspired against such great black leaders as Jesus, Marcus Garvey, and, today, Farrakhan. They participated in the civil rights movement in order to exploit the blacks. They used Hollywood against the blacks. The Jews and the Arab slumlords are "sucking our blood in the black community." The Jews support apartheid. They "raped black women," he said. "What the Jews did. What they did against Nat Turner. It's all in here"—in *The Secret Relationship Between Blacks and Jews*.

But the worst is their lie—this lie of the Jews, which is, in a sense, their essence. The Jews—"the hook-nosed, bagel-eatin', lox-eatin' " Jews—are not in fact Jews. Khalid Muhammad addressed his black audience: "For you are the true Jew. You are the true Hebrew. You are the true ones who are in line with Bible prophecy and scripture, so teaches the Most Honorable Elijah Muhammad and the Honorable Minister Louis Farrakhan."

The speech was venomous but not inarticulate. It outlined a coherent theological interpretation of black suffering: blacks as the people of God against whom the synagogue of Satan has conspired two thousand years. The interpretation was more Christian than Muslim, even if Muhammad was representing the Nation of Islam. It was the kind of speech that, with some of that same language about blood-sucking and crucifixion, Christian Crusaders might have given in A.D. 1095, on their way to slaughter the Jews in the ghettos of Europe. And at Kean College, just as at many other American colleges where Muhammad had appeared, the mostly black audience cheered—though a lone, brave black student, when given the chance to ask a question, politely but firmly likened the speech to Hitlerism.

Then came a national response. On the op-ed page of *The New York Times,* A. M. Rosenthal, Roger Wilkins, and Bob Herbert all banged their fists. The Anti-Defamation League took out a full-page ad, instantly famous, in the *Times* and other papers, quoting Muhammad's speech below the graphic words "You Decide." The United States Senate voted 97–0 to condemn the Kean College speech. The Congressional Black Caucus, having recently announced a "covenant" with Minister Farrakhan, had reason to be embarrassed, and the whole weight of the black political establishment seemed to fall on Farrakhan—at least for a moment. Jesse Jackson and a variety of other political leaders denounced anti-Semitism and called on Farrakhan to act. Farrakhan conferred with the chairman of the Black Caucus, Representative Kweisi Mfume, and then summoned a press conference and demoted Muhammad and chastised him, and praised his "truths." And once again rays of hysteria and hatred beamed outward to the world, this time on CNN.

Farrakhan held up with approval *The Secret Relationship Between Blacks and Jews*. He said that "Talmudic scholars" had caused blacks to suffer "the mental anguish of believing that we are black because of some divine curse." He outdid even his own National Assistant by saying that seventy-five percent of the black slaves in the Old South were owned by . . . Jews! He was raving—our American Zhirinovsky—which did not prevent the National Association for the Advancement of Colored People from declaring itself "satisfied" with Farrakhan's statement. The NAACP's director of communications said the part about slaveowners in the South "may have exaggerated the historical fact," but that it is "a matter for academics to debate."

The counterresponse was another full-page ad in the *Times*, this time placed by People for the American Way. There was shouting on the television talk shows and consternation at the colleges where Farrakhan's National Assistant had been scheduled to speak. Then still another response: Does the world get upset every time some white person unleashes a racist remark about blacks? There was the case of the Jewish comedian Jackie Mason, who managed to make slurs sound funny. There was the argument that demanding a denunciation of anti-Semitism from every black leader in sight was deeply unfair, and that a controversy that had begun with anti-Semitism had turned—so *Time* argued—into "just another kind of bigotry"; namely, antiblack racism. To which A. M. Rosenthal replied— But why go on?

The intensity was startling, but nothing new. The same sparks and flames have been shooting upward every few years for thirty years. The anger and the arguments were no different during the 1968 schoolteachers' strike in New York City, or in 1979, when Andrew Young left Jimmy Carter's administration. The intensity was the same in 1984, when Jesse Jackson made his first run for the presidency and employed Farrakhan's military-looking Fruit of Islam as his personal bodyguards and, that time, pointedly declined to repudiate Farrakhan and instead complained about Jewish persecution. It was the same in the Brooklyn neighborhood of Crown Heights in 1991, when for three days there had been black rioting against the Jews, and again in 1992, after the failure to convict anyone for the murder of a man who had been killed by a Crown Heights mob yelling "Get the Jew!"

Yet during all those years what, exactly, has the argument been about—apart from the words themselves? Have the Jews and the blacks been fighting all this time over political spoils? Not especially. Over economic interests? Some people think so, but economic competition between blacks and Jews is strictly marginal. Has it been a war over neighborhoods? Sometimes, but not consistently. Is it a war between parties, Republicans and Democrats? Or between liberalism and conservatism? Not even that, for at the end of the day the blacks and the Jews have trooped off to the polls and in one national election after another they have, more often than not, voted for the same candidates. So what is it—this fire that burns without logs and never goes out?

One of Freud's first French translators was a man named Jankélévitch, whose son, Vladimir, fought in the French Resistance during the Second World War, taught philosophy for many years at the Sorbonne, was active in the political left— and, by the time he died in 1985, had never stopped complaining bitterly about anti-Semitism. He had encountered it in the ranks of the Resistance. In the year A.D. 3000, Jankélévitch said, people will still be shouting, "Dirty Jew!" And from these several experiences—the Freudian background, the political engagement, the spectacle of anti-Semitism popping up even on the left—he fashioned a theory about hatred and nationality.

His theory was a variation on Freud's idea about the "narcissism of minor differences." Hatred between peoples comes in two varieties, Jankélévitch said. Racism—this is a truism—is a hatred you might feel for people who are different from you: for "the other." But the second kind of hatred is something you might feel for people who, compared with you, are neither "other" nor "brother." It is hatred for the "almost the same." In Jankélévitch's idea, relations with the other tend to be chilly—which doesn't make the hatred any less murderous, given the wrong circumstances. But relations between people who are almost the same tend to be highly charged. He invoked a passage in *Moses and Monotheism* in which Freud observes that "racial intolerance finds stronger expression, strange to say, in regard to small differences than to fundamental ones."

Freud's examples of populations in that kind of relation include the North Germans and the South Germans, the English and the Scotch, and the Spanish and the Portuguese, who have everything in common and can end up hating each other even so. In the 1990s anyone can point to the mass insanity in the former Yugoslavia, where the warring groups resemble one another so closely that most of us in the world beyond the Balkans cannot detect any differences at all. Why do tensions between people who are almost the same heat up into uncontrollable hatred? It is a matter of self-preservation.

To the person whose resemblance to you is close, yet who is not really your double, you might easily end up saying, "You are almost like me. The similarity between us is so plain that in the eyes of the world you are my brother. But, to speak honestly, you are not my brother. My identity, in relation to you, consists precisely of the ways in which I am different from you. Yet the more you resemble me the harder it is for anyone to see those crucial differences. Our resemblance threatens to obliterate everything that is special about me. So you are my false brother. I have no alternative but to hate you, because by working up a rage against you I am defending everything that is unique about me."

Since emotional relations fall under the star of irrationality, people who are almost the same might flip-flop into loving one another, bedazzled by their wonderful point of commonality. Or they might sink into confusion about the intensity of their feelings. "When you are in a state of passion, you don't know if you love or if you hate, like spouses who can neither live together nor live apart," Jankélévitch said.

Does anything in that analysis apply to the predicament of blacks and Jews in America? Not on the face of things. The American Jews and the African-Americans have never looked or sounded alike, and the difference in economic conditions has become ever more pronounced since the days of bedbug-Jewish-tenement poverty. As for the shared history of having someone's boot press on their vulnerable necks, this experience has taken such different forms for blacks and for Jews as to be barely comparable. Any important element of Jewish-and-black almost the sameness, if it existed at all, would have to lie in the zone of the invisible, which is to say the psychological, where all is murk.

Still, I think a fateful trace of such an element does exist, and can even be described, if only vaguely. Many populations have suffered catastrophic defeats; but not all defeats have the same result. The French, having been conquered by the Germans in the Second World War, were subjected to every terrible thing that Jankélévitch and his Resistance comrades worked to destroy; but, even so, the French could think back on their golden centuries of glory, and on that basis they could picture a future of renewed freedom and national self-confidence—maybe a bit chastened.

But there is a second kind of defeat from which you don't really bounce back. The calamity lasts too long; it is overwhelming. People who have undergone that second kind of experience can no longer remember a previous state of healthy self-confidence, except, maybe, in versions that are mythological or religious; and their lack of pleasant secular memories is matched by a lack of any place on earth they can confidently regard as uniquely theirs; and their lack of geography is matched by an almost physical discomfort with their own bodies. Instead of a happy history or a home or a comfortable feeling about themselves, they carry around a memory of their own catastrophe—their "enemy-memory," in Shelby Steele's phrase. They look back and they shudder, and nothing is to be done about it. They might wish sometimes that the old injuries would fade and leave them in peace. But, in another mood, they might discover a treasure in that old frightening enemy-memory of theirs, a spur to all sorts of inventiveness, maybe to hypercreativity or superoriginality—which makes giving up the enemy-memory all the more difficult to do.

Anyone who wants to see an example of that plight in Europe today can wander into the main squares of the cities of Central Europe and contemplate the shabby-looking Gypsies. The majority populations passing on the sidewalk treat the Gypsies with contempt, and the Gypsies glower and skulk and are frightening in return. Let's say a political miracle took place and the oppressed Gypsies suddenly basked in the same rights and esteem as the majority populations, and the doors of opportunity flew open, and the days of Gypsy oppression were over. Just how quickly would the remembered accusations of their enemies stop ringing in Gypsy ears?

Steele, in his book *The Content of Our Character,* reminds us of how much harm these old memories can do—how they can leave people trapped forever in the worst moments of a bygone past, like someone huddling in an air-raid shelter long after the real-life planes have gone away. Yet if you think about the Gypsies it's easy to imagine that the ancient wounds have long ago inscribed themselves in the collective character, and around those wounds have grown all kinds of idiosyncrasies and compensatory works of originality—in music and dance, for instance, just to cite what all the world acknowledged long ago as expressions of a wholly admirable Gypsy genius. Why would the Gypsies want to abandon that? Obviously, the sound and healthy thing would be to adapt their enemy-memory to purposes that are strictly constructive, and to find a way to rid themselves of the hangdog look and the outlaw trades, as the Gypsies have done in the more enlightened democratic countries. But we can suppose that the Gypsies' room for maneuver is not unlimited—unless they want to stop being Gypsies altogether, which is inconceivable.

In the case of the American Jews, a miracle did take place merely by the act of their fleeing from the Old World to the New. The era when superstitious Christians peered into the European ghettos and interpreted the poverty and the stooped Jewish shoulders and the pasty complexions as signs of divine guilt for the long-ago murder of Jesus—this era, for American Jews, slips into the past at a rate that has come to seem positively amusing. "What is the difference between the ILGWU"—the International Ladies' Garment Workers' Union—"and the American Psychiatric Association?" Alfred Kazin once asked. And answered, "One generation." Yet such is the enemy-memory that both the good and the bad in American society keep the last sparks of remembrance from going out. The styles of Jewish New World success follow patterns that were established in the Old World ghettos, and the successes themselves are fated now and then to call up, out of the creepier depths of Christian civilization, the old paranoid accusations about conspiracies and evil.

Even the fat-and-happiest of American Jews has to shudder at the spectacle, which is always taking place, of some eminent person, not only spokesmen of the Nation of Islam, standing up to give the ancient libels a fresh new airing. Then there is the news about the surviving Jewish communities in the Slavic and Muslim worlds and elsewhere, which is never exactly designed to calm American Jewish nerves. Not that many years ago, a large, previously all-but-unknown Jewish tribe was discovered to be living in Ethiopia. Need it be added that the tribe was on the brink of starving to death? And between the memories of the past and what can be seen of the Jewish present outside the happy circle of Western democracy the predicament of the American Jews becomes ever more anomalous.

For the driveway may be long and circular, and the living-room carpet may be thick, but the enemy-memory does not fade—except among the handful of Jews who choose to escape Jewishness altogether. And from the perspective of that memory, to prattle on about kinship between American Jewry and African-Americans seems not so outlandish after all. For anyone can see that, if the Gypsies are a tragic people and the Jews are another, the African-Americans are still another: marked by spectacular defeats; marked, too, by continuing accusations about other than fully human qualities; marked, even—and here the African-American conundrum is classic—by the compensatory feats of supreme cultural brilliance, which all the world has had to acknowledge, and which make the sufferings and the successes almost inextricable. And the whole phenomenon is, from the perspective of Jewish memory, all too familiar.

It's true that to detect invisible similarities you have to peer through a lens capable of revealing them. In a slightly sentimental mood, some American Jews like to imagine that Judaism itself is their lens. That seems to me a dubious claim. If Judaism per se had any such power of insight, there would be two or three hundred years of black-Jewish alliances in the United States by now. But history—real history, not the conspiracy fiend's version—shows nothing of the sort. During slavery times—when Jews counted for half of one percent, or even less, of the American population—a small number of Jews participated in the slave trade, along with vastly larger numbers of Christians and Muslims; and a small number of Jews figured among the South's "master class" of plantation owners (to be precise, Jews constituted one-tenth of one percent of the large plantation owners in the 1830 census). A small number of other Jews participated in the abolitionist movement; and, all in all, the Jews failed to distinguish themselves either as slavers or as antislavers.

Alternatively, it is sometimes said that the European Holocaust is the Jewish lens—though the Holocaust explanation stumbles over the same problem of historical dates. Probably the first important moment in the black-Jewish alliance was the founding of the NAACP, in 1909, long before the Nazi era in Europe. Yet that date—not the exact year but the turn-of-the-century era—does point, I think, to the series of ideas and sentiments that finally allowed a large number of Jews to notice similarities between themselves and the blacks.

No one can feel a boot on the neck for long without dreaming of removing it; but only after the American and the French revolutions did the Old World Jews have the chance to dream along lines of real-life practicality. The Old World Jews had been oppressed by superstition and bigotry, by Christian and Muslim desires to organize society according to religious principles, and by the feudal idea that dynastic landowners (therefore not the homeless Jews) should dominate society. So the new political alternative promoted rationalism and education—against prejudice and superstition. It promised democratic, secular sovereignty—against theocratic domination. And it promised individual rights, equal for all, to be enforced by law—against an exclusively religious or ethnic vision of society.

Enlightenment liberalism was the new idea, and it sliced neatly through the knotty complication of being an unloved minority in a majoritarian world. For the basic unit in the liberal idea was not the exclusive group but the individual person, which opened to the Jews the appealing possibility of taking their place at last as members of a self-selected majority; namely, the grand, all-embracing majority of free and equal individuals. The French Revolution brought these ideas into the open air, and the French and German Jews took them up, and the ideas began a steady eastward push into regions where Jews were more numerous and prejudices more ferocious. The stronger the prejudices and the larger the Jewish population, the more ardent was the enthusiasm with which the new ideas were embraced, until by the time the emancipatory message finally arrived in darkest Poland and the czarist empire it was received almost in the spirit of a religious conversion.

It was the late nineteenth century by then, which was

precisely when the mass emigration of Eastern European Jews got under way. Thus America's Jewish population grew in numbers and in poverty but also in ardor. And this new ardor for an emancipatory liberal vision of a better society now became, circa 1909, the lens through which some of the American Jews began to notice those oddest of their new fellow citizens, the ones with no rights in the land of rights, the victims of majority hatred and outrageous prejudices, their fellows in tragedy: the blacks.

The origin of the Jewish attitude in liberal philosophy accounts, I think, for several of the quirks and oddities of the black-Jewish alliance that now began, very slowly, to emerge. The sympathy for blacks that certain Jews began to feel was not, by and large, a product of personal contact or cultural affinity—except, maybe, in the racially integrated bohemia of jazz and a few other places. The Jews who typically came in contact with blacks during the early and middle twentieth century—the old-time southern Jews and, around the country, the Jewish employers of black workers, the not very rich Jewish housewives who hired black housekeepers and were famous for a lack of genteel courtesy, the landlords and the storekeepers who lingered in northern Jewish neighborhoods after black populations had replaced the Jews—might feel no particular sympathy for the African-American cause. They might even be a little hostile, as a result of irritating face-to-face encounters or in conformity with mainstream American culture. Richard Wright drew quite a few Jewish portraits from the 1920s and '30s in his autobiography, *Black Boy,* and the good, the bad, and the ugly were all represented.

When the Jews did sympathize, it was mostly as a result of abstract political reflection, and the people who indulged in the abstract reflection were not always in a rush to proclaim their own Jewishness. The emancipatory liberalism of the American Jews took an infinity of forms in the twentieth century, and only some of these movements flew a Jewish flag. Many Jews were more likely to proclaim a doctrine of purer universalism and to relegate Jewishness to the sphere of private life, or perhaps to the sphere of things to be abolished someday, along with every other threat to village atheism. From the perspective of people with the universalist idea, humanism and liberalism, not what they conceived of as Jewishness, brought them to the cause of African America. There is an old and slightly peculiar Jewish custom of rebelling against Jewishness by identifying with the most marginal of all possible groups, so as to rebel and still not assimilate into the mainstream; and this, too, played its part in attracting Jews to the black cause.

A black person who judged from his own experience with Jewish storekeepers and with abstractly motivated civil rights supporters who didn't call themselves Jews might easily suppose that Jewish support for black causes was, even in the midcentury heyday of the black-Jewish alliance, either spotty in the extreme or mostly a matter of elite arrangements by a handful of lawyers—and, in either case, not a large and popular tendency. That was how Jewish support did, in fact, begin. The participation of a few Jews in helping to organize the NAACP, the devotion of some Jewish philanthropies to black education (which by the 1930s was benefiting up to forty percent of southern black schoolchildren), the fraternal relations beginning in the 1920s between some top lawyers of the American Jewish Committee and of the NAACP—those were important steps, but they were taken by only a handful of people.

Support for black causes from the Socialist party and its offshoots, during the years when Socialism enjoyed a lot of popularity among poor immigrant Jews, had a bit more sidewalk visibility. Still, Socialist friendliness to the black cause had its ups and downs. As for the Communists, their own support for black causes, eager and important though it proved to be, was no end of peculiar. Even to mention Communism among the currents of Jewish emancipatory liberalism may seem odd—except that, of course, a percentage of American Jews did, in the confusions of the Great Depression, turn to Communism out of the same impulses that led a larger percentage to turn to movements that were democratic. And if, out of the Socialist and the Communist movements, a genuine feeling for racial egalitarianism did emerge, and managed to survive the collapse of both parties into tiny sects, such that quite a few of the white liberal volunteers in the 1950s and '60s heyday of the civil rights movement were actually Jews with backgrounds in the left-wing parties—even so, quirks and inconsistencies survived as well.

What were some of these peculiarities? Sometimes a Jewish snobbism played a part. One handsome check to the NAACP and a proper snob could look down forever on his ordinary American neighbors. It was possible to support black causes out of feelings that had more to do with Jewish origins than with black realities—out of a need to justify a bristly militant liberalism that no longer seemed to make much sense in relation to American Jewish causes. The confusing quality of feeling oneself oppressed and poor yet anomalously burdened with prosperity sometimes led the more addled grandchildren of Polish and Russian peddler Jews to stand up and announce a support for blacks on the basis of a largely imagined Jewish guilt. Jewish cynics who never did express much interest in black causes looked at this heap of contradictory impulses and were beside themselves with scorn. How sappy were the Jewish liberals, how softhearted and daft!

Yet, for all these many twists and inconsistencies (and I could go on listing them, in a spirit of ethnic masochism), some aspect of that sympathy for black causes was authentic, and the aspect went on swelling, until the sentiments that had begun as spotty and unreliable and peculiar had become by the fifties and early sixties a genuine popular enthusiasm among the large percentage of American Jews who considered themselves liberals. It was almost as if to be Jewish and liberal were, by definition, to fly a flag for black America—as if to embark on dangerous Freedom Rides into the Deep South were to live out a supremely Jewish sense of moral action. Jews accounted for almost two thirds of the white volunteers who went south for Freedom Summer, in 1964. Among the people who lacked that kind of physical courage, there was always the possibility of contributing money. Between half and three quarters of the money raised by the civil rights organizations at the height of the movement came from Jewish contributors, which is striking, considering that Jews made up by then less than three percent of the American population.

It was a matter of one population's recognizing another. The liberal Jew said to the black, in effect, "Among all the elements of American society, it is you who are most like me. The similarity between us is so plain that in my own eyes, if not in the eyes of the world, you are my brother. Slavery is Nazism; lynchings are pogroms; Jim Crow is czarist anti-Semitism, American style; Mississippi is Poland; bigotry is bigotry. I am with you! I understand your plight. I understand how it is a worse plight than most people can imagine. I understand it because of who I am, and who I am is someone who fights on behalf of people like you."

There was passion in that statement. And if some kernel of practical self-interest lurked as well—if the higher-ups in the Jewish establishment always knew that people with sheets over their heads were no friends of Jewry, either, and blacks were a good ally to have—that merely shows that idealism and self-interest need not be opposites, in spite of a cheap temptation to assume that they must be. Anyway, the Jewish young people who took up civil rights activism were not thinking of Jewish conditions. They were thinking of justice.

And the differences between the African-Americans and the American Jews? The ones that matter, from a Jankélévitchian perspective, are not the big, obvious disparities but the little motes of disagreement, which, because they burrow within the similarities, are hardest to see. For, in dreaming of a better world, the African-Americans likewise went tit for tat against their own oppression, and, since the horrors inflicted on the blacks resembled in many respects the horrors that had historically been inflicted on the Jews, the proposed black political alternatives naturally bore a resemblance to the liberalism of the Jews. But, just as the sufferings of the blacks were not, in fact, exactly those of the Jews, neither could the proposed alternatives be the same.

African-American political thinking in the twentieth century is usually described as a series of mighty antinomies. Booker T. Washington stands against W.E.B. Du Bois, and Martin Luther King, Jr., against Malcolm X—which is interpreted to mean self-improvement versus the demand for rights, integration versus separatism, nonviolent protest versus what Malcolm coyly described as non-nonviolence. But deeper than all these, I think, lies a still mightier antinomy of African-American political life, which is the conflict between emancipatory liberalism and the philosophy of global anti-imperialism, or Third Worldism.

By black emancipatory liberalism I mean the ideas of democratic socialists like A. Philip Randolph and Bayard Rustin, jurists like Thurgood Marshall, Christian activists like King—all of whom demanded that America live up to its liberal promise. The black liberals were always the people who won the biggest victories for African-Americans, and they were always the people who maintained the closest relations with the Jewish (and non-Jewish) liberals, fellow thinker to fellow thinker. Yet those same blacks always had to contend with a special American complexity, unlike anything in the experience of their Jewish counterparts. The Jews turned to liberalism as the negation of every feudal and theocratic thing that had historically kept them down. But the African-Americans had to struggle against a society that was itself fundamentally liberal—except in connection with them.

Out and out racism was always their main enemy, but racism in the land of Jefferson the slaveowner comes dressed as often as not in a cloak of pieties. Slave masters didn't necessarily defend bondage as such; they defended the democracy of states' rights. Segregationists didn't necessarily defend Jim Crow as such; they defended an individual's right to choose his own associates. And so the black liberals faced a horrendous difficulty. Liberalism in America ought in principle to have offered the blacks the same simple and cheering message that it always offered the Jews. But since in America the liberal words kept slipping away from their own obvious meaning the black liberals were condemned to perform a task of excruciating subtlety: To bang the lectern in a demand for liberal justice while at the same time drawing surgical distinctions between true liberalism and the shoddy variant that was the African-Americans' historic foe. To invoke what Jefferson *should* have said, and distinguish it from what he did say. To thunder while dissecting: a nearly impossible thing to do.

Third Worldism was simpler in every way. The idea of a worldwide revolution by the colonized and nonwhite populations against the European and white imperialists conveyed a good and encouraging message without having to make any delicate distinctions between the true and the shoddy. The message said, "You, the African-Americans, are hopelessly outnumbered within the United States, and this unfortunate reality cannot be wished away by a lot of talk about liberalism and rights. But on a world scale you are no minority at all. The news for you is therefore encouraging. You are many, not few; strong, not weak; time will right your wrongs!"

It's true that for many years Third Worldist ideas among African-Americans were mostly a cultural concept, with little prospect of becoming practical. Yet, just as the politics of Jewish America respond to developments abroad, so do the politics of African America, and, beginning with the anticolonial revolutions after the Second World War, Third Worldism's practicality started to look more convincing.

Were Third Worldism and liberalism at odds with each other? You could look to the anticolonial revolution as a way to achieve the liberal idea of democracy and universal individual rights, and be a liberal and a Third Worldist both. The skinny personage of Mahatma Gandhi incarnated the possibility. Yet liberalism and Third Worldism were not the same. Liberal movements in the Third World could stand up to European imperialism, but so could antiliberal movements. For the basic unit of the Third Worldist idea was not the individual but the group. It was the oppressed national entity, maybe the oppressed race. Dictators cannot fight for individual rights except by committing suicide, but they can fight splendidly on behalf of the group.

Anticolonialism scored its victories around the world in the 1940s and '50s and '60s, and the Third Worldist inspiration did slip from the liberal to the authoritarian. Instead of Gandhi, there was Nasser; instead of individual rights, there were national rights. And, with these shifts going on in the Third World movement, the balance of argument at home in the United States between the black liberals and the black Third Worldists began to shift as well. In 1963, Bayard Rustin stood sufficiently central to African-American politics to serve as chief organizer of that year's historic March on Washington, but by the end of the decade the same person was deemed insufficiently black. And, whatever impact these developments had on African-American circumstances as a whole, the effect on black-Jewish relations was extreme.

There was the matter of affirmative action, which emerged as a practical issue in the middle 1970s. The civil rights organizations came out in favor of affirmative action in order to give reality to the otherwise empty phrases about political equality which had just been adopted as national law—to forestall, in short, the traditional racial hypocrisy of American liberalism. But affirmative action was philosophically ambiguous. It could be supported on a pragmatic ground as a straightforward bit of social engineering, New Deal style. Or it could be interpreted to mean that people should be viewed primarily as members of groups, not as individuals.

The pragmatic interpretation ought to have been acceptable to the pure liberals, Jewish or otherwise. The second interpretation challenged liberalism at its core. But, because the ambiguity never did get cleared up, black activists could go on viewing the program as merely the proper next step for civil rights, regardless of the philosophical intricacies, and could interpret the opposition to affirmative action on the part of certain (not all) leading Jewish groups as a sudden betrayal of the black cause. And the Jewish opponents of affirmative action could view the whole idea as a surprising and dangerous betrayal of liberalism. Affirmative action posed, at least in potential, a threat to all the civil rights achievements that had struck down the right to discriminate against Jews—most notably, the historic anti-Jewish quotas in the universities. So there was a lot of bad blood over affirmative action. And when the second great point of disagreement between a large number of blacks and Jews emerged—the argument over Zionism and the Palestinians—the bad blood turned worse.

In the early years after the Second World War, it was common to regard Israel as a mosquito version of the mammoth state created by Gandhi, distinguished by its democratic ideals and the previously miserable condition of its now liberated population. But, whereas India maintained its prestige, Israel was gradually redefined, within the ranks of the Third World movement, as a European-settler colony.

African-Americans played no part in working up this new, unattractive image of Israel, and in the early years they displayed little interest in it, either. But in the 1960s the new image of Israel came to be accepted by revolutionaries around the world, and the American blacks who wanted to adhere to the Third Worldist idea really had no alternative but to accept at least some part of that view of Israel, and this was easy enough to do. In the rhetoric of Third World revolution, the African-Americans figured among European imperialism's earliest victims, and the Palestinians among the latest. It was sometimes believed that Palestinian skin tone was darker than that of the Israeli Jews, as if in pigmental confirmation of the proposed new link between Palestinians and African-Americans. And if any further sign of brotherhood between Palestinians and African-Americans was needed there was the all too clear reality that, as the years wore on and the Arab boycott against Israel took hold, the old warm relations between Israel and the newly independent countries of black Africa turned chilly, and one of the few African nations with which Israel did succeed in maintaining friendly exchanges was, of all unappealing countries, the land of apartheid. In these ways, the link between Palestinians and African-Americans (and between Israel and white South Africa) came to seem natural, not doctrinal.

The African-American feeling of identification with the Palestinians cast a shadow over Jewish political motives. In Third Worldist eyes, any kind of principled or idealistic position on the Middle East had to mean support for the Palestinians against Israel. Yet here were the same American Jews who claimed to support African-American civil rights supporting Israel, too—quite as if Jewish liberalism were simply another version of the old American racial hypocrisy. Might not the Jewish support for black causes, given its seeming lack of idealism, conceal a deeper exploitation of blacks—or, if not exactly an exploitation, at least an appropriation of the black cause for other uses?

And, with one thing and another, a reasonable black person who began by subscribing to even the smallest portion of the Third Worldist logic could follow a chain of plausible analysis and conclude by saying to the liberal Jew, "You look like my brother—in some respects. You, too, have been persecuted and despised—though not much in this country. You have supported my cause—somewhat. But if you were truly an idealist you would show enthusiasm for affirmative action here at home and for the Palestinians abroad—who are, in regard to racist oppression, my real brothers. Since you do not, your motives appear to be self-serving. And by advancing your interests while pretending to stand for the oppressed you are subtly undermining me. My own suffering has gone on for centuries with very little recognition from the world. Yet, whenever I speak up, you drown me out with your talk of Jewish suffering and your endless disquisitions on the benefits that you have bestowed on me. The more you speak about what we have in common, the harder it is for me to be heard. So you are my false brother. No, I don't hate you. But neither do I feel the ardor that you so strangely claim to feel for me. I am merely cool. Let us see coldly what my interests are, and what yours are, and if we happen to agree on some small point—good."

From the perspective of Jewish liberalism, the argument over affirmative action was bad enough, but the black impulse to support the Palestinians was astonishing. Like the black Third Worldist, the Jewish liberal pictured his own doctrine as no doctrine at all but as simple reality. There might be much to complain about in Israeli policy. But to see Israel as a European colony and an agent of worldwide racism—no, that was inconceivable.

Imperialist? Israel was the self-defense of a tragic minority struggling to achieve a normal existence. White European? Jews were fleeing for their lives from hateful old Europe as well as from the Arab world, where Jewish skins were, by the way, not so light. An affliction to the Arabs? Zionism proposed to be the agricultural modernizer of the Middle East. Unsympathetic to black Africa? No country anywhere in the world had done as much for Africans as had Israel in airlifting the Ethiopian Jews to safety. Let the world's Christians and Muslims make even half that effort! But in the nature of things—so went the liberal-Jewish analysis—when an oppressed minority achieves a bit of power, majority populations everywhere will regard the achievement as an outrage to decency. And so it was when the oppressed Jews succeeded in winning for themselves their modest slice of the enormous region that had been ruled for so many centuries with such cruelty by the genuine imperialisms of Christendom and Islam.

The contempt and enmity of the entire world pushed this new Jewish state into some of the ugliness that has always clung to the despised and the persecuted, and upon this ugliness all the bigotries of the ages had pounced, so that Israel in the age of anti-Zionism was now declared to be a kind of conspiracy for evil, just like the persecuted Jews in the past. Such was the liberal Jewish view.

And so the liberal Jews turned to the African-Americans and said, in effect, "Naturally, we, the American Jews, understand that all over the world majority populations and the partisans of privilege will always look with contempt or outrage on Israel. But surely other peoples who are themselves tragic minorities will recognize in Israel their brother and will rally to its cause, and, weak as they may be in practical terms, will do everything they can to insure that Israel does not end up exterminated by its enemies, as could all too easily happen.

"Surely the African-Americans will understand that Israel is the minority civil rights movement of the Middle East, and the terrorists and tyrants who oppose it are the majority enemies of justice. Surely the African-Americans will understand how, just as poor whites in the American South are eager to attack the southern blacks, so are the poor Arabs in the Middle East eager to pounce on the Jews, and one can even sympathize with the poor Arabs, just as one can perhaps sympathize with the poor southern whites, to a degree. But surely we, the persecuted minorities, can appreciate each other's predicament. Surely the hearts of African-Americans will beat for Israel!"

Those were the thoughts of the liberal Jews. And, of course, Bayard Rustin was not the only black liberal who did view Israel and the Jews in that way. But a sizable portion of black opinion shook its head in dissent.

And at this the Jewish liberal felt almost dizzy with shock. It was the feeling that Jankélévitch defined as a "vertigo"—the vertigo felt by the Jews when they discovered that large parts of the left all over the world were suddenly shifting to an anti-Zionism that had always been the province of Arab monarchists and dictators and other traditional right-wingers. So the Jewish liberal said, in effect, "You, the African-American, look like my brother, because you, too, have been spectacularly oppressed. But when you turn your eyes to the endangered minority population of the Middle East—the Jews—you see with the eyes of a majority oppressor. You are my false brother. And because you look like my brother but are actually my false brother you are undermining me. You are taking away my ability to summon the world's sympathy for the cause of an oppressed people.

"Your own sufferings have given you moral authority, but you are invoking this authority to counter my own. You are making other people think that I, a liberal, am instead merely a Jew, and that Jews are exactly what our enemies have always accused us of being—exploitative and tricky oppressors. You are helping to prepare the moral ground for what may someday turn out to be a new outbreak of anti-Semitic horror in the Middle East. And while you are doing that abroad you are undermining individual rights at home with your new notion of group rights. False brother, you are turning yourself into my enemy."

And now the real slide in relations between blacks and Jews, the avalanche, got under way—from both sides at once. There had always been a strain of folk anti-Semitism in African-American life. There had always been the Christian hostility to Judaism—a hostility that was white, not black, in its southern origins, yet that Richard Wright remembered being taught in a black Sunday school, too. But there was also the unique African-American theology from which Farrakhan's Nation of Islam has taken so many inspirations—the idea that African-Americans are the Hebrews of the Bible, and that biblical epics of slavery and redemption refer to blacks, not to whites. That was never a weak idea in African-American life. It was a beautiful idea; it was a reading of the Bible as living testimony to the present. How much hope and humanity must have clung to that idea in slavery times!

But, once the argument with the American Jews had begun, that ancient African-American theology blossomed into a conflict of identities beyond anything that Jankélévitch had described. For in the minds of the Nation of Islam, and perhaps among some Christians, too, the black was no longer saying to the Jew, "You appear to be my brother, but you are my false brother." The black was saying, "I am you, and you are an impostor. Your history is mine, not yours; and, insofar as people think that you are you, it is because you have stolen my identity. You are more than an enemy; you are a demon. Only Satan could do what you have done!''

Something about those thoughts was touching, as well as despicable. There was a supreme degree of passion, as in the highest form of love: a feeling of complete identity, except in the form of hatred. And once those feelings were out in the open, and skilled orators were touring the college campuses bringing the message, and the idea was popping up in rap music—once that had happened, there was nothing to keep the wildest theories about the Jews from springing up from their ancient bed of myth, superstition, and theology.

The theories about Jews as a conspiracy to damage blacks via the slave trade and the movies, about evil Jewish doctors who infect blacks with AIDS (this was another theory that the Kean College speaker seemed to defend), about Jewish intentions to miseducate black children through the public school system—all these gained a visibility they had never before enjoyed. And to combat those theories became, for anyone in the black community except a rigorous and consistent liberal, ever harder to do.

Even the great black majority who felt no hatred at all for Jews had to wonder if the wilder theories were really expressions of bigotry, as the liberals kept insisting. What *is* bigotry, after all, and whose definition should be followed? By a liberal definition, the views of a Farrakhan or a Professor Leonard Jeffries are bizarre and reprehensible. But those same views are not at all bizarre or viewed as reprehensible in the intellectual atmosphere of Middle Eastern anti-Zionism.

Didn't the United Nations itself declare that Zionism was in fact racism? So a cloud of Third Worldist confusion settled over these questions. Maybe the weird theories about Jewish evil were anti-Semitic, maybe not. But no one could doubt that to speak up against those theories was to break the solid front of black political protest, which some brave souls were always willing to do. But not every soul is brave. Or clear thinking. And so throughout the 1970s and '80s the liberal voices within African America grew quieter, and the Third Worldist voices grew louder; and from within the Third Worldist chorus could be heard the tones of old-fashioned prejudice; and prejudice led to prejudice, against Jews or against Asians; and the bigotries got ever more extreme, until a few lone loony voices were hitting the Hitlerian note, and the lone voices were authentically audible.

"He was wickedly great," Farrakhan's National Assistant said about Hitler—which was merely a quotation from Farrakhan himself. And whether that kind of language would excite a vigorous black response was hard to predict. For there had been an intellectual collapse. It was the collapse that made someone like Farrakhan's assistant a popular lecturer on the college campuses. It was, in the field of political thought, the equivalent of what had happened socially and culturally to the lower class in the poorest American ghettos: a collapse into self-destruction and dangerousness, into hatred and self-hatred, which the black liberals were, at least for the moment, hard-pressed to restrain.

The Jewish version of the downhill slide was not exactly parallel. The growth of Jewish neoconservativism in the seventies and eighties was not itself an example of rightist extremism or of racist demagogy. Yet the Jewish neoconservatives did urge the liberal Jews to give up their pro-black sympathies. They endowed the Reagan coalition with a kind of intellectual sophistication that had never figured among the strengths of the southern California GOP. They became, in short, black America's political antagonists, and powerful ones, at that, which no important faction of Jewish politics had been before. They never did win over a Jewish electoral majority. But they whittled away—from "above," let us say—at the old Jewish attitudes that had once done so much to support the African-American cause.

Another kind of whittling occurred from "below." Across the country, the modest neighborhoods of the working-class and lower-middle-class Jews turned out to be, of all the neighborhoods in a given city, some of the only districts that proved halfway receptive to black migration, for reasons that did not exclude the traditional liberalism of the old Jewish working-class movements. So the blacks moved in, and the moment in which they moved was precisely the moment in which, for a thousand reasons having nothing to do with black-Jewish relations, the black lower class entered into its calamitous decline. The Jewish poor and not so poor, the schoolteachers and the shopkeepers who remained behind, found themselves beset by the violence of the social disaster. And, between the neoconservative criticisms from "above" and the sidewalk experiences from "below," the old liberal ideas underwent the kind of silent evolution in which the words remain the same but the tone of voice turns cold. Then came the discovery about black anti-Semitism, and the experience was devastating.

Jews who still called themselves liberals ended up obsessing about black street crime, whether the crime statistics were up or down. Every phrase uttered by a black writer or leader on Jewish topics—even when the phrase was intended to be friendly—came to feel like a dagger thrust. A litany of invidious comparison took the place of the older litany of sympathetic comparison. *We* got over our original poverty, went the new Jewish argument, and we took advantage of the public schools and colleges, and we flourished, and we are the cat's meow. Why aren't you? And in these ways the differences between the American Jews and the rest of the white population regarding race began to narrow, even if the narrowing was not expressed at the polls.

It is a little unfair to take the 1991 fighting in Crown Heights as a symbol of the larger dispute. The Lubavitcher Jews of Crown Heights are members of a peculiar sect that never did join in the mass Jewish embrace of liberal ideas, and the blacks of Crown Heights are in large numbers immigrants from the Caribbean with no background in the history of black-and-Jewish alliances in America. Still, a shocking scene is a shocking scene. A murderous black mob dashing through the streets shouting slogans in favor of Hitler is no small thing to contemplate. A mob of Hasidic Jews marching around the neighborhood dressed in the costumes of eighteenth-century Poland, chanting (peacefully—but still) in Yiddish-inflected accents that blacks should go back to Africa: that does make a piquant tableau. The faces above bigotry's most vulnerable necks were howling bigotry's favorite phrases.

It was a Jankélévitchian moment. And, with rage and idiocy awash in the Brooklyn streets, blacks and Jews everywhere in America—not just the crazies or the religious sectarians—could say, as if in chorus, except with fingers pointed at each other's chests, "You *look* like an oppressed minority. But it is I who belong to the true minority. You are yourself part of the oppressive majority. It is I who deserve the sympathy of others. But it is you who receive it. Not only are you oppressing me; you are making it harder for the world to appreciate the cruelty that has historically been done to me. And, because my tragic history is a crucial part of who I am, you are denying me my recognition as a human being. You are turning me into nobody. The war between us is therefore total."

The first stage of the relation described by Jankélévitch was an acknowledgment of similarity, and the second stage was an acknowledgment that similarity contains a difference, thereby funneling a broad passion into a narrow spout of rancor. Now we enter a third stage, which turns out to follow Jankélévitch's analysis exactly, except that its causes have more to do with outer events than with inner dynamics.

The revolutions of 1989–91 around the world were liberalism's greatest moment of triumph probably in all history. But triumph meant exhaustion. And these two factors—liberalism and fatigue—are almost guaranteed, as I see it, to transform the black-Jewish relation. Without Soviet backing, the air went out of the Third Worldist revolutionary idea in a matter of months. The international pressures that made it more or less mandatory for African-Americans, if they wanted to take their place within the Third World revolutionary movement, to endorse—or, at least, abide—the anti-Zionist cause disappeared almost overnight. The evolution in Jesse Jackson's descriptions of Zionism—from "a kind of poisonous weed" (in a speech to an

American Palestinian group in 1980) to an estimable "liberation movement" (in a speech to the World Jewish Congress in 1992)—no doubt reflected a personal development, but man and zeitgeist have always been intertwined in the person of Jesse Jackson. And, with Third Worldism in defeat, the radical criticism of liberalism, not just on the question of Israel but on all questions, lost its force.

I don't question that outright anti-Semites will keep turning up among black campus lecturers or that the old animosities will linger among the sidewalk booksellers and among some of the less distinguished black studies departments, or that the chain of influence which descends from anti-Semitic professors through demagogic street activists to the young kids with knives in the poor neighborhoods will still be visible. But there was a time when these things looked like a wave of the future. Today they seem like a strange misshapen thing left over from the past. Already, in the early 1990s, a new generation of liberal black intellectuals began to make themselves heard. Here and there a liberal politician began to speak up a bit louder. There was reason to hope that liberalism was reviving, a little shakily, perhaps. But even the shakiest liberalism, if it goes on growing, will eventually allow larger numbers of African-Americans to look on their old, frustrating Jewish allies of the past with less anger and prejudice in the future, if not in every case with warmth.

Will liberalism among the American Jews similarly become a little stronger? Many regimes collapsed when the Soviet Union collapsed, and Jewish neoconservatism was among them. But then, among the American Jews, political emotions in the future are likely to remain a little cool. The twentieth century was not only the worst century in the history of the Jews but also, within the Jewish world, one of the most passionate centuries, and the passions have been expended chiefly on projects of emancipatory liberalism, not just for the Jews, that have proved to be less than successful. Socialism as a worldwide movement did not deliver universal emancipation. Communism turned out to be a fiasco in which the Jews themselves ended up prominent among the victims. In the Middle East, Zionism's loftiest dream was obliged to sink to the undreamy level of merely surviving, no matter what the price.

The effort of the Jewish liberals in the United States to perfect American democracy by supporting the cause of African-Americans was just one more among these several universalist campaigns, and it ended with some successes but also with a pathetic aspiration that went no further than hoping that anti-Semitism among blacks could be contained. And, in the wintry atmosphere that has followed on these failures, the old-fashioned ideas of emancipatory liberalism are not about to burst into renewed bloom among Jews in America or anywhere else, and the moral grandeur of the Jewish political movements of the twentieth century does not seem likely to be matched in the twenty-first.

What, then, will be the ground for either hostility or fraternity between African-Americans and American Jews in that century? I can guess. The blacks and the Jews will remember their old alliances and their old fights. They will forgive some old injuries, forget none.

But there is a little joke at the end of this story. Judaism allows divorce, and the mainstream black church, in its Protestant denominations, likewise permits it. But the relation between Jews and blacks does not allow divorce. The American Jews and the African-Americans are who they are because of long centuries of a past that can be put to different uses but cannot be overcome. It was the past that made the blacks and the Jews almost the same, and the past has the singular inconvenience of never going away.

Jankélévitch knew this. His idea of almost-the-same populations pictured "spouses who can neither live together nor live apart." That is the situation today. Separate beds, separate rooms; the same house. Love, hatred; a wobbling back and forth from one to the other. A slightly irrational relation, as all emotional relations are irrational. An intensity that never quite evaporates—all of it destined to go on as long as polyglot America goes on.

LITERARY
BATTLES
PAST AND
PRESENT

James Baldwin

Negroes Are Anti-Semitic Because They're Anti-White

James Baldwin (1924–1987), one of the most accomplished essayists in American literature, was the author of more than twenty books of fiction and nonfiction. This essay, which was prompted by a 1966–1967 debate among Harlem writers and editors, first appeared in The New York Times Magazine, *April 9, 1967.*

■ **W**hen we were growing up in Harlem our demoralizing series of landlords were Jewish, and we hated them. We hated them because they were terrible landlords and did not take care of the building. A coat of paint, a broken window, a stopped sink, a stopped toilet, a sagging floor, a broken ceiling, a dangerous stairwell, the question of garbage disposal, the question of heat and cold, of roaches and rats—all questions of life and death for the poor, and especially for those with children—we had to cope with all of these as best we could. Our parents were lashed down to futureless jobs, in order to pay the outrageous rent. We knew that the landlord treated us this way only because we were colored, and he knew that we could not move out.

The grocer was a Jew, and being in debt to him was very much like being in debt to the company store. The butcher was a Jew, and yes, we certainly paid more for bad cuts of meat than other New York citizens, and we very often carried insults home, along with the meat. We bought our clothes from a Jew and, sometimes, our secondhand shoes, and the pawnbroker was a Jew—perhaps we hated him most of all. The merchants along 125th Street were Jewish—at least many of them were; I don't know if Grant's or Woolworth's are Jewish names—and I well remember that it was only after the Harlem riot of 1935 that Negroes were allowed to earn a little money in some of the stores where they spent so much.

Not all of these white people were cruel—on the contrary, I remember some who were certainly as thoughtful as the bleak circumstances allowed—but all of them were exploiting us, and that was why we hated them.

But we also hated the welfare workers, of whom some were white, some colored, some Jewish, and some not. We hated the policemen, not all of whom were Jewish, and some of whom were black. The poor, of whatever color, do not trust the law and certainly have no reason to, and God knows we didn't. "If you *must* call a cop," we said in those days, "for God's sake, make sure it's a white one." We did not feel that the cops were protecting us, for we knew too much about the reasons for the kinds of crimes committed in the ghetto; but we feared black cops even more than white cops, because the black cop had to work so much harder—on *your* head—to prove to himself and his colleagues that he was not like all the other niggers.

We hated many of our teachers at school because they so clearly despised us and treated us like dirty, ignorant savages. Not all of these teachers were Jewish. Some of them, alas, were black. I used to carry my father's union dues downtown for him sometimes. I hated everybody in that den of thieves, especially the man who took the envelope from me, the envelope which contained my father's hard-earned money, that envelope which contained bread for his children. "Thieves," I thought, "every one of you!" And I know I was right about that, and I have not changed my mind. But whether or not all these people were Jewish, I really do not know.

The army may or may not be controlled by Jews; I don't

know and I don't care. I know that when I worked for the army I hated all my bosses because of the way they treated me. I don't know if the post office is Jewish but I would certainly dread working for it again. I don't know if Wanamaker's was Jewish, but I didn't like running their elevator, and I didn't like any of their customers. I don't know if Nabisco is Jewish, but I didn't like cleaning their basement. I don't know if Riker's is Jewish, but I didn't like scrubbing their floors. I don't know if the big, white bruiser who thought it was fun to call me "Shine" was Jewish, but I know I tried to kill him—and he stopped calling me "Shine." I don't know if the last taxi driver who refused to stop for me was Jewish, but I know I hoped he'd break his neck before he got home. And I don't think that General Electric or General Motors or RCA or Con Edison or Mobiloil or Coca-Cola or Pepsi-Cola or Firestone or the Board of Education or the textbook industry or Hollywood or Broadway or television—or Wall Street, Sacramento, Dallas, Atlanta, Albany, or Washington—are controlled by Jews. I think they are controlled by Americans, and the American Negro situation is a direct result of this control. And anti-Semitism among Negroes, inevitable as it may be, and understandable, alas, as it is, does not operate to menace this control, but only to confirm it. It is not the Jew who controls the American drama. It is the Christian.

The root of anti-Semitism among Negroes is, ironically, the relationship of colored peoples—all over the globe—to the Christian world. This is a fact which may be difficult to grasp, not only for the ghetto's most blasted and embittered inhabitants, but also for many Jews, to say nothing of many Christians. But it is a fact, and it will not be ameliorated—in fact, it can only be aggravated—by the adoption, on the part of colored people now, of the most devastating of the Christian vices.

Of course, it is true, and I am not so naive as not to know it, that many Jews despise Negroes, even as their Aryan brothers do. (There are also Jews who despise Jews, even as their Aryan brothers do.) It is true that many Jews use, shamelessly, the slaughter of the 6 million by the Third Reich as proof that they cannot be bigots—or in the hope of not being held responsible for their bigotry. It is galling to be told by a Jew whom you know to be exploiting you that he cannot possibly be doing what you know he is doing because he is a Jew. It is bitter to watch the Jewish storekeeper locking up his store for the night, and going home. Going, with *your* money in his pocket, to a clean neighborhood, miles from you, which you will not be allowed to enter. Nor can it help the relationship between most Negroes and most Jews when part of this money is donated to civil rights. In the light of what is now known as the white backlash, this money can be looked on as conscience money merely, as money given to keep the Negro happy in his place, and out of white neighborhoods.

One does not wish, in short, to be told by an American Jew that his suffering is as great as the American Negro's suffering. It isn't, and one knows that it isn't from the very tone in which he assures you that it is.

For one thing, the American Jew's endeavor, whatever it is, has managed to purchase a relative safety for his children, and a relative future for them. This is more than your father's endeavor was able to do for you, and more than your endeavor has been able to do for your children. There are days when it can be exceedingly trying to deal with certain white musical or theatrical celebrities who may or may not be Jewish—what, in show business, is a name?—but whose preposterous incomes cause one to think bitterly of the fates of such people as Bessie Smith or King Oliver or Ethel Waters. Furthermore, the Jew can be proud of his suffering, or at least not ashamed of it. His history and his suffering do not begin in America, where black men have been taught to be ashamed of everything, especially their suffering.

The Jew's suffering is recognized as part of the moral history of the world and the Jew is recognized as a contributor to the world's history: this is not true for the blacks. Jewish history, whether or not one can say it is honored, is certainly known: the black history has been blasted, maligned and despised. The Jew is a white man, and when white men rise up against oppression, they are heroes: when black men rise, they have reverted to their native savagery. The uprising in the Warsaw Ghetto was not described as a riot, nor were the participants maligned as hoodlums: the boys and girls in Watts and Harlem are thoroughly aware of this, and it certainly contributes to their attitude toward the Jews.

But, of course, my comparison of Watts and Harlem with the Warsaw Ghetto will be immediately dismissed as outrageous. There are many reasons for this, and one of them is that while America loves white heroes, armed to the teeth, it cannot abide bad niggers. But the bottom reason is that it contradicts the American dream to suggest that any gratuitous, unregenerate horror can happen here. We make our mistakes, we like to think, but we are getting better all the time.

Well, to state it mildly, this is a point of view which any sane or honest Negro will have some difficulty holding. Very few Americans, and this includes very few Jews, have the courage to recognize that the America of which they dream and boast is not the America in which the Negro lives. It is a country which the Negro has never seen. And this is not merely a matter of bad faith on the part of Americans. Bad faith, God knows, abounds, but there is something in the American dream sadder and more wistful than that.

No one, I suppose, would dream of accusing the late Moss Hart of bad faith. Near the end of his autobiography, *Act One,* just after he has become a successful playwright, and is riding home to Brooklyn for the first time in a cab, he reflects:

I stared through the taxi window at a pinch-faced ten-year-old hurrying down the steps on some morning errand before school, and I thought of myself hurrying down the streets on so many gray mornings out of a doorway and a house much the same as this one. My mind jumped backward in time and then whirled forward, like a many-faceted prism—flashing our old neighborhood in front of me, the house, the steps, the candy store—and then shifted to the skyline I had just passed by, the opening last

night, and the notices I still hugged tightly under my arm. It was
possible in this wonderful city for that nameless little boy—for
any of its millions—to have a decent chance to scale the walls and
achieve what they wished. Wealth, rank, or an imposing name
counted for nothing. The only credential the city asked was the
boldness to dream.

But this is not true for the Negro, and not even the most
successful or fatuous Negro can really feel this way. His journey
will have cost him too much, and the price will be revealed in
his estrangement—unless he is very rare and lucky—from other
colored people, and in his continuing isolation from whites.
Furthermore, for every Negro boy who achieves such a taxi
ride, hundreds, at least, will have perished around him, and not
because they lacked the boldness to dream, but because the
Republic despises their dreams.

Perhaps one must be in such a situation in order really to
understand what it is. But if one is a Negro in Watts or Harlem,
and knows why one is there, and knows that one has been
sentenced to remain there for life, one can't but look on the
American state and the American people as one's oppressors.
For that, after all, is exactly what they are. They have corralled
you where you are for their ease and their profit, and are doing
all in their power to prevent you from finding out enough
about yourself to be able to rejoice in the only life you have.

One does not wish to believe that the American Negro can
feel this way, but that is because the Christian world has been
misled by its own rhetoric and narcotized by its own power.

For many generations, the natives of the Belgian Congo,
for example, endured the most unspeakable atrocities at the
hands of the Belgians, at the hands of Europe. Their suffering
occurred in silence. This suffering was not indignantly reported
in the Western press, as the suffering of white men would have
been. The suffering of this native was considered necessary,
alas, for European Christian dominance. And, since the world
at large knew virtually nothing concerning the suffering of this
native, when he rose he was not hailed as a hero fighting for

his land, but condemned as a savage, hungry for white flesh. The Christian world considered Belgium to be a civilized country; but there was not only no reason for the Congolese to feel that way about Belgium; there was no possibility that they could.

What will the Christian world, which is so uneasily silent now, say on that day which is coming when the black native of South Africa begins to massacre the masters who have massacred him so long? It is true that two wrongs don't make a right, as we love to point out to the people we have wronged. But *one* wrong doesn't make a right, either. People who have been wronged will attempt to right the wrong; they would not be people if they didn't. They can rarely afford to be scrupulous about the means they will use. They will use such means as come to hand. Neither, in the main, will they distinguish one oppressor from another, nor see through to the root principle of their oppression.

In the American context, the most ironical thing about Negro anti-Semitism is that the Negro is really condemning the Jew for having become an American white man—for having become, in effect, a Christian. The Jew profits from his status in America, and he must expect Negroes to distrust him for it. The Jew does not realize that the credential he offers, the fact that he has been despised and slaughtered, does not increase the Negro's understanding. It increases the Negro's rage.

For it is not here, and not now, that the Jew is being slaughtered, and he is never despised, here, as the Negro is, *because* he is an American. The Jewish travail occurred across the sea and America rescued him from the house of bondage. But America *is* the house of bondage for the Negro, and no country can rescue him. What happens to the Negro here happens to him *because* he is an American.

When an African is mistreated here, for example, he has recourse to his embassy. The American Negro who is, let us say, falsely arrested, will find it nearly impossible to bring his case to court. And this means that *because* he is a native of this country—"one of our niggers"—he has, effectively, no recourse and no place to go, either within the country or without. He is a pariah in his own country and a stranger in the world. This is what it means to have one's history and one's ties to one's ancestral homeland totally destroyed.

This is not what happened to the Jew and, therefore, he has allies in the world. That is one of the reasons no one has ever seriously suggested that the Jew be nonviolent. There was no need for him to be nonviolent. On the contrary, the Jewish battle for Israel was saluted as the most tremendous heroism. How can the Negro fail to suspect that the Jew is really saying that the Negro deserves his situation because he has not been heroic enough? It is doubtful that the Jews could have won their battle had the Western powers been opposed to them. But such allies as the Negro may have are themselves struggling for their freedom against tenacious and tremendous Western opposition.

This leaves the American Negro, who technically represents the Western nations, in a cruelly ambiguous position. In this situation, it is not the American Jew who can either instruct him or console him. On the contrary, the American Jew knows just enough about this situation to be unwilling to imagine it again.

Finally, what the American Negro interprets the Jew as saying is that one must take the historical, the impersonal point of view concerning one's life and concerning the lives of one's kinsmen and children. "We suffered, too," one is told, "but we came through, and so will you. In time."

In whose time? One has only one life. One may become reconciled to the ruin of one's own life, but to become reconciled to the ruin of one's children's lives is not reconciliation. It is the sickness unto death. And one knows that such counselors are not present on these shores by following this advice. They arrived here out of the same effort the American Negro is making: They wanted to live, and not tomorrow, but today. Now, since the Jew is living here, like all the other white men living here, he wants the Negro to wait. And the Jew sometimes—often—does this in the name of his Jewishness, which is a terrible mistake. He has absolutely no relevance in this context as a Jew. His only relevance is that he is white and values his color and uses it.

He is singled out by Negroes not because he acts differently from other white men, but because he doesn't. His major distinction is given him by that history of Christendom, which has so successfully victimized both Negroes and Jews. And he is playing in Harlem the role assigned him by Christians long ago: he is doing their dirty work.

No more than the good white people of the South, who are really responsible for the bombings and lynchings, are ever present at these events, do the people who really own Harlem ever appear at the door to collect the rent. One risks libel by trying to spell this out too precisely, but Harlem is really owned by a curious coalition which includes some churches, some universities, some Christians, some Jews, and some Negroes. The capital of New York is Albany, which is not a Jewish state, and the Moses they sent us, whatever his ancestry, certainly failed to set the captive children free.

A genuinely candid confrontation between Negroes and American Jews would certainly prove of inestimable value. But the aspirations of the country are wretchedly middle-class and the middle class can never afford candor.

What is really at question is the American way of life. What is really at question is whether Americans already have an identity or are still sufficiently flexible to achieve one. This is a painfully complicated question, for what now appears to be the American identity is really a bewildering and sometimes demoralizing blend of nostalgia and opportunism. For example, the Irish who march on St. Patrick's Day do not, after all, have any desire to go back to Ireland. They do not intend to go back to live there, though they dream of going back there to die. Their lives, in the meanwhile, are here, but they cling, at the same time, to those credentials forged in the Old World, credentials which cannot be duplicated here, credentials which the American Negro does not have. These credentials are the abandoned history of Europe—the abandoned and romanticized history of Europe. The Russian Jews here have no desire to return to Russia either, and they have not departed in great clouds for Israel. But they have the authority of knowing it is there. The Americans are no longer Europeans, but they are still living, at least as they imagine, on that capital.

That capital also belongs, however, to the slaves who created it here; and in that sense, the Jew must see that he is part of the history of Europe, and will always be so considered by the descendant of the slave. Always, that is, unless he himself is willing to prove that this judgment is inadequate and unjust. This is precisely what is demanded of all the other white men in this country, and the Jew will not find it easier than anybody else.

The ultimate hope for a genuine black-white dialogue in this country lies in the recognition that the driven European serf merely created another serf here, and created him on the basis of color. No one can deny that the Jew was a party to this, but it is senseless to assert that this was because of his Jewishness. One can be disappointed in the Jew—if one is romantic enough—for not having learned from his history; but if people did learn from history, history would be very different.

All racist positions baffle and appall me. None of us is that different from one another, neither that much better nor that much worse. Furthermore, when one takes a position one must attempt to see where that position inexorably leads. One must ask oneself, if one decides that black or white or Jewish people are, by definition, to be despised, is one willing to murder a black or white or Jewish baby: for *that* is where the position leads. And if one blames the Jew for having become a white American, one may perfectly well, if one is black, be speaking out of nothing more than envy.

If one blames the Jew for not having been ennobled by oppression, one is not indicting the single figure of the Jew but the entire human race, and one is also making a quiet breathtaking claim for oneself. I know that my own oppression did not ennoble me, not even when I thought of myself as a practicing Christian. I also know that if today I refuse to hate Jews, or anybody else, it is because I know how it feels to be hated. I learned this from Christians, and I ceased to practice what the Christians practiced.

The crisis taking place in the world, and in the minds and hearts of black men everywhere, is not produced by the Star of David, but by the old, rugged Roman cross on which Christendom's most celebrated Jew was murdered. And not by Jews.

Cynthia Ozick

Literary Blacks and Jews

*Cynthia Ozick, the novelist, short-story writer, and essayist,
is the author of, among other books,* The Shawl *and* Art &
Ardor, *in which the essay "Literary Blacks and Jews"
appeared. The essay was originally published in* Midstream
in 1972.

█ ██n 1958, in his celebrated collection *The
Magic Barrel,* Malamud published a short story about a Negro
and a Jew. It was called "Angel Levine," and it contrived for
Manischevitz, a Job-like figure who has "suffered many re-
verses and indignities," the promise of redemption through a
magical black man. Manischevitz has already lost his cleaning
establishment through fire, his only son through war, his
only daughter through a runaway marriage with a "lout."
"Thereafter Manischevitz was victimized by excruciating back-
aches and found himself unable to work. . . . His Fanny, a
good wife and mother, who had taken in washing and sewing,
began before his eyes to waste away . . . there was little hope."

A black man appears. His idiom is elaborate in Father
Divine style: "If I may, insofar as one is able to, identify
myself, I bear the name of Alexander Levine." Manischevitz at
first doubts that this derby-hatted figure is a Jew, but the Negro

says the blessing for bread in "sonorous Hebrew" and declares himself to be a "bona fide angel of God," on probation. Of this Manischevitz is not persuaded. "So if God sends to me an angel, why a black?"

The angel departs, rebuffed by Manischevitz's distrust. Then "Fanny lay at death's door," and Manischevitz, desperate, goes "without belief" in search of the black angel. In a Harlem synagogue he witnesses a small knot of Negro worshipers in skullcaps bending over the Scroll of the Law, conducting something very like a Baptist theology session: "On de face of de water moved de speerit. . . . From de speerit ariz de man." Passing through a lowlife cabaret, Manischevitz is jeered at: "Exit, Yankel, Semitic trash." When at last he finds the black Levine, he is broken enough to burst out with belief: "I think you are an angel from God." Instantly Fanny recovers, and as a reward Levine is admitted to heaven. "In the flat Fanny wielded a dust mop under the bed. . . . 'A wonderful thing, Fanny,' Manischevitz said. 'Believe me, there are Jews everywhere.' "

A distinction must be made. Is it the arrival of a divine messenger we are to marvel at, or is it the notion of a black Jew? If this is a story with a miracle in it, then the only miracle it proposes is that a Jew can be found among the redemptive angels. And if we are meant to be "morally" surprised, it is that—for once—belief in the supernatural is rewarded by a supernatural act of mercy. But the narrative is altogether off-hand about the question of the angel's identity: Levine is perfectly matter-of-fact about it, there is nothing at all miraculous in the idea that a black man can also be a Jew. In a tale about the supernatural, this is what emerges as the "natural" element—as natural-feeling as Manischevitz's misfortunes and his poverty. Black misfortune and poverty have a different resonance—Manischevitz's wanderings through Harlem explain the differences—but, like the Jews' lot, the blacks' has an everyday closeness, for Manischevitz the smell of a familiar fate. To him—and to Malamud at the end of the fifties—that black and Jew are one is no miracle.

A little more than a decade later, with the publication of *The Tenants*,* the proposition seems hollow. Again Malamud offers a parable of black and Jew culminating in fantasy, but now the fantasy has Jew slashing with ax, black with saber, destroying each other in a passionate bloodletting. The novel's last paragraph is eerily liturgical—the word "mercy" repeated one hundred and fifteen times, and once in Hebrew. Nevertheless *The Tenants* is a merciless book. Here are the two lines which are its last spoken exchange:

> "Bloodsuckin Jew Niggerhater."
> "Anti-Semitic Ape."

It took the narrowest blink of time for Malamud, who more than any other American writer seeks to make a noble literature founded on personal compassion, to come from "Believe me, there are Jews everywhere" to this. How was the transmutation from magical brotherhood to ax murder wrought? Is it merely that society has changed so much since the late 1950s, or is it that the author of "Angel Levine" was, even then, obtuse? If the difference in Malamud's imaginative perception lies only in our own commonplace perception that the social atmosphere has since altered in the extreme—from Selma to Forest Hills—then "Angel Levine," far from being a mythically representative tale about suffering brothers, is now no more than a dated magazine story. One test of the durability of fiction is whether it still tells even a partial truth ten years after publication. The conclusion of *The Tenants* seems "true" now—i.e., it fits the current moment outside fiction. But a change in social atmosphere is not enough to account for the evanescence or lastingness of a piece of fiction. There are other kinds of truth than sociological truth. There is the truth that matches real events in the world—in *The Tenants,* it is the black man and the Jew turning on each other—and there is the truth that accurately describes what can only be called aspiration.

*Farrar, Straus and Giroux, 1971.

Even in the world of aspiration, it is a question whether "Angel Levine" remains true. And on the last page of *The Tenants,* when Jew and black cut sex and brains from each other, Malamud writes: "Each, thought the writer, feels the anguish of the other." This is the truth of invisible faith, and it is a question whether this too can survive.

"The anguish of the other" is a Malamudic assumption, endemic in his fiction. The interior of many of Malamud's fables resounds with the injunction that for the sake of moral aspiration one must *undergo.* Yakov Blok of *The Fixer* is an ordinary man with ordinary failings, born a Jew but not yet an accountable Jew until he has undergone, in his own flesh, the terror of Jewish fate. In *The Assistant* Morris Bober's helper, the Italian Frank Alpine, formerly a hold-up man, becomes a Jew through gradually taking on the obligations of a Jew, ultimately even undergoing painful but "inspiring" circumcision. The idea of the *usefulness* of submitting to a destiny of anguish is not a particularly Jewish notion; suffering as purification is far closer to the Christian ethos. Jewish martyrs are seen to be only martyrs, not messiahs or even saints. Malamud's world often proposes a kind of hard-won, eked-out saintliness: suffering and spiritual goodness are somehow linked. The real world of humanity—which means also the real world of the Jews—is not like this. "Bad" Jews went up in smoke at Auschwitz too—surely embezzlers as well as babies, not only zaddikim but misers too, poets as well as kleptomaniacs. Not one single Jew ever deserved his martyrdom, but not every martyr is a holy man. For Malamud all good men are Job.

Nevertheless there remains a thin strand of connection between Malamud's visionary "Angel Levine" and a commonplace of Jewish temperament, between the messianic insistence on the anguish of the other and the common sense of ordinary, "bad," Jews. The sociological—the "real"—counterpart of Malamud's holy fables is almost always taken for granted by Jews: it is, simply put, that Jews have always known hard times, and are therefore naturally sympathetic to others who are having, or once had, hard times. The "naturally" is what is important.

It is a feeling so normal as to be unrelated to spiritual striving, self-purification, moral accountability, prophecy, anything at all theoretical or lofty. This plain observation about particularized suffering requires no special sensitiveness; *naturally* there are Jews everywhere, and some of them are black.

But what has surprised some Jews, perhaps many, is that this Jewish assumption—this quiet tenet, to use a firmer word, that wounds recognize wounds—is not only *not* taken for granted by everyone else, especially by blacks, but is given no credibility whatever. Worse, to articulate the assumption is to earn the accusation of impudence. Nowadays the accusers would include numbers of Jews who point out how thoroughly racism has infiltrated the life of Jewish neighborhoods and institutions; Jews, they say, are as racist as anyone—maybe more so, in view of (the litany begins) those Jewish shopkeepers who have traditionally been the face-to-face exploiters of the black ghetto. For all these accusers, "Angel Levine" must seem not just dated, obsolete, a sentimental excrescence of that remote era when Jews were as concerned with CORE as they were with UJA—but *wrong.* And many young blacks writing today would regard its premise not only as not a moral hope, but as a hurtful lie. Or else would see Manischevitz's salvation as simply another instance of Jewish exploitation, this time of black benevolence.

Black distrust of this heritage of Jewish sympathy is obviously a social predicament, but it is, curiously, a literary one as well. If the distrust has caused a blight on the sympathy, it turns out also that the distrust antedates the withering of that sympathy. The historical weight of "Angel Levine" was this: Negroes are not goyim, not in the full oppressive meaning of that word. How could they be? Anti-Semitism is not properly a Negro appurtenance—it is not historically black, any more than plantation-slave guilt is properly a Jewish burden. Thirteen years later *The Tenants* appears to reply: but no, the black man is a goy after all; and perhaps always was. Between these contradictory and irreducible formulations, Jewish astonishment came to fruition. It was as improbable for the Jew to imagine himself in the role of persecutor—or even indifferent bystander—as it was for him to imagine the black man in that same role. Yet by the late sixties Jews and blacks were recognizable, for and by one another, in no other guise. In a 1966 symposium in *Midstream* on the relations between blacks and Jews, the sociologist C. Eric Lincoln wrote: "One could argue the expectation that if the Jews are not especially moved by faith, then they ought to be moved by experience. Perhaps so. But the best way to forget an unpleasant experience is not by becoming implicated in someone else's troubles." If this sounded like a sensible generality, it was nevertheless shocking to Jews because it was so thoroughly contrary to the way Jews had been experiencing their own reality, their own normality.

But 1966 counts as almost recent; it is, anyway, midway in time between the redemptiveness of "Angel Levine" and the murderous conclusion of *The Tenants*—the corrosion of relations had already begun. It began perhaps not so much because of the emergence of black political violence and Jewish fear of that violence, and not even because anti-Semitism had again become the socialism of the militant masses, but more fundamentally out of the responsiveness of America itself: the Jews have been lucky in America, the blacks not. Manischevitz's daughter—we can imagine it—moves out of the foul old neighborhood to Long Island; the black Levine, according to Malamud, has no place green to go but heaven.

Jews are nowadays reminded that this difference—America felt simultaneously as Jewish Eden and black inferno—has always been exactly the thing that called into question the authenticity of Jewish sympathy, that this disparity from the beginning made the Jews suspect to resentful blacks, that Jewish commitment to black advancement, much less black assertion, *had* to be undermined by the Jews' pleasure in an America open and sweet to them. The statement "The blacks have not been lucky in America" is used now as a reproof to these luckier Jews for the impudence of their empathy, and to show it up as a lie—an ineluctable time-bomb sort of lie: if Jewish identification with black causes was after all not intended to be traitorous, then it was destined by Jewish success to become so. That most American Jews are themselves less than eighty years distant from their own miseries in the Russian Pale is said to be wiped out by their American good luck, and all at once; Jews who lay claim to historical memory are ridiculed as pretentious or bullying—present security is taken for a mandatory form of amnesia.

But this very formulation—the hell of being black in America—that is today raised against Jews to chide them for the vanity and presumptuousness of assuming historical parallels, is nevertheless not tolerated when Jews themselves proffer it. Either it is taken as still another meaningless white mea culpa, or else as a sign of greenhorn uppityness: the Jew putting on airs in the pretense of a mea culpa he hasn't been around long enough to earn. Lack of sympathy is an obvious offense; sympathy turns out to be more offensive yet. The point is surprising but unsubtle. If the current wound-licking withdrawal of Jews is now seen as an outrage or an expected betrayal, what of that earlier, poignantly spontaneous Jewish concern? In the very hour of its freest, most impassioned expression, it was judged as a means to take the Negro's humanity away from him—even then. To illustrate this astounding statement one must turn from the social side to the literary.

Sociologists—I hope I am permitted this fractionally unfair jibe—arrive at their preconceptions cautiously and soberly, but it is the smoothness of their preconceptions they are all the while aiming for. Literary minds work rawly and unashamedly through their beliefs, and have the skeptical grace to arrive at no-man's-land. Both Jew and black in *The Tenants* are literary men. Their war is a war of manhood and of art. The book has no conclusion and stops in the middle of an incoherency. Eight years before the publication of *The Tenants,* five years after the appearance of "Angel Levine," at the absolute height of "Jewish concern" for the condition of being black in America, a Jew and a black, both literary men, acted out an adumbration of the tragic discord (this phrase is not too grandiose) of *The*

Tenants. Their war was a war of manhood (what does it mean to be human) and of art (what are a writer's most urgent sources). Their clash led to no tangible conclusion and stopped in the middle of a double questioning: "How it seems to Ellison I cannot really say," Irving Howe wrote at the last, "though I should like very much to know." "You should not feel unhappy about this or think that I regard you either as dishonorable or an enemy. I hope," Ralph Ellison had already written, "you will come to view this exchange as an act of, shall we say, 'antagonistic cooperation'?"

("Each, thought the writer, feels the anguish of the other.")

The exchange is seminal and ought to be republished all in one place for its superb documentary value—a collision rich in felt honesty and therefore somehow strange, hurtful and agonizing, eluding decent summarization. Ellison's side in particular is a remarkably useful notation in the history not so much of black as of Jewish self-understanding. That there is space here only to give the argument with the sort of crude speed one would ordinarily eschew is probably, for purposes of illuminating a single point, all to the good—that single point being the response of one profoundly gifted black writer to "Jewish concern."

It ought to be made instantly clear that nothing in Howe's "Black Boys and Native Sons"—the essay that triggered the debate with Ellison, first published in *Dissent* (Autumn 1963)—was overtly written from the viewpoint of a Jew. The essay was, first of all, a consideration of Baldwin and Wright, and finally of Ellison himself. Baldwin, Howe observed, had at the start of his career backed off from Wright's "nightmare of remembrance," hoping to " 'prevent myself from becoming *merely* a Negro; or even, merely a Negro writer.' " And Ellison, Howe noted, was the "Negro writer who has come closest to satisfying Baldwin's program." Appraising Ellison's novel *Invisible Man,* Howe marveled at "the apparent freedom it displays from the ideological and emotional penalties suffered by Negroes in this country," but at the same time admitted he was troubled by "the sudden, unprepared, and implausible assertion of unconditioned freedom with which the novel ends." "To write simply about 'Negro experience' with the aesthetic distance urged by the critics of the fifties, is a moral and psychological impossibility." Howe charged, "for plight and protest are inseparable from that experience." And while acknowledging that "the posture of militancy, no matter how great the need for it, exacts a heavy price from the writer," Howe set his final sympathies down on the side of Wright's "clenched militancy" and Baldwin's ultimately developed "rage."

As against Ellison's affirmation of America as a place of "rich diversity and . . . almost magical fluidity and freedom," Howe wrote:

> What, then, was the experience of a man with a black skin, what *could* it be in this country? How could a Negro put pen to paper, how could he so much as think or breathe, without some impulsion to protest, be it harsh or mild, political or private, released or buried? The "sociology" of his existence formed a constant pressure on his literary work, and not merely in the way this might be true for any writer, but with a pain and a ferocity that nothing could remove.

Afterward Ellison was to characterize these phrases as "Howe, appearing suddenly in blackface." The reply to Howe, an essay of great flexibility and authority, came in the pages of *The New Leader* the following winter, and what Ellison made plain was that he was first of all a writer and a man, and took his emotional priorities from that: "Evidently Howe feels that unrelieved suffering is the only 'real' Negro experience, and that the true Negro writer must be ferocious. . . . One unfamiliar with what Howe stands for would get the impression that when he looks at a Negro he sees not a human being but an abstract embodiment of living hell."

In coming out for the autonomy of art, Ellison seemed to leave Howe stuck with all the disabilities, crudenesses, and ingenuousness of the militant Protest Novel. Yet in almost the next breath here is Ellison defending his own militancy as unassailable: "I assure you that no Negroes are beating down my door, putting pressure on me to join the Negro Freedom Movement, for the simple reason that they realize that I am enlisted for the duration. . . . Their demands, like that of many whites, are that I publish more novels. . . . But then, Irving, they recognize what you have not allowed yourself to see: namely that my reply to your essay is itself a small though necessary action in the Negro struggle for freedom." Here Ellison suddenly seems to be giving Howe a victory. Even in *not* writing the Protest Novel he is protesting; *by virtue of being black* his heart is instantly recognizable—by fellow blacks—as being in the right place, "enlisted."—And had not Howe argued, "But even Ellison cannot help being caught up with the *idea* of the Negro"?

This part of the argument—complex and blazing, essentially the classic quarrel between critic and imaginative artist, and between the artist's own two selves, the "aesthetic" and the "engaged"—is also an uncanny fore-echo of one of Malamud's preoccupations in *The Tenants*. There, however, it is the Jew who assumes Ellison's overall position of the free artist committed first of all to the clean fall of his language, and the black man who expresses Howe's implacability. What this reversal portends we shall see in a moment, but first it is necessary to look at Ellison's consideration of Howe as Jew. It comes very suddenly—and I think justly—in his reply, and points to the absence anywhere in Howe's remarks of the admission that he is a Jew. Whether or not Howe himself thought this relevant is not the issue; what is important is that Ellison thought it relevant, and scornfully rounded on Howe for having called himself a "white intellectual."

> . . . in situations such as this [Ellison wrote] many Negroes, like myself, make a positive distinction between "whites" and "Jews." Not to do so could be either offensive, embarrassing, unjust, or even dangerous. If I would know who I am and preserve who I am, then I must see others distinctly whether they see me so

or no. Thus I feel uncomfortable whenever I discover Jewish intellectuals writing as though *they* were guilty of enslaving my grandparents, or as though the *Jews* were responsible for the system of segregation. Not only do they have enough troubles of their own, as the saying goes, but Negroes know this only too well.

The real guilt of such Jewish intellectuals lies in their facile, perhaps unconscious, but certainly unrealistic, identification with what is called the "power structure." Negroes call that "passing for white." . . . I consider the United States freer politically and richer culturally because there are Jewish Americans to bring it the benefit of their special forms of dissent, their humor, and their gift for ideas which are based upon the uniqueness of their experience.

The statement reads admirably. But if Ellison wants to "see others distinctly," including Howe's distinctiveness as a Jewish rather than a "white" intellectual, he must not object to Howe's seeing *him* distinctly, as a man participating in a certain social predicament—i.e., getting born black in America. Defining an individual's social predicament does not automatically lead to stripping him of his personal tastes and talents, as Ellison assumes earlier in his essay, when he speaks of "prefabricated Negroes . . . sketched on sheets of paper and superimposed upon the Negro community." Jews also have their predicament, or call it their destiny, as Jews; but destiny is something profoundly different from a stereotype.

The second part of Ellison's remarks, ringing though they are, is where the real difficulty lies. If Ellison thought Howe obtuse because he visualized the black as a man in perpetual pain, if Ellison thought Howe was distorting his own more open perception of the effect on blacks of their civil inequities ("matters," Ellison wrote, "about which I could do nothing except walk, read, hunt, dance, sculpt, cultivate ideas")—what could a Jew think of Ellison's Jewish projections? What could be "special" about forms of Jewish dissent that do not include dissent on behalf of others?* What else, in the eye of history, could "special forms of dissent" *mean* if not the propensity to be enlisted in social causes not intimately one's own? What could be the purpose of ideas based upon the uniqueness of Jewish experience if that uniqueness did not signify at least in part a perennial victimization, and if that experience did not extend itself beyond compassion into identification? How then does it happen that Ellison, in attributing so many useful and distinctive things to Jews, has it all add up to nothing less ugly than "passing for white"?

The trouble, I think, is a simple one. At bottom it is Ellison, not Howe, who fails to nail down the drift of distinctive experience, who imagines the Jew as naturally identifying with the white "power structure." Ellison has some of the psychology right, to be sure—it *was* a case of "perhaps unconscious" identification, but in a way Ellison was curiously unable to conceive of, except for the instant it took for him to ridicule the idea: "Howe, appearing suddenly in blackface." But Howe's call for the "impulsion to protest" was not a matter of burnt cork—he was not coming on as a make-believe Negro (and certainly not as a make-believe member of the "power structure"), but rather as a Jew responding implicitly and naturally—i.e., vicariously—to an urgent moment in history, applying to that moment the "benefit of [his] special form of dissent." That the "identification" was authentic, the vicariousness pragmatic, the dissent genuinely felt, untouched by manipulativeness or cynicism, the next several years in America rapidly made clear, the proof being the rise of black programs of "ferocity," both political and literary—which, interestingly enough, a Jewish critic was able to foretell through the exercise of his own familial sensibility.

In this interpretive retelling, I have perhaps made Howe out

---

*Howe has written elsewhere that he became a socialist through realization of what poverty was. And it was the poverty of the rural South that brought it home to him, though at the very moment he was reading about it he was himself an impoverished youth living wretchedly in a Bronx tenement in the middle of the Depression. (That the connection was made through *reading* is perhaps also to the point.)

to be too much the prototypical Jew. This may be unfair to him. I do not know his personal views or whether he would welcome this characterization. But the exchange with Ellison, at this distance and after so many reversals in the putative black-Jewish alliance (how long ago that now seems, how unreal the very phrase), has taken on the power, and some of the dread, of a tragic parable. Ellison's inability to credit the Jew with a plausible commitment was, as it turned out, representative not only of what was to come, but of what had long been. From the Ellisonian point of view, "Angel Levine" never *was* true: impossible for black man and Jew to share the same skin and the same pair of eyes out of which to assess reality. Ellison's side of the argument, it seems to me, utterly undermines the "sociological" premises of "Angel Levine"— black and Jew are not, will never be seen to be, mutually salvational. But it is not only the nonfictive referents of the tale that are undermined. Little by little even the moral truthfulness begins to seep out of the vision itself—what was radiant, if illusioned, hope at the time "Angel Levine" was conceived has disintegrated into a kind of surrealism, an arbitrary act of art, set apart from any sources of life. Literature (even in the form of fantasy) cannot survive on illusion.

This is perhaps why Malamud went forward from the failed dream of "Angel Levine" to the warlike actualities of *The Tenants*. Ellison, meanwhile, is revealed by the passage of time to be not simply representative but prophetic. Society becomes for the black, if not yet magically fluid, then not nearly so much of a shut box as it is for Malamud's Jew in the claustrophobic world of *The Tenants,* or for the Jew in an America now seen to be inhabited by black as well as white goyim, with few temperamental allies. Black political fluidity has increased immeasurably since Ellison wrote, expressing itself in a kind of overall ascendancy of purpose, while Jewish political self-consciousness is static, confined to a handful of Congressional constituencies. But even then, while acknowledging the chasm between himself and the power structure, Ellison made it plain that he was at home in America in the most comfortable sense of country-culture. In the very same essay addressed to Howe there is an account of quail hunting in snowy Ohio fields, and a note of gratitude to Hemingway for having written so well on wing shooting "that I could keep myself and my brother alive during the 1937 recession by following his descriptions." Few Jews, even of the third or fourth generation, will recognize in themselves this sort of at-homeness with the land, whereas even urban Poles and Italians have land-memory to draw upon. What emerges from the encounter with Howe is that Ellison has a gentile ease in America—an easier scorn, even, for its blemishes—that Howe and Malamud, with their bookish moral passion, have not. "I could do nothing except walk, read, hunt, dance, sculpt, cultivate ideas." It is almost as if the Jew can do nothing but cultivate ideas.

What happened between Ellison and Howe (behind the back, as it were, of literature) was bound to be seized on by the larger metaphor of the novel. In my own case I have not found it possible to think about *The Tenants* without first turning Howe-Ellison round and round; together they make a bemusing artifact in a reverse archaeology. Dig them up and discover, in genteel form, the savage future.

I came to rehearse their exchange because, in my first reading of *The Tenants,* I was, like many readers, rabidly discontent with Malamud's conception of his black character, Willie Spearmint, later called Spear. Willie Spear is a black writer who has the flavor of an Eldridge Cleaver rather than an Ellison; and this seemed to matter. Malamud, it appeared, had deliberately chosen—for novelistic bite and drama—an unruly spear carrier, when he might have chosen a poised aristocrat of prose. And up against Spear he set the Jewish writer Harry Lesser, a man almost too fastidious in his craft. The balance was unequal, the antagonists unfairly matched, the Jew too hesitant and disciplined, the black too spontaneous and unschooled.

That the antagonists *have* to be a match for each other at first strikes one as important, because *The Tenants* is partly, despite its directness of language and gesture, a theater piece designed as stately discourse. Though I admit the comparison is inflated, nevertheless one is put in mind of the eye-to-eye feud of Elizabeth and Mary, Queen of Scots, in Schiller's *Maria Stuart;* or of Shaw's Joan at her trial, another example of an elevated contest of societal interpretation. *The Tenants* is obviously barer and coarser than these—airless and arid, a flat plain pitting philosopher-king against philosopher-king. Except for these two figures—the Jew and the black—the book is, by and large, unpeopled. The two writers meet in an almost empty tenement about to be torn down. Lesser still lives in his old apartment, refusing to move out until his novel is finished. Already ten years of his life have gone into trying to finish it. Willie is a squatter—hauls in a typewriter, rustles up an old table and chair, and begins.

The friendship that springs up between them is not really a writers' friendship. In a literary sense it is the relation of higher and lower. Lesser is always the pro, the polisher, authority, patron of opinion; he has published before, one book is moderately famous. Willie, out of the ghetto, is the rough-hewn disciple. Lesser is the cultivated representative of Society-at-Large, and when he speaks as writer he speaks not as a Jew but as a clear-cut descendant of the American literary tradition from Hawthorne to James—that very James, in fact, who, visiting the Lower East Side in 1904, worried about the effect of Yiddish-influenced impurities on his clean ancestral English. Lesser too feels himself superior: a natural inheritor, like James, of the language, while Willie is only a crude aspirant, likely to damage his material by clumsiness. Lesser observes:

> He has not yet mastered his craft. . . . What can I say to a man who's suffered so much personal pain, so much injustice, who clearly finds in his writing his hope and salvation, who defines himself through it? He comes in the end, as in the old slave narratives, to freedom, through his sense of writing as power—it flies up and carries him with it—but mainly in his belief that he can, in writing, help his people overthrow racism and economic inequality. That his freedom will help earn theirs. The Life he

writes, whatever he calls it, moves, pains, inspires, even though it's been written before, and better, by Richard Wright, Claude Brown, Malcolm X, and in his way, Eldridge Cleaver. Their self-discoveries have helped Willie's. Many black men live the same appalling American adventure, but it takes a unique writer to tell it uniquely, as literature. To make black more than color or culture, and outrage larger than protest or ideology. . . . Lesser sees irrelevancy, repetition, underdeveloped material; there are mistakes of arrangement and proportion, ultimately of focus.

Reading this, it is easy to think: Ah, but this is unjustly conceived. Willie is a straw man. Why not a black writer who is not only fully literate, but *accomplished*? Suppose Malamud had given us Ellison instead of Willie—then what? Lesser, like Ellison, believes first of all in the primacy, the loveliness, of the sentence; for him literature is the personal courage by which the language is seized. Beyond that lies propaganda. Granted that two-literary-intellectuals-talking-to-each-other does not make a novel (Mann and the Russians excepted), or, at least, would not make *this* novel, Malamud seems to be asking for the sort of resentment that would soon come to surround his formulation: Jewish Intellectual versus Tough Black Militant. Unequal warfare in the Republic of Letters. Could it not—for fairness—somehow have been contrived as Jewish Intellectual versus Black Intellectual?

There were, of course, good novelistic reasons why it could not. For instance, the conflict that eventually interposes itself between Lesser and Willie is not intellectual but rawly sexual. Willie has a Jewish girlfriend, Irene, whom Lesser covets and ultimately wins. Irene is unfortunately a fiction device and lives only intermittently. Her narrative task is to convert the two writers into enemies through sexual jealousy. Lesser's importuning landlord, Levenspiel, is also a fiction device—he is there to give us the novel's pivotal "problem," to put time pressure on a stubborn Lesser—but Levenspiel, by contrast, manages to live vividly: "Have a little mercy, Lesser, move out so I can break up this rotten house that weighs like a hunch on my back. . . . *Hab rachmones,* Lesser, I have my own ambition to realize." All this is beside the point. Levenspiel and Irene and Willie's black friends who slide in and out from the wings are all interruptions in the dialogue between Lesser and Willie; they are pretexts for necessary "action," for novelistic progress. They are not what the book fundamentally intends.

If *The Tenants* progresses, it is not through plot but through revelation. The revelation is one-sided: it happens inside Lesser. We do not really know what happens inside Willie. And what happens inside Lesser is this: The clear realization that the black writer who shares his quarters and also his literary hopes is, more than he is writer, more than he is lover, more even than he is fleshly human being, a ferocious, a mythic, anti-Semite.

It is a revelation to Lesser because, at the start of their closeness, it did not "show." When Willie is angry at Lesser he says "white," he says "ofay," he does not yet see distinctly into his rage at the Jew. Lesser, himself a failing writer, views Willie as a possibly ascending one. All that is in Willie's way is technique. He tells Willie, "Not that you don't work hard but there has to be more emphasis on technique, form. . . ." They discuss form:

> Lesser asks Willie to grant him goodwill. "I know how you feel, I put myself in your place."
>
> In cold and haughty anger the black replies. "No ofay motherfucker can put himself in *my* place. This is a *black* book we talkin about that you don't understand at all. White fiction ain't the same as *black*. It *can't* be."
>
> "You can't turn black experience into literature just by writing it down."
>
> "Black ain't white and never can be. It is once and for only black. It ain't universal if that's what you are hintin up to. What I feel you feel different. You can't write about black because you don't have the least idea what we are or how we feel. Our feelin chemistry is different than yours. Dig that? It *has* to be so. I'm writin the soul writin of black people cryin out we are still slaves

in this fuckn country and we ain't gonna stay slaves any longer. How can you understand it, Lesser, if your brain is white?"

"So is your brain white. But if the experience is about being human and moves me then you've made it my experience. You created it for me. You can deny universality, Willie, but you can't abolish it."

"Bein human is shit. It don't give you any privileges, it never gave us any."

"If we're talking about art, form demands its rights, or there's no order and maybe no meaning. What else there isn't I think you know."

"Art can kiss my juicy ass. You want to know what's really art? *I* am art. Willie Spearmint, *black man*. My form is *myself*."

Up to the moment of Willie's conclusion—"*I* am art"—this exchange is only another chapter of Howe-Ellison, with Willie as Howe, speaking in behalf of "being caught up with the *idea* of the Negro," and Lesser as Ellison, speaking in behalf of the universal values of art and humanity. But the two positions, Ellison's and Willie's, intermingle somewhat. Willie, like Ellison, does not trust his antagonist to "know how you feel, . . . [to] put myself in your place." Addressing Howe, Ellison simultaneously denies and affirms universality: as a black man he considers himself first of all a man, one who despite external disabilities is pleased to walk, read, hunt, etc., like all men; but again as a black he denies that anyone not black can creditably take into himself the day-to-dayness of the black predicament. Willie accepts only the denial: only a black can know what it is to be black, no one else. As for "being human," not only does Willie reject the term "universal," but he sees himself as almost physiologically different ("Our feelin chemistry is different than yours"), and he goes further yet—he freezes himself into the image of a totem, a *"black man."* The statement "My form is *myself*" is beyond humanity, beyond even art. It stands for something more abstract than either: a political position taken at its most absolute. For a totem *is* an absolute politics: an object, an artifact, a *form* representing an entire people, together with its interests, its cult, its power, its history, and fate. The totem has no fluidity, its being is its meaning. Willie has turned the politics of a group into an object—himself, *black man*. In Willie Art is Politics, Politics is Art.

This is why it would not have served Malamud's deepest intention if he had chosen not Willie, but a more "realistic," pragmatic, literate, humane, relatively apolitical, less symbolic black for the novel. In *not* choosing an Ellison, of course, Malamud took on himself both a risk and a certainty. The certainty was the charge of "stereotype" and "blacklash," to which *The Tenants* has already been preeminently subject. The risk—a "stereotype" having indeed been chosen—was the failure of the novel as art. To a degree this *has* happened—to the very degree that Willie's stereotyped expectations lead to banalities masking as passions. Something was necessary to stimulate Willie's active vengeance, so we are given a plot fulcrum, Willie's girl Irene. In return for Lesser's stealing his girl, Willie destroys Lesser's work of ten years; the war is on. Irene exists to accommodate neither Willie nor Lesser, but the exigencies of a made fiction. All this is too obviously and distractingly schematic—even the lineaments of "parable" cannot contain it—and if I seem to be bringing it up again now, it is only to contrast it with the novel's authentic passions. These are in the mimicry of Willie's writing. I will come to them in a moment.

Suppose, though, Malamud *had* chosen an Ellison-like character to confront his Lesser. The first advantage would have been safety in the world external to the novel: with equal contenders, fewer readers might have cried bigot. And internally, also, there would have been an advantage: the contenders might have met and if necessary separated on the *cultural* issues, as Howe and Ellison did, not on the extraneous ones of purloined women and violated manuscripts. ("But," Malamud might counter, "purloined women and violated literature are the stuff of Willie's culture.") It might even be argued that, if novelistic conflict was what was wanted, if dramatic misunderstanding and distrust were what was wanted, a fictionalized

Howe-Ellison clash could have provided them as surely as Lesser-Willie, and with the black man's "humanity" intact, all stereotypes avoided and averted. Inside the air of Malamud's novel, Ellison—or, rather, "Ellison"—would still have found Jewish literary empathy suspect, as the actual Ellison did in the more open world of nonfictional debate; and there would not have occurred, between two civilized beings, the perilous contrast between the "civilized" Jew Lesser and the "savage" Willie. (As the book now stands, though, there is nothing to choose at the end between Willie's and Lesser's savagery.) And not only this: with "Ellison" instead of Willie to do battle with Lesser, the novel would have been intellectually richer, thicker, clearer, the parable more perfect, the fright more frightening because in seemingly safer hands.

With so much to lose from Willie, with so much to gain from "Ellison," why did Malamud opt for what is so plainly a grossness, a caricature, above all a stereotype?

Here is Willie at his grossest:

". . . You tryin to kill off my natural writin by pretendin you are interested in the fuckn form of it though the truth of it is you afraid of what I am goin to write in my book, which is that the blacks have to murder you white MF's for cripplin our lives." He then cried out, "Oh, what a hypocrite shitass I am to ask a Jew ofay for advice how to express *my* soul work. Just in readin it you spoil what it says. I ought to be hung on a hook till some kind brother cuts off my white balls."

Ellison had complained to Howe (implying Howe was guilty of it too) that nonblack writers tend to create "prefabricated Negroes . . . sketched on sheets of paper and superimposed upon the Negro community." Surely this quotation from Willie fits Ellison's imputations; Willie is unabashedly "prefabricated."

But the real question is: Who cast this die, who prefabricated Willie? Not Malamud. The source of a stereotype is everything. When, in the late 1890s, William Dean Howells praised the black poet Paul Dunbar's dialect verse for having "the charming accents of the Negro's own version of our [sic] English," chiefly because it exploited "the limited range of the race," which was "the range between appetite and emotion," the stereotype imposed on Dunbar by a white critic killed the poet and the man; he died in bitterness at thirty-four, wretched over the neglect of what he regarded as his real work—"But ah, the world, it turned to praise / A jingle in a broken tongue." In the sixty or so years since Dunbar's death, the "jingle in a broken tongue" has entered the precincts of "soul," and the notion of "our English," when espoused by blacks, receives serious pedagogical and linguistic consideration as a legitimate alternative, a separate language with a distinctive grammar. The stereotype, emerging from Howells, was an insult and a misappropriation; emerging from black pride, it begins to gather the honors of honest coinage.

Malamud did not make Willie. He borrowed him—he mimicked him—from the literature and the politics of the black movement. Willie is the black dream that is current in our world. Blacks made him. Few blacks disavow him. The black middle class, which is ambivalent about Willie, nevertheless does not disavow him—not simply out of loyalty to the underclass (the loyalty is what is in doubt), but out of covert gratitude.* Almost no black writer has disavowed Willie. Ellison is the exception: ". . . what an easy congame for ambitious, publicity-hungry Negroes this stance of 'militancy' has become!" he exclaimed to Howe, but that was eight years ago, and since then, though Willie has grown louder and published amply (he is famous as LeRoi Jones, for instance), Ellison has had nothing to say about him. Surely Baldwin does not disavow Willie; he has become him.

*Orde Coombs wrote some years back in *Harper's* (January 1972), "The thirty-to-forty-year-old black who holds down a good job in the North must know that his present success is a direct result of past tumult. All his talent, all his effort would not have otherwise given him a toehold in television, in consulting firms, in brokerage firms, in advertising, and in publishing. . . . Many of these black men know they owe their livelihoods to their poorer, more militant brethren. . . . *In fact, only one group has really benefited from the turbulence; and that is the middle class.*" (Coombs's emphasis.)

In short, Willie is what he intends himself to be (which is also what he is intended to be by those blacks who do not deny him): a totem, emblem of a community unified in and through Willie's spirit, what he calls his "form"—not man, as Ellison would have it, but *black man*.

What is the meaning of Willie in his self-declared "form"? Willie's form takes up not freedom and fluidity, but unmovable hatred and slavish vengeance. His vengeance is "literary" in two ways: the burning of Lesser's book, and the creation of his own—but "his own" ends as a travesty and spoliation of all humane literary values. Only through the destruction of Jewish culture, says Willie's form, can black culture arise. Lesser finds Willie's notes: "I have got to write better. Better and better. Black but better. Nothing but black. Now or never." And whereas earlier—before the pivotal jealousy episode—writing "black" for Willie had for the most part meant telling the poignant and honest story of his ruined, scarred, and panicked childhood in the ghetto,★ now, writing black for vengeance, Willie dreams pogroms. For him literature serves politics—not as propaganda consciously does, as an "arm" or partner or extension or tool of politics—but intrinsically, below the level of rational motivation. Willie's only politics is coextensive with nearly the whole of his literary imagination; it is the politics and the imagination of anti-Semitism.

Lesser finds another of Willie's notes:

> It isn't that I hate the Jews. But if I do any, it's not because I invented it myself but I was born in the good old U. S. of A. and there's a lot of that going on that gets under your skin. And it's also from knowing the Jews, which I do. The way to black freedom is against them.

Now that Willie has stopped seeing Lesser as a more experienced writer and can think of him only as a Jew, Lesser too

---

★Malamud has mastered the idiom typical of this fiction. For anyone doubtful about Malamud's ear—or, rather, literary eye—an anthology called *What We Must Be: Young Black Storytellers* (Dodd, Mead, 1971) is instructive.

alters. He is rewriting his lost manuscript in fear and anguish, but the vision slips from him, he is in terror of Willie. "I treated you like any other man," he tells Willie. Willie replies, "No Jew can treat me like a man," and Lesser, afraid for his life, turns as savage as Willie, with this difference: ". . . it sickened him deeply"; he remains self-conscious. Nevertheless he gets an ax and chops up Willie's typewriter. On that typewriter Willie had written pages of anti-Semitic (some of it "anti-Zionist") poetry and prose, fantasying the murder of Jews. The work of the two writers is contrasted. Lesser's destroyed book is about a writer's struggle to love. The writer is named Lazar Cohen; he is much like Malamud's Fidelman, an artist with a Jewish name who conceives of himself only as artist, almost never as Jew. Willie's stories are about blacks torturing Jews. In one of them, "a Jew slumlord in a fur-collar coat, come to collect his blood-money rents," is stabbed and killed by three blacks, who strip his corpse naked and propose to eat it, but change their minds. "He tastes Jewtaste, that don't taste like nothin good." The story, as Lesser finds it in Willie's notes, ends:

> Then they [the murderers] go to a synagogue late at night, put on yarmulkes and make Yid noises, praying.
> In an alternate ending the synagogue is taken over and turned into a mosque. The blacks dance hasidically.

With the apparition once again of a black synagogue, with the word "hasidically," Malamud suddenly and astonishingly blows in a whiff of "Angel Levine"—are his blacks becoming Jews again? Lesser has a fantasy: In a mythical Africa there is a double tribal wedding. A rabbi presides. The chief's son, who turns out to be Willie, is marrying a Jewish girl, who is Irene. Lesser is marrying a black woman. The rabbi exhorts the couples, "Someday God will bring together Ishmael and Israel to live as one people. It won't be the first miracle." Inside his dream Lesser says critically of it, "It's something I imagined, like an act of love, the end of my book, if I dared."

But Malamud himself does not dare. "Angel Levine" is not merely out of date, it is illusion; at the close of *The Tenants* Malamud explicitly acknowledges that it is illusion. Lesser's ax—it is the final vision of the novel—sinks into Willie "as the groaning black's razor-sharp saber, in a single boiling stabbing slash, cut[s] the white's balls from the rest of him." It is curious, horrible, and terrifying to take in what Malamud in *The Tenants* openly posits: that the Jew in America, beginning as Howe did with a cry of identification with black suffering, is self-astonished to find himself responding now in the almost forgotten mood of *zelbsbuts*—the shtetl's term for weaponry stored against the fear of pogroms. Lesser, a hesitant intellectual, is driven to hauling an ax. But *The Tenants* insist on more than this. Like much of Malamud's work, and specifically like *The Assistant* and *The Fixer,* it offers the metaphoric incarnation of a Malamudic text: Whoever wants to kill the Jew has already killed the human being in himself.

It is not only no failing, it is the best achievement of the novel that Willie, its black militant, is a stereotype devoid of any easy humanity. The clichés appropriate for a political strategy are unsuitable for describing the soul of a living person. Given the extraliterary truth that black militancy, in and out of print, has now come to define itself if not largely then centrally through classical anti-Semitism, to bestow on a fictional Willie a life beyond his bloody fantasies would have been a savagery akin to Willie's own. To put it another way: To have ascribed to Willie the full and continuing aspects of a decent breathing human being *but for his hatred of Jews* would have been to subvert the meaning of human.

The Tenants is a claustrophobic fable: its theme is pogrom. It remarks the minutiae of a single-handed pogrom so closely that the outer world is shut out. There is almost no city beyond Lesser's tenement, and there are no white Gentiles in the novel, no faint indication of that identification with the Gentile power structure Ellison claimed Jewish intellectuals were seeking. In *The Tenants* the Jew has no allies. Jew and black fight alone in an indifferent world.

There is no means, at this juncture, of determining whether its current worldly truths will one day seep out of *The Tenants,* as the moral radiance of "Angel Levine" had ultimately, through subversion by history, to ebb into falsehood. But—for the moment—Malamud has abandoned the hopefulness of "Angel Levine" and drawn a parable of political anxiety. "Each, thought the writer, feels the anguish of the other" is the last flicker of that hopefulness but does not convince. Willie is Lesser's doom—Lesser, dreaming of love, rigorously apolitical, isolated in his aesthetics, becomes the inescapable victim of an artist whose art is inseparable from butchery.

Yevtushenko, declaiming at the Felt Forum that bombs and balalaikas are in essence always separate,* nevertheless speaks not for Lesser but for Willie. Yevtushenko's poem condemning the bombing of Hurok's office, and the death of a secretary there, moved everyone, who could disagree? But the poem is a cheat. To be horrified at the bombing is not automatically to assent to the purity of art. Mozart was played at Auschwitz, and it is a ruse to pretend that any natural "separation" of art keeps it unblemished by political use. Malamud, in plucking Willie out of the black writing that made him, has not invented the politicization of fiction. And in inventing *The Tenants,* Malamud ironically follows Willie—he has written a tragic fiction soaked in the still mainly unshed blood of the urban body politic.

AFTERWORD (1993)

Rereading "Literary Blacks and Jews," an essay somewhat under a quarter of a century old, I am shocked to see that it is

---

*Yevgeny Yevtushenko, the Soviet poet, gave a reading in New York City the day after a New York group had bombed the offices of Sol Hurok, the agent responsible for booking Soviet cultural events in the United States. A young Jewish woman, a secretary in Hurok's office, was killed. Yevtushenko overnight wrote a poem of commemoration; it compared the girl's death to the gassing of Jews in Auschwitz, and declared that art and politics must be kept separate. The poem noticeably subverted its own thesis.

more up-to-date now than it was then. What for Malamud was a fiction of blows—blows not yet realized in actual human flesh at the time his novel appeared, and therefore still confined to the safety of metaphor—has become, in the last decade of the twentieth century, a reality of the New York streets. In 1971, when *The Tenants* was published, Crown Heights was a potentiality locked in words. Now those words have assumed their deadly incarnation. "There is no means at this juncture," I wrote over two decades ago, "of determining whether its current worldly truths will one day seep out of *The Tenants*." The rawest mistake in that sentence is the "seep." What happened in Crown Heights was flood.

But what I failed to notice then—the habit was not yet so systemic or so systematic as it has since become—was that Malamud's ultimate premise did not hold. His premise was equal culpability: what has long been termed, in political language, the moral equation issue. The enraged Jew, Malamud's tale insists, can turn out to be, even if defensively, as violent in America as the enraged black; at the end of the day there is nothing to choose between the two for savagery. Yet if, in the light of black hostility current then and later, Malamud got Willie Spear right, he anyhow got Lesser wrong. He conceived the Jew as less than he was—a thing that, given the name "Lesser," may have been deliberate. The point is this: Jews as a body have never raised a persecutor's hand against African-Americans. Lesser hauls an ax only in the ferocities of Malamud's imagination.

If *pogrom* means mass murder, then what occurred in Crown Heights was not a pogrom; only two Jews died, one stomped and stabbed by a gang of assailants shouting "Kill the Jew," the other a suicide (an elderly Holocaust survivor who, reliving old horrors, threw herself out of her apartment window). And since only one man was murdered, perhaps the better word would be lynching, if lynching includes, as I think it does, the simultaneous terrorizing of an entire section of the population. As for Malamud's equation of Willie and Lesser at the close of *The Tenants:* there was no physical or moral equality in Crown Heights. Blacks came after Jews, not vice versa. It was Jews, not blacks, who cowered behind their doors—doors marked and made vulnerable by mezuzahs. Equality in Crown Heights was equality of the eye. If blacks are easy targets for hate because they are visually recognizable, so were these Hasidim: you could tell who the Jews were by their distinctive dress and by the capsules containing Scripture affixed to their doorposts. And, I would add, by their civic peaceableness in the wake of angry disappointment. Los Angeles was torched after Rodney King. No one burned Brooklyn after Lemrick Nelson.*

This same presumption of equal culpability was what was really the matter with Art Spiegelman's *New Yorker* cover cartoon of the hot-lips Hasid giving a love smack to the cute black chick. Since Spiegelman's "valentine to New York" had the advantage of offending the inmost dignity of two groups of the citizenry at once, probably caricature is not the best means of peacemaking. But that was the smaller—the Lesser—part of the problem. When people are asked to kiss and make up, it is being suggested that there has been a falling out, and that a fairly equal measure of blame attaches to both sides. But there was no falling out. The Hasidim are a famously private and insular community, sectarians isolated not only from society at large but from other Jews (even from devoutly Orthodox Jews, and often even from other Hasidic groupings), and from modernism in general. Like the Amish (and costumed not very differently), they are turned harmlessly inward; their children are profoundly regulated. No one has heard of Amish lynching Presbyterians and Methodists on the ground of social and theological differences, and it is likely no one ever will. No one has heard of Hasidim running in mobs after blacks for purely racist reasons, and it is likely no one ever will. This is not to

*Rodney King's first trial ended in the acquittal of the Los Angeles police officers accused of excessive force in his arrest, following a nationwide viewing of a videotape of that beating. Lemrick Nelson, whose culpability in the Crown Heights murder of Yankel Rosenbaum was similarly hard to doubt, was acquitted by a jury, members of which later partied with Nelson's defense lawyer.

say that the Hasidim of Crown Heights are necessarily sensitive to the condition of being black in America, or for that matter in Brooklyn. But they do not commit mob violence. To be sure, their spokesmen are sometimes charged with local politicking—a sign that certain citizenly assimilationism can penetrate any group, no matter how socially isolated—but engaging in neighborhood political jockeying is precisely the reverse of engaging in neighborhood violence. Consequently Malamud's—and Spiegelman's—ultimate equation cannot stand. As the Israeli novelist and activist Amos Oz has memorably noted, the sixties slogan, "Make Love Not War," has always been off the mark. The opposite of war is not love, and certainly not lovemaking. It is living in peace. And even to say "war" is a mistake. In war, there are two contending parties, equally menacing. Both are armed. Both go out of the house. If Crown Heights was not a pogrom (and speaking quantitatively it was not), neither was it a war. Only one side did the stabbing. Only one side went into the streets.

"But obviously there is Jewish racism," someone (a Jew) said to me as I was beginning this afterword. He reminded me that a Hasid in Crown Heights had yelled "Go back to Africa." One may presume the Hasid had never heard of Marcus Garvey. And yes, and yes, immigrant Jews new to English, and sometimes their native-born daughters and sons, used to call Negroes (when that was the acceptable American term) *schwartzes,* Yiddish for blacks. As certain as I am that the term was simply and neutrally descriptive, in the (foreign) language of the household, with no intent to demean, I can anyhow surmise that almost no one will care to believe this; so I will not press a sociolinguistic point. I have no interest in Jewish apologetics. It goes without saying that there are Jews who have been hurtful (the yelling Hasid mean-spirited and aggressive) and careless and insensitive. Incontrovertibly there are Jews who, like other urban folk, have a street-smarts fear of young black males in sneakers, often enough unjustifiably. There may be Jews who openly espouse the inferiority of blacks. (So far, though, in writing at least, only one such person, bristling with statistically oriented theories, has surfaced in the public press.) Jews like all the other peoples have never yet been confirmed as a community of saints (as any quick look into Isaiah and Jeremiah will demonstrate). In short—and obviously—there are Jewish racists.

But distinctions are called for. That there are racists among Jews does not mean there is Jewish racism. The history of Jewish relations with blacks in this country—I mean the heart and soul and spirit and passion of Jewish attention to and engagement with black suffering and aspiration—is light-years beyond the commitment of any other group of Americans. That may be an old fact by now, and for whatever reasons arising out of the perplexity of human feeling it may be a hated and resented fact, or even a disbelieved fact; but it is a fact. No amount of skepticism can dissolve it. American Jews as a collectivity are not racist; to say so—no matter who says so—is a canard. And to compound such a canard with an "obviously" is to seek to deepen an injury already rooted in falsehood. Racism is a wholesale act of the body politic, established in law and custom. Racism is a majority manifestation. Racism is a mob on the prowl. Racism is the tic or reflex of the benighted. Racism is the Ku Klux Klan. Racism is a movement, complete with leaders and followers. Racism is a widespread common belief in the deficiency of certain classes of human beings. Racism is a lie that has taken on the public appearance of a social axiom. Racism has visible and vocal community promoters. Above all, racism is measured by the proportion of its adherents in any society, or in any element of a society.

So *The Tenants has* come true, but only halfway. "The way to black freedom is against them," Willie says, meaning the Jews. Willie is recognizably in our world, and not only among the unsophisticated or the deprived. Louis Farrakhan heads a popular religious movement. Leonard Jeffries is a tenured professor in a university. Jesse Jackson was a widely admired presidential candidate when he ventured into political anti-Semitism (however reformed or reborn his politics may be nowadays). Leadership of this kind has had its successes. WLIB, an African-American radio outlet in New York, attracts vox populi, and its call-in lines crackle with anti-Semitism. As for Lesser, where is he to be found? Not, as we have seen, among the terrified Hasidim of Crown Heights. And with regard to the question of leadership, no American Jewish political figure or head of any American Jewish organization has ever been charged with a single syllable or gesture of insensitiveness toward African-Americans. The opposite is true; everyone knows this. I am not now referring to long-ago black-Jewish political alliances, or to the hugely disproportionate participation of Jews in the civil rights movement. I mean that everyone knows what representative Jewish attitudes *at this very hour* are. The mainstream Jewish organizations were silent during the Crown Heights disturbances in order not to appear to be putting pressure of any kind on blacks. It was the dread of giving hurt that prevailed, even in the face of a murder. In New York last year, The Jewish Museum mounted a strenuously peacemaking exhibit stressing the affinities of Jewish and black history and aspiration. In Los Angeles, a new Holocaust Museum has opened, with programs explicitly designed to teach against hate. On the Jewish side, then, *The Tenants* has turned out to be false prophecy. In 1992, however, Farrakhan's Nation of Islam published a three-hundred-page volume called *The Secret Relationship Between Blacks and Jews,* the inflammatory thesis of which is that the slave trade was dominated by Jews.

Ironically, it is "Angel Levine" that has come true altogether, and always was true. There *are* black Jews. There have been black Jews for millennia. We in our provincialism were drawn to notice them only when Israel's rescue effort brought home thousands of Ethiopian Jews. Black synagogues are not a Malamudian fantasy. Black Jews can be seen giggling and wriggling in any cluster of Israeli schoolchildren. The marriages between Ashkenazi and Ethiopian have begun. Yet curiously, African-Americans have shown virtually no interest in this pleasing and deeply mutual embrace; perhaps it is seen only as the reunion of coreligionists, with no wider relevance. More likely, though, this dismissal of, or indifference to, the improving lives of these desperate refugees from Ethiopia is rooted in the fact that they are fervent and unconditional Zionists acting on an ancient and undying dream of Jerusalem. Vilification of the State of Israel has unfortunately become the foreign policy of black anti-Semitism, and "Zionist" a major jibe in its diplomatic vocabulary. But for American Jews there is no question that—policy arguments aside—the fate of Israel is a sine qua non. I will not speak here of African-American enthusiasm for the ANC's alliance with the PLO, or of African-American blindness to the acutely fragile situation of South African Jews; but it is enough to note that uninformed assaults on Israel by black Americans (who are certainly not alone in this), and a willed misunderstanding of Middle Eastern events since 1967, have done more to destroy Jewish confidence in black goodwill and fairness than any number of homegrown "Hymietown" quips.

In the wake of all the foregoing, I nevertheless feel a certain optimism about the future relations of blacks and Jews in the welter of our ever more diversifying society—an optimism faint but *there*. Evolving new positions among some black intellectuals stimulate persuasive grounds for hope. I tend to put my faith in braininess—by which I mean, really, principled reason, principled inspiration. I am radically uneasy when I write "the blacks," "the Jews." "The blacks" who rioted and killed a man in Crown Heights are not stand-ins for an abstract African-American collectivity; they are criminals implicated in a discrete crime. Similarly, Hasidic insularity is a way of life apart from ninety-nine percent (if not more) of more typically civic-oriented American Jews. Principled inspiration for whole peoples lies elsewhere.

It will be discovered, in part, in that new generation of African-American intellectuals I am thinking of—though unquestionably they are indebted for their legacy of conscientious independent-mindedness to such eminent older figures as Bayard Rustin and Thurgood Marshall, as well as, notably, Ralph Ellison. What they have achieved is no more and no less than intellectual autonomy—the sloughing off of the consolations,

and safety, of group predictability; the inner force of a willingness to arrive at conclusions apart from established grooves. In
light of the collegial resentments these fresh thinkers (Shelby
Steele, Stanley Crouch, Henry Louis Gates, Jr., et al.) are
sometimes subject to, it will not be surprising if black intellectual discourse soon becomes as contentious as the Jewish variety—not an altogether admirable thing, since quarrelsomeness
and the often rough angers of divided opinion are hard to
praise; but a case can be made that noisy communal argument,
including washing one's dirty linen in public, is healthier than
so-called "solidarity." When Henry Louis Gates, Jr., published
an op-ed piece in *The New York Times* repudiating black anti-
Semitism, he won the gratitude of American Jews; and from
the Jewish point of view it was a brilliant step forward toward
reconciliation. But from the black point of view—I acknowledge the temerity of my trying to imagine this—it was at
bottom much more significant than merely a gesture in recognition of historic Jewish fears. Surely it ought to have been seen
as what it magnificently was: the latest declaration of black
freedom. After all, it isn't the being unjustly hated that keeps
the human mind in chains; it is the impulse to hate unjustly.

And the proposition that black solidarity ought to override
black anti-Semitism is, to be blunt, pernicious. If the means to
a politically strong black collectivity is the naming of "traitors"
(i.e., coercion under the rubric of unity) or the toleration of
anti-Semitism, what then? Farrakhan may indeed be a model
fighter for black entrepreneurialism and against drugs, but to
overlook or underplay his anti-Semitism is no different from
saying that Mussolini made the trains run on time, or that
Hitler built the Autobahn; and no different from admiring the
Jewish Simone Weil as a saint of humanism despite the anti-
Semitism in her writing and in her life. Solidarity without
principle hardly deserves the name; it is only another form of
insecure huddling—whereas genuine solidarity is open communal purpose, the consensus of good that ascends out of the
storm of contending ideas. Anti-Semitism is a fraud and an
indignity, not an idea. An idea, I take it, adheres to the

principle of distinction making, which can separate out communal purpose from the muck and dross of contempt.

It was the rising reality of black anti-Semitism that ended the era of passionate Jewish identification with the black condition in America. Even Ralph Ellison, in that distant and relatively uncontroversial period of the black-Jewish "coalition," could not credit that passion; one must wonder whether any black ever did credit it. As for now, Jewish concern clearly remains, but the ardor of Jewish identification* is over. In any case, Jewish passion, since it was not trusted to be what it naively was, must have been felt as intrusion; there was possibly something obtuse in so much Jewish emotionalism.

And there are, I know, black positions resentful of current Jewish emotionalism—i.e., Jewish reaction to black anti-Semitism. "Do you think all we have to worry about are the feelings of Jews? We've got bigger problems of our own!" And this, too, rings true; nor is it a defense of anti-Semitism. Yet Gates, and other African-American intellectuals who declined to be outraged by his public airing of intramural flaws, have cleared the way for an honesty to be claimed by all hands. "I don't like people who like me because I'm a Negro," the early, preideological James Baldwin wrote in 1955; "neither do I like people who find in the same accident grounds for contempt." Neither hot love nor cold retreat; no grasping for affection, no turning disgustedly away. Neither holds out hope for honesty between American Jews and American blacks. Except for that reductive "accident" (which nearly dismisses history), this

---

*I am ready, by the way, to yield to Irving Howe in what I am told is his continuing insistence that in his exchange with Ellison he was not approaching their discussion from any Jewish standpoint. Reflecting on that exchange in 1972, and noting "the absence anywhere in Howe's remarks of the admission that he is a Jew," I commented: "Whether or not Howe himself thought this relevant is not the issue; what is important is that Ellison thought it relevant, and scornfully rounded on Howe for having called himself a 'white intellectual.' " I also said: "I have perhaps made Howe out to be too much the prototypical Jew. This may be unfair to him. I do not know his personal views or whether he would welcome this characterization." My understanding today is that Howe indeed did not welcome it in that context. Then let me conscientiously add now that people ought to be permitted to look through the lenses they freely choose.

simple formulation, applicable to both blacks and Jews, seems to me right now to be, if not definitive, then certainly useful and clarifying. It obviates intrusion and weeds out condescension. It is austerely unsentimental. It sounds a note both personal and communal. It shuts out—no, throws out—the monoliths of lockstep ideology. It allows for disagreement and for breathing space. It is a good place to begin again.

Norman Podhoretz

My Negro Problem— and Ours

Norman Podhoretz is the editor in chief of Commentary, *where this essay first appeared in 1963. He is also the author of six books, including* Making It *and* Doings and Undoings: The Fifties and After in American Writing *(in which "My Negro Problem—and Ours" was reprinted).*

If we—and . . . I mean the relatively conscious whites and the relatively conscious blacks, who must, like lovers, insist on, or create, the consciousness of the others—do not falter in our duty now, we may be able, handful that we are, to end the racial nightmare, and achieve our country, and change the history of the world.

James Baldwin

Two ideas puzzled me deeply as a child growing up in Brooklyn during the 1930s in what today would be called an integrated neighborhood. One of them was that all Jews were rich; the other was that all Negroes were persecuted. These ideas had appeared in print; therefore they must be true. My own experience and the evidence of my senses told me they were not true, but that only confirmed what a daydreaming boy in the provinces—for the lower-class neighborhoods of New York belong as surely to the provinces as any rural town in North Dakota—discovers very early: *his* experience is unreal and the evidence of his senses is not to be trusted. Yet even a boy with a head full of fantasies incongruously synthesized out of Hollywood movies and English novels cannot altogether deny the reality of his own experience—especially when there is so much deprivation in that experience. Nor can he altogether gainsay the evidence of his own senses—especially such evidence of the senses as comes from being repeatedly beaten up, robbed, and in general hated, terrorized, and humiliated.

And so for a long time I puzzled to think that Jews were supposed to be rich when the only Jews I knew were poor, and that Negroes were supposed to be persecuted when it was the Negroes who were doing the only persecuting I knew about—and doing it, moreover, to *me*. During the early years of the war, when my older sister joined a left-wing youth organization, I remember my astonishment at hearing her passionately denounce my father for thinking that Jews were worse off than Negroes. To me, at the age of twelve, it seemed very clear that Negroes were better off than Jews—indeed, than *all* whites. A city boy's world is contained within three or four square blocks, and in my world it was the whites, the Italians and Jews, who feared the Negroes, not the other way around. The Negroes were tougher than we were, more ruthless, and on the whole they were better athletes. What could it mean, then, to say that they were badly off and that we were more fortunate? Yet my sister's opinions, like print, were sacred, and when she told me about exploitation and economic forces I believed her. I believed her, but I was still afraid of Negroes. And I still hated them with all my heart.

It had not always been so that much I can recall from early childhood. When did it start, this fear and this hatred? There was a kindergarten in the local public school, and given the character of the neighborhood, at least half of the children in my class must have been Negroes. Yet I have no memory of being aware of color differences at that age, and I know from observing my own children that they attribute no significance to such differences even when they begin noticing them. I think there was a day—first grade? second grade?—when my best friend Carl hit me on the way home from school and announced that he wouldn't play with me any more because I had killed Jesus. When I ran home to my mother crying for an explanation, she told me not to pay any attention to such foolishness, and then in Yiddish she cursed the goyim and the *schwartzes*, the *schwartzes* and the goyim. Carl, it turned out, was a *schwartze*, and so was added a third to the categories into which people were mysteriously divided.

Sometimes I wonder whether this is a true memory at all. It is blazingly vivid, but perhaps it never happened: can anyone really remember back to the age of six? There is no uncertainty in my mind, however, about the years that followed. Carl and I hardly ever spoke, though we met in school every day up through the eighth or ninth grade. There would be embarrassed moments of catching his eye or of his catching mine—for whatever it was that had attracted us to one another as very small children remained alive in spite of the fantastic barrier of hostility that had grown up between us, suddenly and out of nowhere. Nevertheless, friendship would have been impossible, and even if it had been possible, it would have been unthinkable. About that, there was nothing anyone could do by the time we were eight years old.

Item: The orphanage across the street is torn down, a city housing project begins to rise in its place, and on the marvelous vacant lot next to the old orphanage they are building a playground. Much excitement and anticipation as opening day draws near. Mayor LaGuardia himself comes to dedicate this great gesture of public benevolence. He speaks of neighborliness and borrowing cups of sugar, and of the playground he says that children of all races, colors, and creeds will learn to live together in harmony. A week later, some of us are swatting flies on the playground's inadequate little ball field. A gang of Negro kids, pretty much our own age, enter from the other side and order us out of the park. We refuse, proudly and indignantly, with superb masculine fervor. There is a fight, they win, and we retreat, half whimpering, half with bravado. My first nauseating experience of cowardice. And my first appalled realization that there are people in the world who do not seem to be afraid of anything, who act as though they have nothing to lose. Thereafter the playground becomes a battleground, sometimes quiet, sometimes the scene of athletic competition between Them and Us. But rocks are thrown as often as baseballs. Gradually we abandon the place and use the streets instead. The streets are safer, though we do not admit this to ourselves. We are not, after all, sissies—that most dreaded epithet of an American boyhood.

Item: I am standing alone in front of the building in which I live. It is late afternoon and getting dark. That day in school the teacher had asked a surly Negro boy named Quentin a question he was unable to answer. As usual I had waved my hand eagerly ("Be a good boy, get good marks, be smart, go to college, become a doctor") and, the right answer bursting from my lips, I was held up lovingly by the teacher as an example to the class. I had seen Quentin's face—a very dark, very cruel, very Oriental-looking face—harden, and there had been enough threat in his eyes to make me run all the way home for fear that he might catch me outside.

Now, standing idly in front of my own house, I see him approaching from the project accompanied by his little brother who is carrying a baseball bat and wearing a grin of malicious anticipation. As in a nightmare, I am trapped. The surroundings are secure and familiar, but terror is suddenly present and there is no one around to help. I am locked to the spot. I will not cry out or run away like a sissy, and I stand there, my heart wild, my throat clogged. He walks up, hurls the familiar epithet ("Hey, mo'f——r"), and to my surprise only pushes me. It is a violent push, but not a punch. A push is not as serious as a punch. Maybe I can still back out without entirely losing my dignity. Maybe I can still say, "Hey, c'mon Quentin, whaddya wanna do *that* for? I dint do nothin' to *you*," and walk away, not too rapidly. Instead, before I can stop myself, I push him back—a token gesture—and I say, "Cut that out, I don't wanna fight, I ain't got nothin' to fight about." As I turn to walk back into the building, the corner of my eye catches the motion of the bat his little brother has handed him. I try to duck, but the bat crashes colored lights into my head.

The next thing I know, my mother and sister are standing over me, both of them hysterical. My sister—she who was later to join the "progressive" youth organization—is shouting for the police and screaming imprecations at those dirty little black bastards. They take me upstairs, the doctor comes, the police come. I tell them that the boy who did it was a stranger, that he had been trying to get money from me. They do not believe me, but I am too scared to give them Quentin's name. When I return to school a few days later, Quentin avoids my eyes. He knows that I have not squealed, and he is ashamed. I try to feel proud, but in my heart I know that it was fear of what his friends might do to me that had kept me silent, and not the code of the street.

Item: There is an athletic meet in which the whole of our junior high school is participating. I am in one of the seventh-grade rapid-advance classes, and "segregation" has now set in with a vengeance. In the last three or four years of the elementary school from which we have just graduated, each grade had been divided into three classes, according to "intelligence." (In the earlier grades the divisions had either been arbitrary or else unrecognized by us as having anything to do with brains.) These divisions by IQ, or however it was arranged, had resulted in a preponderance of Jews in the "1" classes and a corresponding preponderance of Negroes in the "3's," with the Italians split unevenly along the spectrum. At least a few Negroes had always made the "1's," just as there had always been a few Jewish kids among the "3's" and more among the "2's" (where Italians dominated). But the junior high's rapid-advance class of which I am now a member is overwhelmingly Jewish and entirely white—except for a shy lonely Negro girl with light skin and reddish hair.

The athletic meet takes place in a city-owned stadium far from the school. It is an important event to which a whole day is given over. The winners are to get those precious little medallions stamped with the New York City emblem that can be screwed into a belt and that prove the wearer to be a distinguished personage. I am a fast runner, and so I am assigned the position of anchor man on my class's team in the relay race. There are three other seventh-grade teams in the race, two of them all Negro, as ours is all white. One of the all-Negro teams is very tall—their anchor man waiting silently next to me on the line looks years older than I am, and I do not recognize him. He is the first to get the baton and crosses the finishing line in a walk. Our team comes in second, but a few minutes later we are declared the winners, for it has been discovered that the anchor man on the first-place team is not a member of the class. We are awarded the medallions, and the following day our home-room teacher makes a speech about how proud she is of us for being superior athletes as well as superior students. We want to believe we deserve the praise, but we know we could not have won even if the other class had not cheated.

That afternoon, walking home, I am waylaid and surrounded by five Negroes, among whom is the anchor man of the disqualified team. "Gimme my medal, mo'f——r," he grunts. I do not have it with me and I tell him so. "Anyway, it ain't yours," I say foolishly. He calls me a liar on both counts and pushes me up against the wall on which we sometimes play handball. "Gimme my mo'f——n' medal," he says again. I repeat that I have left it home. "Let's search the li'l mo'f——r," one of them suggests, "he prolly got it *hid* in his mo'f——n' *pants.*" My panic is now unmanageable. (How many times had I been surrounded like this and asked in soft tones, "Len' me a nickel, boy." How many times had I been called a liar for pleading poverty and pushed around, or searched, or beaten up, unless there happened to be someone in the marauding gang like Carl who liked me across that enormous divide of hatred and who would therefore say, "Aaah, c'mon, le's git someone else, *this* boy ain't got no money on 'im.") I scream at them through tears of rage and self-contempt, "Keep your f——n' filthy lousy black hands offa me! I swear I'll get the cops." This is all they need to hear, and the five of them set upon me. They bang me around, mostly in the stomach and on the arms and shoulders, and when several adults loitering near the candy store down the block notice what is going on and begin to shout, they run off and away.

I do not tell my parents about the incident. My teammates, who have also been waylaid, each by a gang led by his opposite number from the disqualified team, have had their medallions taken from them, and they never squeal either. For days, I walk home in terror, expecting to be caught again, but nothing happens. The medallion is put away into a drawer, never to be worn by anyone.

Obviously experiences like these have always been a common feature of childhood life in working-class and immigrant neighborhoods, and Negroes do not necessarily figure in them. Wherever, and in whatever combination, they have lived together in the cities, kids of different groups have been at war, beating up and being beaten up: micks against kikes against wops against spicks against polacks. And even relatively homogeneous areas have not been spared the warring of the young: one block against another, one gang (called in my day, in a pathetic effort at gentility, an "SAC," or social-athletic club) against another. But the Negro-white conflict had—and no doubt still has—a special intensity and was conducted with a ferocity unmatched by intramural white battling.

In my own neighborhood, a good deal of animosity existed between the Italian kids (most of whose parents were immigrants from Sicily) and the Jewish kids (who came largely from East European immigrant families). Yet everyone had friends, sometimes close friends, in the other "camp," and we often visited one another's strange-smelling houses, if not for meals, then for glasses of milk, and occasionally for some special event like a wedding or a wake. If it happened that we divided into warring factions and did battle, it would invariably be halfhearted and soon patched up. Our parents, to be sure, had nothing to do with one another and were mutually suspicious and hostile. But we, the kids, who all spoke Yiddish or Italian at home, were Americans, or New Yorkers, or Brooklyn boys:

we shared a culture, the culture of the street, and at least for a while this culture proved to be more powerful than the opposing cultures of the home.

Why, *why* should it have been so different as between the Negroes and us? How was it borne in upon us so early, white and black alike, that we were enemies beyond any possibility of reconciliation? Why did we hate one another so?

I suppose if I tried, I could answer those questions more or less adequately from the perspective of what I have since learned. I could draw upon James Baldwin—what better witness is there?—to describe the sense of entrapment that poisons the soul of the Negro with hatred for the white man whom he knows to be his jailer. On the other side, if I wanted to understand how the white man comes to hate the Negro, I could call upon the psychologists who have spoken of the guilt that white Americans feel toward Negroes and that turns into hatred for lack of acknowledging itself as guilt. These are plausible answers and certainly there is truth in them. Yet when I think back upon my own experience of the Negro and his of me, I find myself troubled and puzzled, much as I was as a child when I heard that all Jews were rich and all Negroes persecuted. How could the Negroes in my neighborhood have regarded the whites across the street and around the corner as jailers? On the whole, the whites were not so poor as the Negroes, but they were quite poor enough, and the years were years of Depression. As for white hatred of the Negro, how could guilt have had anything to do with it? What share had these Italian and Jewish immigrants in the enslavement of the Negro? What share had they—downtrodden people themselves breaking their own necks to eke out a living—in the exploitation of the Negro?

No, I cannot believe that we hated each other back there in Brooklyn because they thought of us as jailers and we felt guilty toward them. But does it matter, given the fact that we all went through an unrepresentative confrontation? I think it matters profoundly, for if we managed the job of hating each other so well without benefit of the aids to hatred that are supposedly at the root of this madness everywhere else, it must mean that the madness is not yet properly understood. I am far from pretending that I understand it, but I would insist that no view of the problem will begin to approach the truth unless it can account for a case like the one I have been trying to describe. Are the elements of any such view available to us?

At least two, I would say, are. One of them is a point we frequently come upon in the work of James Baldwin, and the other is a related point always stressed by psychologists who have studied the mechanisms of prejudice. Baldwin tells us that one of the reasons Negroes hate the white man is that the white man refuses to *look* at him: the Negro knows that in white eyes all Negroes are alike; they are faceless and therefore not altogether human. The psychologists, in their turn, tell us that the white man hates the Negro because he tends to project those wild impulses that he fears in himself onto an alien group which he then punishes with his contempt. What Baldwin does *not* tell us, however, is that the principle of facelessness is a two-way street and can operate in both directions with no difficulty at all. Thus, in my neighborhood in Brooklyn, *I* was as faceless to the Negroes as they were to me, and if they hated me because I never looked at them, I must also have hated them for never looking at *me*. To the Negroes, my white skin was enough to define me as the enemy, and in a war it is only the uniform that counts and not the person.

So with the mechanism of projection that the psychologists talk about: it too works in both directions at once. There is no question that the psychologists are right about what the Negro represents symbolically to the white man. For me as a child the life lived on the other side of the playground and down the block on Ralph Avenue seemed the very embodiment of the values of the street—free, independent, reckless, brave, masculine, erotic. I put the word *erotic* last, though it is usually stressed above all others, because in fact it came last, in consciousness as in importance. What mainly counted for me about Negro kids of my own age was that they were "bad boys." There were plenty of bad boys among the whites—this was, after all, a neighborhood with a long tradition of crime as a career open to aspiring talents—but the Negroes were *really* bad, bad in a way that beckoned to one, and made one feel inadequate. *We* all went home every day for a lunch of spinach-and-potatoes; *they* roamed around during lunch hour, munching on candy bars. In winter *we* had to wear itchy woolen hats and mittens and cumbersome galoshes; *they* were bareheaded and loose as they pleased. *We* rarely played hooky, or got into serious trouble in school, for all our street-corner bravado; *they* were defiant, forever staying out (to do what delicious things?), forever making disturbances in class and in the halls, forever being sent to the principal and returning uncowed. But most important of all, they were *tough;* beautifully, enviably tough, not giving a damn for anyone or anything. To hell with the teacher, the truant officer, the cop; to hell with the whole of the adult world that held *us* in its grip and that we never had the courage to rebel against except sporadically and in petty ways.

This is what I saw and envied and feared in the Negro: this is what finally made him faceless to me, though some of it, of course, was actually there. (The psychologists also tell us that the alien group which becomes the object of a projection will tend to respond by trying to live up to what is expected of them.) But what, on his side, did the Negro see in me that made me faceless to *him?* Did he envy me my lunches of spinach-and-potatoes and my itchy woolen caps and my prudent behavior in the face of authority, as I envied him his noontime candy bars and his bare head in winter and his magnificent rebelliousness? Did those lunches and caps spell for him the prospect of power and riches in the future? Did they mean that there were possibilities open to me that were denied to him? Very likely they did. But if so, one also supposes that he feared the impulses within himself toward submission to authority no less powerfully than I feared the impulses in myself toward defiance. If I represented the jailer to him, it was not because I was oppressing him or keeping him down: it was because I symbolized for him the dangerous and probably

pointless temptation toward greater repression, just as he symbolized for me the equally perilous tug toward greater freedom.
I personally was to be rewarded for this repression with a new
and better life in the future, but how many of my friends paid
an even higher price and were given only gall in return.

We have it on the authority of James Baldwin that all
Negroes hate whites. I am trying to suggest that on their side
all whites—all American whites, that is—are sick in their
feelings about Negroes. There are Negroes, no doubt, who
would say that Baldwin is wrong, but I suspect them of being
less honest than he is, just as I suspect whites of self-deception
who tell me they have no special feeling toward Negroes.
Special feelings about color are a contagion to which white
Americans seem susceptible even when there is nothing in their
background to account for the susceptibility. Thus everywhere
we look today in the North, we find the curious phenomenon
of white middle-class liberals with no previous personal experience of Negroes—people to whom Negroes have always been
faceless in virtue rather than faceless in vice—discovering that
their abstract commitment to the cause of Negro rights will
not stand the test of a direct confrontation. We find such people
fleeing in droves to the suburbs as the Negro population in the
inner city grows; and when they stay in the city we find them
sending their children to private school rather than to the
"integrated" public school in the neighborhood. We find them
resisting the demand that gerrymandered school districts be
rezoned for the purpose of overcoming de facto segregation;
we find them judiciously considering whether the Negroes (for
their own good, of course) are not perhaps pushing too hard;
we find them clucking their tongues over Negro militancy; we
find them speculating on the question of whether there may
not, after all, be something in the theory that the races are
biologically different; we find them saying that it will take a
very long time for Negroes to achieve full equality, no matter
what anyone does; we find them deploring the rise of black
nationalism and expressing the solemn hope that the leaders of

the Negro community will discover ways of containing the impatience and incipient violence within the Negro ghettos.

But that is by no means the whole story; there is also the phenomenon of what Kenneth Rexroth once called "crow-jimism." There are the broken-down white boys like Vivaldo Moore in Baldwin's *Another Country* who go to Harlem in search of sex or simply to brush up against something that looks like primitive vitality, and who are so often punished by the Negroes they meet for crimes that they would have been the last ever to commit and of which they themselves have been as sorry victims as any of the Negroes who take it out on them. There are the writers and intellectuals and artists who romanticize Negroes and pander to them, assuming a guilt that is not properly theirs. And there are all the white liberals who permit Negroes to blackmail them into adopting a double standard of moral judgment, and who lend themselves—again assuming the responsibility for crimes they never committed—to cunning and contemptuous exploitation by Negroes they employ or try to befriend.

And what about me? What kind of feelings do I have about Negroes today? What happened to me, from Brooklyn, who grew up fearing and envying and hating Negroes? Now that Brooklyn is behind me, do I fear them and envy them and hate them still? The answer is yes, but not in the same proportions and certainly not in the same way. I now live on the Upper West Side of Manhattan, where there are many Negroes and many Puerto Ricans, and there are nights when I experience the old apprehensiveness again, and there are streets that I avoid when I am walking in the dark, as there were streets that I avoided when I was a child. I find that I am not afraid of Puerto Ricans, but I cannot restrain my nervousness whenever I pass a group of Negroes standing in front of a bar or sauntering down the street. I know now, as I did not know when I was a child, that power is on my side, that the police are working for me and not for them. And knowing this I feel ashamed and guilty, like the good liberal I have grown up to be. Yet the twinges of fear and the resentment they bring and the self-contempt they arouse are not to be gainsaid.

But envy? Why envy? And hatred? Why hatred? Here again the intensities have lessened and everything has been complicated and qualified by the guilts and the resulting over-compensations that are the heritage of the enlightened middle-class world of which I am now a member. Yet just as in childhood I envied Negroes for what seemed to me their superior masculinity, so I envy them today for what seems to me their superior physical grace and beauty. I have come to value physical grace very highly, and I am now capable of aching with all my being when I watch a Negro couple on the dance floor, or a Negro playing baseball or basketball. They are on the kind of terms with their own bodies that I should like to be on with mine, and for that precious quality they seem blessed to me.

The hatred I still feel for Negroes is the hardest of all the old feelings to face or admit, and it is the most hidden and the most overlarded by the conscious attitudes into which I have succeeded in willing myself. It no longer has, as for me it once did, any cause or justification (except, perhaps, that I am constantly being denied my right to an honest expression of the things I earned the right as a child to feel). How, then, do I know that this hatred has never entirely disappeared? I know it from the insane rage that can stir in me at the thought of Negro anti-Semitism; I know it from the disgusting prurience that can stir in me at the sight of a mixed couple; and I know it from the violence that can stir in me whenever I encounter that special brand of paranoid touchiness to which many Negroes are prone.

This, then, is where I am; it is not exactly where I think all other white liberals are, but it cannot be so very far away either. And it is because I am convinced that we white Americans are—for whatever reason, it no longer matters—so twisted and sick in our feelings about Negroes that I despair of the present push toward integration. If the pace of progress were not a factor here, there would perhaps be no cause for despair: time and the law and even the international political situation are on the side of the Negroes, and ultimately, therefore, victory—of a sort, anyway—must come. But from everything we have learned from observers who ought to know, pace has become as important to the Negroes as substance. They want equality and they want it *now*, and the white world is yielding to their demand only as much and as fast as it is absolutely being compelled to do. The Negroes know this in the most concrete terms imaginable, and it is thus becoming increasingly difficult to buy them off with rhetoric and promises and pious assurances of support. And so within the Negro community we find more and more people declaring—as Harold R. Isaacs recently put it in these pages*—that they want *out*: people who say that integration will never come, or that it will take a hundred or a thousand years to come, or that it will come at too high a price in suffering and struggle for the pallid and sodden life of the American middle class that at the very best it may bring.

The most numerous, influential, and dangerous movement that has grown out of Negro despair with the goal of integration is, of course, the Black Muslims. This movement, whatever else we may say about it, must be credited with one enduring achievement: it inspired James Baldwin to write an essay† which deserves to be placed among the classics of our language. Everything Baldwin has ever been trying to tell us is distilled here into a statement of overwhelming persuasiveness and prophetic magnificence. Baldwin's message is and always has been simple. It is this: "Color is not a human or personal reality; it is a political reality." And Baldwin's demand is correspondingly simple. color must be forgotten, lest we all be smited with a "vengeance that does not really depend on, and cannot really be executed by, any person or organization, and that cannot be prevented by any police force or army: historical vengeance, a cosmic vengeance based on the law that we

*"Integration and the Negro Mood," *Commentary*, December 1962.
†Originally published in *The New Yorker* under the title "Letter from a Region in My Mind," subsequently published in book form (along with a new introduction) under the title *The Fire Next Time*.

recognize when we say, 'Whatever goes up must come down.' " The Black Muslims Baldwin portrays as a sign and a warning to the intransigent white world. They come to proclaim how deep is the Negro's disaffection with the white world and all its works, and Baldwin implies that no American Negro can fail to respond somewhere in his being to their message: that the white man is the devil, that Allah has doomed him to destruction, and that the black man is about to inherit the earth. Baldwin of course knows that this nightmare inversion of the racism from which the black man has suffered can neither win nor even point to the neighborhood in which victory might be located. For in his view the neighborhood of victory lies in exactly the opposite direction: the transcendence of color through love.

Yet the tragic fact is that love is not the answer to hate—not in the world of politics, at any rate. Color is indeed a political rather than a human or a personal reality and if politics (which is to say power) has made it into a human and a personal reality, then only politics (which is to say power) can unmake it once again. But the way of politics is slow and bitter, and as impatience on the one side is matched by a setting of the jaw on the other, we move closer and closer to an explosion and blood may yet run in the streets.

Will this madness in which we are all caught never find a resting-place? Is there never to be an end to it? In thinking about the Jews I have often wondered whether their survival as a distinct group was worth one hair on the head of a single infant. Did the Jews have to survive so that six million innocent people should one day be burned in the ovens of Auschwitz? It is a terrible question and no one, not God himself, could ever answer it to my satisfaction. And when I think about the Negroes in America and about the image of integration as a state in which the Negroes would take their rightful place as another of the protected minorities in a pluralistic society, I wonder whether they really believe in their hearts that such a state can actually be attained, and if so *why* they should wish to survive as a distinct group. I think I know why the Jews once wished to survive (though I am less certain as to why we still do): they not only believed that God had given them no choice, but they were tied to a memory of past glory and a dream of imminent redemption. What does the American Negro have that might correspond to this? His past is a stigma, his color is a stigma, and his vision of the future is the hope of erasing the stigma by making color irrelevant, by making it disappear as a fact of consciousness.

I share this hope, but I cannot see how it will ever be realized unless color does *in fact* disappear: and that means not integration, it means assimilation, it means—let the brutal word come out—miscegenation. The Black Muslims, like their racist counterparts in the white world, accuse the "so-called Negro leaders" of secretly pursuing miscegenation as a goal. The racists are wrong, but I wish they were right, for I believe that the wholesale merging of the two races is the most desirable alternative for everyone concerned. I am not claiming that this alternative can be pursued programmatically or that it is immediately feasible as a solution; obviously there are even greater barriers to its achievement than to the achievement of integration. What I am saying, however, is that in my opinion the Negro problem can be solved in this country in no other way.

I have told the story of my own twisted feelings about Negroes here, and of how they conflict with the moral convictions I have since developed, in order to assert that such feelings must be acknowledged as honestly as possible so that they can be controlled and ultimately disregarded in favor of the convictions. It is wrong for a man to suffer because of the color of his skin. Beside that clichéd proposition of liberal thought, what argument can stand and be respected? If the arguments are the arguments of feeling, they must be made to yield; and one's own soul is not the worst place to begin working a huge social transformation. Not so long ago, it used to be asked of white liberals, "Would you like your sister to marry one?" When I was a boy and my sister was still unmarried, I would certainly have said no to that question. But now I am a man, my sister is already married, and I have daughters. If I were to be asked today whether I would like a daughter of mine "to marry one," I would have to answer: "No, I wouldn't *like* it at all. I would rail and rave and rant and tear my hair. And then I hope I would have the courage to curse myself for raving and ranting, and to give her my blessing. How dare I withhold it at the behest of the child I once was and against the man I now have a duty to be?"

POSTSCRIPT (1993)

This book is not the first time "My Negro Problem—and Ours" has been treated as an event in the history of black-Jewish relations. Yet even though I spoke explicitly as a Jew throughout, and even though in the concluding section I drew a comparison between blacks and Jews, I was writing not as a Jew but as a white liberal; and it was as a statement about liberal feeling in general, rather than about Jewish feeling in particular, that the essay was generally read upon its original publication in 1963. In later years, with the spread of black anti-Semitism, "My Negro Problem" began being cited as evidence that "the Jews" were hypocritical in their professions of support of black aspirations and demands. This was in fact an egregious and slanderous misrepresentation of the American Jewish community, which (even in the face of the rising tide of black hostility to Jews) has to this day remained far more sympathetic to blacks than any other white ethnic group. It was also a distortion of what I was saying—though that distortion, and the political purposes it has served, may be one of the factors which has kept the essay alive.

Other factors which may have kept it alive have served other purposes. When "My Negro Problem" first came out, a critic said that there was something in it to offend everyone. He was right. Integrationists, white and black alike—who were the dominant force in the civil rights movement at the time—took offense at my prediction that integration was not going to work. Black nationalists—who were mounting an increasingly influential challenge to the integrationists—took offense at my slighting references to the history and culture of their people as nothing more than a "stigma." And Jews were offended by my willingness to entertain the possibility that the survival of the Jewish people might not have been worth the suffering it had entailed.

As the years wore on, however, a curious reversal occurred. Now it began to seem that "My Negro Problem" had something in it to please, if not everyone, then a growing body of sentiment both among blacks and whites. This something was the idea that all whites were incorrigibly racist. To be sure, I had not exactly endorsed that idea. What I had actually said was that all whites were sick and twisted in their feelings about blacks. But to most readers, it seems, this formulation was the functional equivalent of a charge of universal white racism. It thereby lent itself nicely to the view that *the* "Negro problem"—indeed the only Negro problem—was external oppression, and that nothing blacks themselves did or failed to do made, or could ever make, more than a trivial difference.

The almost complete abdication of black responsibility and the commensurately total dependence on government engendered by so obsessive and exclusive a fixation on white racism has been calamitous. It has undermined the very qualities that are essential to the achievement of independence and self-respect, and it has spawned policies that have had the perverse effect of further discouraging the growth of such qualities. It has thereby contributed mightily to the metastasis of the black underclass—a development which, in addition to destroying countless black lives, has subjected more and more whites to experiences like the ones I described going through as a child in "My Negro Problem."

In 1963 those descriptions were very shocking to most white liberals. In their eyes Negroes were all long-suffering and noble victims of the kind who had become familiar through the struggles of the civil rights movement in the South—the "heroic period" of the movement, as one of its most heroic leaders, Bayard Rustin, called it. While none of my white critics went so far as to deny the truthfulness of the stories I told, they themselves could hardly imagine being afraid of Negroes (how could they when the only Negroes most of them knew personally were maids and cleaning women?). In any case they very much disliked the emphasis I placed on black thuggery and aggression.

Today, when black-on-white violence is much more common than it was then, many white readers could easily top those stories with worse. And yet even today few of them would be willing to speak truthfully in public about their entirely rational fear of black violence and black crime. Telling the truth about blacks remains dangerous to one's reputation: to use the now famous phrase I once appropriated from D. H. Lawrence in talking about ambition, the fear of blacks has become the dirty little secret of our political culture. And since a dirty little secret breeds hypocrisy and cant in those who harbor it, I suppose it can still be said that most whites are sick and twisted in their feelings about blacks, albeit in a very different sense from the way they were in 1963.

The opening section of "My Negro Problem," then, is perhaps even more relevant today than it was then. I cannot, however, say the same for other parts of the essay. Obviously I was for the most part right in predicting that integration as it was naively envisaged in those days (blacks, with discriminatory barriers lowered, more and more moving on their own individual merits into the middle class and working and living harmoniously together with whites in all areas of society) would not come about in even the remotely foreseeable future. The one and perhaps the only institution in which the old integrationist ideal has been fully realized is—to the surprise and chagrin of many liberals—the army. Almost everywhere else—to my own surprise and chagrin—a diseased mutation of integrationism, taking the form of a quota system and euphemistically known as affirmative action, went on to triumph in the end.

It has been a bitter triumph, attained at the cost of new

poisons of white resentment and black self-doubt injected into the relations between the races. True, more blacks are economically better off today than they were in 1963, and the black community has more political power than it did then. But at the same time relations between whites and blacks have deteriorated. Gone on the whole are the interracial friendships and the interracial political alliances that were very widespread thirty years ago. In their place we have the nearly impassable gulfs of suspicion and hostility that are epitomized by the typical college dining hall of today where black students insist on sitting at tables of their own and whites either are happy to accept this segregated arrangement or feel hurt at being repulsed.

Then there is the other great cost—the damage done to the precious American principle (honored though it admittedly once was more in the breach than in the observance) of treating individuals as individuals rather than as members of a group. The systematic violation of that principle as applied to blacks has opened the way to its violation for the sake of other "disadvantaged minorities" (a category that now includes women, who are a majority, and is beginning to include homosexuals, who are as a group economically prosperous). And so the dangerous and destructive balkanization of our culture and our society proceeds.

With respect to blacks, this development grew out of the unexpected cooptation of black-nationalist passions by the ideology of reverse discrimination. The Black Muslims are still out there preaching separatism, but their old driving force—the call for "black power"—is now firmly harnessed to the integrationist mutation. This mutated integrationism, moreover, has gone beyond demanding that blacks be force-fed by government coercion into jobs and universities and professional schools in proportion to their numbers in the population. It now demands that districts be gerrymandered to ensure the election of black legislators; and the next step seems to be government coercion to ensure that these black legislators will be "authentic" (i.e., committed to the endless extension of reverse discrimination). Like meritocratic standards, elections may soon be denounced as subtle instruments of "institutional racism."

Failing to anticipate these developments in "My Negro Problem," I found no escape from the trap I was describing except the wholesale merging of the two races. And because my objective in writing the essay was to speak the truth as I saw it and to go where it took me no matter what the consequences, it would have been a cowardly betrayal to shrink from the conclusion to which my analysis inexorably led. Yet if I did the right thing from the perspective of intellectual coherence and literary fitness, I was wrong to think that miscegenation could ever result in the elimination of color "as a fact of consciousness," if for no other reason than that (as Ralph Ellison bitingly remarked to me) the babies born of such marriages would still be considered black.

Why, then, have I permitted "My Negro Problem—and Ours" to be reprinted here, as I have dozens of times before, without revision? The answer, frankly, is that I have always been proud of it as a piece of writing (and I like to believe that its virtues as a literary essay have been another, and possibly even the main, factor in keeping it alive). It is in the nature of a successfully realized literary work that it achieves an existence independent of its author, and so it is with "My Negro Problem—and Ours." Long ago it ceased belonging to me, and for better or worse I feel that I have no right to tamper with it or to kill it off. I do, however, hope to write at length about all these issues again someday—if, that is, I can ever muster the kind of nerve that came very hard even to my much younger and more reckless self.

Joe Wood

The Problem Negro and Other Tales

Joe Wood is the editor of Malcolm X: In Our Own Image *and is a columnist for* The Village Voice. *He wishes to thank Dan Abrahamson, Lisa Kennedy, and Adolph Reed for reading drafts of this essay.*

 I.

We were the end of the line. We were the children of the immigrants who had camped at the city's back door, in New York's rawest, remotest, cheapest ghetto, enclosed on one side by the Canarsie flats and on the other by the hallowed middle-class districts that showed the way to New York. "New York" was what we put last on our address, but first in thinking of the others around us. *They* were New York, the Gentiles, America; we were Brownsville—*Brunzvil*, as the old folks said—the dust of the earth to all Jews with money, and notoriously a place that measured all success by our skill in getting away from it. So that when poor Jews left, even Negroes, as we said, found it easy to settle on the margins of Brownsville. . . .

—Alfred Kazin, *A Walker in the City*

Dan watches *L.A. Law* and I turn my glass around and around. I go over the events once more. I remember being a smart black boy on winter break from private school: I read a lot during school breaks; I was a curious and obedient boy who paid close attention to his parents' exhortations about the improvement of the race—I had a role to play. My parents were determined to see their children become doctors or lawyers or captains of industry or something to help black people be proud, so I tried hard, very hard—I brought all my books to bed. My mother drove my sister and me to the library and my father drove us to private school and when I lay down I would open the books, the pages covering my feet and legs and stomach like new bandages, leaves from the Bible, Edith Wharton, Malcolm X, *The New Republic,* James Joyce, Yukio Mishima, Gerard Manley Hopkins, James Baldwin, Spider Man, Tom Wolfe, *Playboy,* Maya Angelou, John le Carré, *The New York Times,* Kurt Vonnegut—they would wrap my limbs and torso like gauze.

I recall: beneath a sheet of open pages when I reached for a volume of essays for high school students and then I opened to the contents page and found the one called "My Negro Problem—and Ours" by Norman Podhoretz. It was the late 1970s and the essay was strictly '63 so it was old news by the time my young mind got to it but it was still relevant I found out soon as I turned the crisp pages and began to read and began to think and this is where another kind of *black* comes in. I had a pillow in the small of my back, I was feeling safe from the cold, with the winter outside and the warm yellow light from my lamp, and a few minutes later as the words, sentences, paragraphs flowed on I began to notice the black blotch hiding in this essay like a fly in the soup, underneath the ordered surface: a black madness. Easy to overlook at first, but it persisted—you could almost smell it, the monster, it had menaced Podhoretz; I watched it rise again and use its black fists on the young Norman, young and innocent: how *white* it made young Norman, white with fear and the strange virtue brutality lends its victims, white as Fay Wray; how *white* it made the older, "liberal" Podhoretz, this black thing haunting his thoughts, how white it made the reader as we witnessed and read about our Negro problem, our public madness, how white it made you and me.

I love Dan. He lives in Seattle now and that's the main reason I'm out here as I write to you, gentle reader. This place is not like New York, the city where Podhoretz and I grew up. Seattle is unabashedly clean and nice with fresh-faced happy residents and green and flowery gardens for trimming—even the ghettos here seem pleasant and charming and on the best days only a little haunted. There is next to no evidence of black people anywhere. Negroes either keep silent or are kept so, which could also be said of Asians or Jews or most any other demographic category, with the exception of that humongous and empty standard, "white." How plain a contrast to the city where Podhoretz wrote and I first read his essay, where Jew versus black and black versus Jew was the featured story of our last mayoral campaign. This afternoon, as I read Podhoretz's essay a second time after so many years, Seattle's clean and fresh whiteness made New York smell sharp. I could sense on the xeroxed pages the odor of my great city, and it filled the room, and now Norman Podhoretz's Jewishness was very apparent indeed.

Let me explain. There I was: lying on my bed in my parents' home in December underneath the books and warm light when I first received Podhoretz's revelation about the threat posed by blacks. I remember considering my own ability to threaten others physically. I had never been gifted in this regard; I was not very good at sports, even the ones I played. Senior year my soccer coach named me captain despite the votes of my teammates. I am not sure why he did this and I never worked up the courage to ask; the captainship marked the peak of my sporting life and I wasn't eager to know anything that would compel me to give up the honor, earned or not. Maybe being captain signified strength, or someone's recognition of my physical strength—this was important to me, a boy who had one eye on college, who wanted to be well-rounded for the recruiters at Yale and Harvard and Princeton. My second eye was firmly locked on myself. I was a boy who chose to model myself on the boys I saw on television and in the neighborhood and in my home: I thought myself a defender and warrior-boy who would become a man someday.

It was foolishness but it was me. I never did much fighting with my fists; early on I learned how effective words can be in determining the course of a physical fight, how they can take away someone's will to fight: this skill was taught by friends, all black, from my neighborhood. We prized the power of mean talk. I carried this knowledge across town to school, secretly, and kept it close while I sat in my nearly all-white classes and half-readied for some apocalyptic showdown. I waited. Which may sound strange coming from a fairly popular student at the top of his class, but it's true: I was never so weak as to let myself get beaten up by anyone at that school. In third grade I promised myself I would never be fucked up by a whiteboy because *I* had the strength since I was black and I could always tap that strength if I had to, that blackness, cupped in my mind as one protects a flame or a personal god, my precious blackness.

Gentle reader, I do realize the irony in this cupping—yes, I certainly was trying to use Massa's tools to take apart Massa's house. Please consider the absurdity of my situation. I believed my parents when they warned of racism even though I hoped and hoped they were wrong. Surely you understand why I monitored white hostility only in secret, even from myself. I couldn't have survived at Riverdale for ten years constantly contemplating my schoolmates' unspoken fears. The extent to which most whites feared black people and in particular black males remained invisible to me—I blindly absorbed the dreadful blackness they had in their minds and I blended it with my parents' pride and I worshiped this amalgam. My blindness was ensured by other factors: our family's Protestant prudery, my own sexual inexperience, my interest in the frippery of machismo. The bottom line, though, was a perfect blindness, and it kept me from facing for a long time what a big deal some whites made of the blackness of my dick.

Please be patient. I'm only trying to remember myself: this talk about my black dick—how unnecessary! Where does it lead?! Here: The digression serves a small point. I didn't quite understand how fervently some Americans worshiped the black dick until I read Podhoretz in my room on my bed that winter night and suddenly the astonishing specter of a black monster appeared beating Norman with his black fists and chasing him to whiteness. That monster was the very person I had never let myself be, and really couldn't perfectly be, a true captain of physical might, and now Norman was showing him to his reader, me, and you, as a con man would a stash of iron pyrites; this beast I had been given by my classmates, this thing I had transformed, secretly, was now being stuck by the writer directly in my face:

There is no question that the psychologists are right about what the Negro represents symbolically to the white man. For me as a child the life lived on the other side of the playground and down the block seemed the very embodiment of the values of the street—free, independent, reckless, brave, masculine, erotic. I put the word *erotic* last, though it is usually stressed above all others, because in fact it came last, in consciousness as in importance. What mainly counted for me about Negro kids of my own age was that they were "bad boys." There were plenty of bad boys among the whites—this was, after all, a neighborhood with a long tradition of crime as a career open to aspiring talents—but the Negroes were *really* bad, bad in a way that beckoned to one, and made one feel inadequate. *We* all went home every day for a lunch of spinach-and-potatoes; *they* roamed around during lunch hour, munching on candy bars. In winter *we* had to wear itchy woolen hats and mittens and cumbersome galoshes, *they* were bare-headed and loose as they pleased. *We* rarely played hooky, or got into serious trouble in school, for all our street-corner bravado; *they* were defiant, forever staying out (to do what delicious things?), forever making disturbances in class and in the halls, forever being sent to the principal and returning uncowed. But most important of all, they were *tough;* beautifully, enviably tough, not giving a damn for anyone or anything. To hell with the teacher, the truant officer, the cop; to hell with the whole of the adult world that held *us* in its grip and that we never had the courage to rebel against except sporadically and in petty ways.

This is what I saw and envied and feared in the Negro: this is what finally made him faceless to me. . . .

Podhoretz's faceless, tough god was, like mine, a black boy—an attractive, supermasculine and supertough figure who is, ultimately, indomitable. The power of this black boy's penis is so great, in fact, that later in the essay the writer practically gives his daughter away to it ("If I were to be asked today whether I would like a daughter of mine 'to marry one' . . ."). What was I, an actual black boy, to make of this portrait Podhoretz had drawn? The essay was the most articulate expression of white phallic anxiety I'd ever seen—I knew the moment I put it down that my blind days were over. Read "My Negro Problem" and you will, I assure you, recognize plenty of worn-out stuff: its puerile blend of macho white nationalism and embarrassed homoeroticism is nothing you haven't encountered before. Phallic panic is, of course, nothing new either; my interest in it then was as self-concerned as I've described, and as superficial. But what I suddenly noticed about the essay now, in Seattle, is less obvious, I think. For in looking at it here and smelling its New York odor I have come to believe that all of Podhoretz's pseudopsycho confessional stuff is a ruse, a prurient distraction he's presented to keep you from looking at what's really, for him, a much more important issue: the problem of his Jewishness.

Norman Podhoretz was born in 1930 in Brooklyn, in the wake of a great discussion about the course of Zionism, and more generally, the future of Jewry. Around the turn of the century, Jewish thinkers in Europe turned to the subject of Jewish "muscle," or physical strength, and its utility. Some intellectuals, influenced by the theories of German romanticists, argued for a less rationalistic, more physically attractive muscle; others for a more militaristic brawn; still others for a mystical tapping of Old Testament essence. Although ap-

proaches varied, a consensus for strength developed, and this
became a consistent element of Jewish thought. Targeting old
stereotypes of the emaciated and overintellectual Jew—lowly
inhabitant of the shtetl and the ghetto—Jewish thinkers basically agreed that a dose of toughness would help transform the
Jews into a modern people.

The consensus would not be confined to the narrow precincts of Europe's Jewish intelligentsia. Boats sent the new
thinking to America in the notebooks of students and activists;
the ideas surfaced in the cafeterias and subways and libraries
and kitchens of New York's Jewish ghettos. Anti-Semitism
flourished in America during the first decades of this century,
and Jewish muscularism was one way of responding to the
hostility; by 1942, as news of Nazi death camps started to
appear in the papers, ideas about Jewish strength influenced
almost everyone, left or right.

The thing I find most interesting about "My Negro Problem" today is how Podhoretz, putatively discussing his personal
anxiety about black men, does not so much as mention contemporary Jewish discourse on strength. Podhoretz seems to
suggest that his Jewish identity has next to nothing to do with
his thinking on race, but given the centrality of Jewishness
in Podhoretz's work (the essay was originally published in
Commentary), the omission is very strange. Perhaps when he
was young, Norman Podhoretz was not at all affected by ideas
about Jewish muscularism or the news of the death camps;
perhaps his memories of his youth and body were not subsequently shaped by these ideas, either. Anything is possible,
after all, and I would like to give Podhoretz the benefit of
the doubt.

But I can't. Podhoretz grew up reading everything, and
taking seriously the talk in the cafeterias and subways and
libraries and kitchens he visited—we know this. In the beginning of "My Negro Problem," Podhoretz remembers his sister
lecturing "about [the] exploitation and economic forces" menacing black people. He even says he believed her. . . . What we
don't know is what other talk he believed and how it informed

his "Negro problem." "To me, at the age of twelve, it seemed very clear that Negroes were better off than Jews—indeed, than all whites. A city boy's world is contained within three or four square blocks, and in my world it was the whites, the Italians and Jews, who feared the Negroes, not the other way around," he reports. Since this passage appears so early in the essay, one might reasonably expect the author to use some of the remainder of the piece relating his child's eye view of the conversation of local adults. What his parents said might explain how he could believe his sister and still consider black people "better off." Was it simply a boyish equation of physical strength with social might? It couldn't have been only that, though Podhoretz seems to say so. He gives a curiously decontextualized itemization of beatings at the hands of black boys; this list is supposed to explain why he hates blacks, and it constitutes the bulk of the essay. Toward the end Podhoretz admits that he still hates black people: witness "the insane rage that [is stirred] at the thought of Negro anti-Semitism." Many have, gentle reader, called "My Negro Problem" honest, but suspect with me that Norman chose and held on to his ideas about black people for reasons he does not confess in this essay, or other essays about black problems, or in his political memoirs, *Making It* and *Breaking Ranks*. There *is* a dark unsaid thing haunting "My Negro Problem"—and it demands that we shine light between the lines.

My theory is impossible to prove—it's impossible to determine Podhoretz's intentions. I can, however, compare his "honest" observations of history with history. Podhoretz was the son of immigrants who were only recent converts to whiteness. Stepping off the boat at Ellis Island with the sun settling into purple bloom behind and now the Statue of Liberty ahead, the Irish or Sicilians or the Eastern Jews who trekked here knew little about the notions "white" or "Negro." What they did know was how low they'd been back home and why they'd left in the first place. The Jews especially—they returned to Europe in the smallest numbers because they'd been pogrommed dispersed ghettoized despised all over the continent—they'd been the blacks of the Old World, and America promised a chance to be strong and free. This country, of course, had a long past of its own, which could not be easily understood from the portholes of a ship. Would the Jews be despised here, too? The newcomers could not be certain, but as they walked past the queues and saw who was lifting and pushing and carting things on the city shore, they *could* see that black Americans were, to some extent, still slaves.

Today, more than seventy-five years after the height of the great wave of immigration from Eastern Europe, Podhoretz's neoconservative heirs celebrate assimilation as a relatively simple process: you came here, you worked hard, you got your reward. This story fails utterly to describe the complicated journey of our present moment's quintessential American immigrants. When they first arrived in numbers, Jews were considered congenitally weak, criminal, dirty, and so on, and therefore unassimilable. Those who settled in New York's ghettos were even deemed embarrassing by many of their more established German counterparts. What's more, many immigrants weren't sure they wanted to be assimilated. Getting used to the new country took time. "[It] should be remembered," reports Irving Howe in *World of Our Fathers,* "[that the move to the new neighborhoods] left behind a majority of the Jewish immigrants, who remained workers and petty tradesmen to the end. Only in the second and third generations— native-born, well educated, and free of many of their parents' constraints—would the climb out of poverty and subjection be largely completed." Like the first large wave of Irish, most newcomers did not themselves make it to middle-class, white America—the "we" to which "My Negro Problem" ostensibly refers. Yet, for all the difficulties, this country's promise of upward mobility gave *the children* of the immigrants hope. Success, they sensed, would come in time: anti-Semitism and the strangeness of these shores eventually would not keep Jews from being full citizens in large part because it couldn't take their white skin away.

Throughout "My Negro Problem," Podhoretz unwittingly gives readers a glimpse of the peculiar blend of desire, anxiety, and racism that informed Jewish American discourse during the Depression. This collision of impulses is never better revealed than in the writer's discussion of a black playmate named Carl. "I think there was a day—first grade? second grade?—when my best friend Carl hit me on the way home from school and announced he wouldn't play with me any more because I had killed Jesus. When I ran home to my mother crying for an explanation, she told me not to pay any attention to such foolishness, and then in Yiddish she cursed the goyim and the *schwartzes*, the *schwartzes* and the goyim." It is here that Podhoretz comes closest to describing how his boyhood world shaped his ideas about black people. The scrape with Carl is perfectly typical of New York City, where ethnic clashes are routine, but the incident also condenses nicely a worldview peculiar to immigrant Jews at the time, which can be boiled down to a question: With goyim slamming you from above, and blacks threatening from below, what is a person to do?

Though Podhoretz never says so directly, it's clear that such reasoning became the basis of his own view of black people. My Negro problem, and *ours*—the Negroes especially, their presence in America really made life precarious for many Jews. African-Americans were, after all, Christian goyim and also, mysteriously, black. This equation: Did Mom express her opinions of blacks before and after the incident? Did any of the white boys ever threaten Norman in the same anti-Semitic fashion Carl did? How much did Norman make up? "Sometimes," Podhoretz reflects, "I wonder whether this is a true memory at all: can anyone really remember back to the age of six?" He may no longer be sure exactly what happened (and we can't know, either), but it's certain the little boy did mind his mother's curses, because now he mutters them, too: *The insane rage that is stirred in me at the thought of Negro anti-Semitism . . .*

  It would be absurd to say that Podhoretz *couldn't* like Carl because of his own Jewishness—that's not my theory. I'm only suggesting that he picked up his attitudes on blacks from people such as his mother, and that his feelings were also shaped by the problems blacks pose for Jewish identity. It's plain enough to see—look again, this time at Podhoretz the writer and not the little boy. In choosing to open his essay with a spotty memory of a black boy whose most notable feature is moral equivalence to goyim, Podhoretz dismisses the idea of a special black moral station. It is an understandable move. African-Americans' history of subjugation bestowed a moral authority historically reserved for Jews *by Jews* in Christian Europe. (In both cases, victimhood's "authority" was often contested by outsiders, and promoted vigorously by certain interests within.) Since Jewish Americans could basically be themselves without the kind of penalties they had suffered in Europe, a Jewish identity based on that oppression made no sense. One way to deal with the resultant confusion was to hate the displacers, the blacks. While Carl never hits Norman, the boy's verbal attack serves as a prelude to an itemized series of physical contests, each of which ends in the writer's (desired?) brutalization: Carl, and all blacks, are as oppressive and bad as white Christians.

Or worse. Remember: "The Negroes were *really* bad, bad in a way that beckoned to one, and made one feel inadequate." This sentiment is more than an instance of boyhood panic. It is a permission slip for hating Negroes in the here-and-now, especially in the enraged, nationalist, physicalized variety James Baldwin had recently described in *The Fire Next Time*. If whites were endangered by black badness, Jews—who had been victims of goyim for centuries, and were, consequently, the moral *whitest*—were most endangered. For this reason the words also demonstrate, I think, the writer's *Jewish* concern about physical vulnerability. Here it is very important to note that Podhoretz never acknowledges any ethnic dimension to his white anxiety. Not until later in his writings does he openly champion Jewish physical toughness as a way of handling enemies. In this essay, written in 1963, Podhoretz only obliquely reveals familiarity with ideas he would later pursue like a zealot.

Return with me, gentle reader, for a second look at the great wave. Hand me the light—from the hour the immigrants stepped off the boat, the challenge was to become American. There were misgivings about *how* to remain a Jewish community, but most Jews never questioned *whether* to be Jewish. Jews, unlike other European immigrants, had no homeland of their own—they had always adapted to lands that were, in varying degrees, inhospitable. Given their memories of European oppression, and the worries of the ghettos in America, most people must have been dizzied by the new country—exchanging anxieties about physical safety for the liberty of whiteness must have seemed dangerous, especially considering the various forms of anti-Semitism in the air during the Depression. But America's bottom line was, in fact, real. It promised all white individuals that their mental strength and effort would be rewarded with riches; eventually, opposition to Jews waned and Jewish children flourished. Jewish discourse about physical strength shifted accordingly. In this country, physical prowess had, at least since the turn of the century, been under discussion, whether explicitly by members of WASP elites (such as Theodore Roosevelt) in their quest for the strenuous life, or covertly by white Americans of all classes who, as Podhoretz put it, saw the blacks as "*tough;* beautifully, enviably tough." Physical strength, as a defining group characteristic, was a complicated business—muscularism, as such, could plainly not function as a direct route to a modern, Jewish American identity.

It was a thorny problem—precisely how was one to become an *American* Jew? The hankerings for physical strength did not disappear, not completely. They remained part of the fabric of Jewishness, encouraged by the stories parents told about the long years of Jewish subjugation, the hostility Jewish children faced in schools and industry, the recent European Holocaust. For some the desires would continue to be a source of contention with blacks no matter how much Jewish circumstances changed. I suspect Podhoretz was such a person, though I'm certain he'd deny it:

> I think I know why the Jews once wished to survive (though I am less certain as to why we still do): they not only believed that God had given them no choice, but they were tied to a memory of past glory and a dream of imminent redemption. What does the American Negro have that might correspond to this? His past is a stigma, and his vision of the future is the hope of erasing the stigma by making color irrelevant, by making it disappear as a fact of consciousness.

Podhoretz is barking from the shadows, gentle reader. Don't be afraid—read the record and see for yourself: remember how much the writer envied Negro strength, notice how he fails to mention the millennia of "stigma" between Jewish "past glory" and "imminent redemption," notice how easily his lunatic description of black experience could be used to describe Jewish experience. Then dare to follow my reasoning to its unattractive and obvious conclusion. At bottom, a profound self-hatred menaces in "My Negro Problem": each time Podhoretz reveals his weakness, as whiteness, he is confessing how much he hates his weakness, as Jewishness, gentle reader.

So you and I aren't fooled by Podhoretz's tricks. And when we look between the lines of " Our Negro Problem" again we might reach still further, beyond his Jewish problem, to a sad paradox: Podhoretz, I think, is fighting with his family. All children love and hate their forebears; the urge to fear one's family is as ancient and selfish as the first child. Podhoretz the son is sick of the way his parents sound and smell and look—he wants them in his own image, naturally, but he doesn't know what his own image is: his sense of himself depends entirely on what he thinks of them. The writer's many faceless ancestors, with *their* real Jewishness, their precious *blackness,* are an insistent speaking mirror—listen as Podhoretz screams and curses and tries not to hear: *What, Norman, will you make of us?*

II.

For Jack was no ordinary singer of ragtime. Those dark eyes of his might have been the ecstatic eyes of a poet in the days when the Chosen People lived sedately in the land of Canaan. They might have been prophetic eyes, stern and stirring, in the years of Zedekiah, son of Josiah, King of Judah, when Jerusalem "knew not its God." They might have been deep wells of lamentation even one generation ago had his lyric voice been born to cry the sorrows of Israel in a Russian synagogue.

—Samson Raphaelson, *The Day of Atonement*, basis of *The Jazz Singer*

The preacher begins the tale.

You are black and proud and you will remember that somewhere along the way some of the people in our line were made very low and not tough at all. I recall: We laughed at the whites when their backs were turned and our mother spit out the lemon seeds like babies under the porch because she said someday a tree with its natty leaves would lick light there long after we moved to the city. We were slaves then and maybe we are still today, slaves, our blackness a badge of terrifying knowledge, a certificate of human accomplishment, its possibility and strength, like a god or a flame inside cupped hands, not something to flee from like a dead body or a bad smell.

The preacher reads some history.

While Jews, who along with Italians and the Irish have in most of the century's renderings of American history been assigned the role of "immigrant," and as such, are permitted a history *before* America, Negroes were made in America. That left us with a blank place where a history should be: no place to put our peoplehood and few ways to understand the situation. So we patched our wound with the pages of the Bible. So in church, our hospital, we tell the tale over and over again: how much we resemble the ancient Jews, how we too are slaves awaiting deliverance. We hold this tale more dear than did the Pilgrims, who made us slaves—but what then to make of the Jews, who would certainly want their story back?

The preacher cautions us, and proffers an explanation.

Think of yourself as swimmers in the great flow of Western

thought. We were slipped certain wrong images of the Jew as crafty weakling and the Jew with a tail like the great Satan who killed Christ and stole young babies and seduced good women and the Jew as parasite. While we could see (if we stopped to think) that many Jews had roughly been "blacks"; and, though we considered ourselves Jews, we didn't have much special sympathy for them because we were also swimmers, and we were entitled to hate Jews as much as other Americans such as Ernest Hemingway, Henry Ford, Pat Buchanan, or any average beat cop in Boston, Chicago, or New York City, and we almost did.

But we couldn't. For the subterranean fact is that we loved and hated Jews like a second child does the first: we were their betters before the Son and only their closest rivals before the Father. We had to fight with the ones who had once owned our new clothes, precisely because they wore them first, and didn't deserve them. An example: There are literal-minded Negroes selling wooden jewelry on 125th Street who will tell you the Jews aren't *even* the real Jews, brother, no—those recessive freaks are not it, not in America. *We are the oppressed.* There are American Africans too who will sell you books detailing how we are the real Jews and the real Egyptians at the same time and your sisters and brothers don't even see the irony—it's almost enough to make you laugh until you remember the beautiful desire like a nerve underneath, ceaselessly working through the pages and words and memories, to find and love the self.

It was simple and plain. You'd heard the Jews controlled jazz, the media, the Democratic party, the civil rights movement, and Harlem real estate: and you wondered. You knew this didn't explain why the police beat you up or why the public education system was a mess or why your neighborhood was without cable and regular garbage pickup but still you wondered. Like when you saw the names on the masthead of *The New York Times* and on the credits of those Hollywood films you would talk about it everywhere even though you never saw anybody on a talk show speak about that and you knew why: everybody's an expert on black people and especially the Jews who claim they are our friends but how come everyone can talk about the blacks but no one can talk about Jews, you said.

"Don't let them call you an anti-Semite, sista, you'll never work again," he said.

"Jewish people do run the *Times*," you said.

"Definitely," he said. "All you have to do is look at the names on the masthead to see that."

"And Jewish people do control most of the major studios in Hollywood. Just like they ran the teachers' unions, just like the Italians controlled carting and construction, and now the Koreans run those fruit markets. That's the way it works—why can't I say that?"

"You know why."

"The real question is what you do with the information. How you interpret it. I'm not out to get Jewish people."

"That don't matter."

"I know."

"The Jews got it sewed up. They got the shit sewed up," he said. "And can't admit it. I'm tired of reading about Israel and the Holocaust. And about how they worked in the civil rights movement. They did that because the white boys didn't want them living one house over. My theory is they produced the civil rights movement and they pumped up King and all them preachers as a public relations diversion so no one would notice them buying mortgages."

"Well," you said, scratching your nose. You felt guilty whenever someone talked about "the Jews." "I think it's more that Jewish editors are not going to say anything bad about Jews. Just like if it was Irish editors there you wouldn't hear anything about the Irish."

"Telling the truth is not anti-Semitic. Am I right?"

You didn't say anything.

He picked up the slack. "I read where the Anti-Defamation League said the white boys are the ones running around writing

'Heil Hitler' and 'Jewboy' and shit on the synagogues. They didn't report *that*. Desecrating graves and shit. Niggas got better sense than that."

"Yeah," you said. "We're spending too much time shooting each other down."

"We're getting a lot of help, sista."

"True. But I'm not worried. Minister Farrakhan's going to lead us through."

He laughed. "Menace-ter Farrakhan. You know they're scared of his loud mouth. And love to talk about him, too. Like he's got power. Like he's got the *Times* and CBS and the media. Like those boys at the foot of the Brooklyn Bridge in the cold with their papers are thinking about Jews all the time."

"Yes, you thought. Every time I see them in their pitiful bow ties I think about how so many black men are just plain bored. And desperate to do something positive."

"Some of them brothers crazy, too," he said.

"But they *do* know how to straighten people out."

"Farrakhan busy in his palatial mansion getting instructions directly from the Mothership."

"Last issue I bought they saw it hovering over Bolivia or Peru!"

"Sheeeeeeit!" he laughed. "Farrakhan is something. But did you read about the grand rebbe in Crown Heights? Schneerson and them—serious lunatics, sista. My theory is the Holocaust messed them up. The Lubavitchers are just the fringe version of a big psychosis they all got over the Holocaust. Notice how no matter how comfortable life starts to feel, no matter all the power they have, they're always bringing back the Nazis. Either that or they're using the Nazis as an excuse to beat down niggas."

"Six million is a lot of million," you said, in a light voice.

"I'm telling you. Holocaust got them psychotic. But I want to hear them talk about how many million of us died getting here. Six million's only a drop in the ocean compared to what we went through. I want to know how many of us died on their slave ships. They never teach about that Holocaust. They prefer to call us *schwartzes* and forget about it."

Then he continued. "You don't hate them sometimes?"

Very quickly you said "No."

"Good. Well, I do. I'll be honest. I hate them sometimes. Because they were the minstrels. Al Jolson was a Jew and the Beastie Boys are Jews. Somebody even told me Elvis was a Jew. They bought our shit for a dime and made a mint off it. Fats Waller to Billie Holiday to Chuck Berry to all them rappers—it's the Jews making the money. They act like your friend but they're the number one pimps of niggas. You got to admit that."

"Jewish people definitely don't have a monopoly on that."

"But the Jews were the ones who made Hollywood: Selznick and Goldwyn and Mayer—Jews. You said that yourself. How many times you seen a big-nosed, money-grubbing cat named Goldberg up there on the screen, and how many times you seen an ignorant can't-talk Gremlin-acting nigga? So how you going to say they're not responsible for that? It's a fact. Undeniable. Now it's to the point where they don't even have to slander us anymore. They got their Negro minstrels to say what they want in their papers and magazines and then they give 'em a dollar and a prize and it's nothing but Negro smiles. You know what I'm saying—think about the *Times*. They hate niggas because they know we got their number."

You felt the pull of the words. Down. Down—you took a sip of water before you spoke. "It's like nothing is more pathetic to me than a Jewish person—with all the Jews the Germans killed—calling somebody a *schwartze*. But I still have to keep telling myself it's not *only* them. Because it's not."

"I ain't saying *only* but I will say the Jews have done a majority of the thieving from us. It'd be lying to yourself not to admit it. Look at your history: they got us like Jesus *and* they're selling tickets to the show! Smart! Those Germans didn't kill them for nothing."

"What?"

"I don't mean they should have killed them."

"I know you didn't."

"What I meant was the Jews must have done something."

"But that could sound like you're saying we deserved slavery."

"I'm not saying that."

"So what are you saying?"

"I'm not saying they deserved to die. Nobody deserves that. All's I'm saying, sista, is it's different. Because you have to remember that we weren't living in the same society as *our* oppressors. They didn't know us, but the Germans knew the Jews."

Oh.

But you said "Uh-huh" and let it slide.

"I know you think I hate them," he said in a muffled voice, as if from under water. "But I don't. Only sometimes. And not all of them. Only the ones who use us."

And then you showed some teeth, guilty inside, because you wanted to say something more, to separate yourself, and you couldn't. Not then. No, you were going down there, too—so you smiled—there was a limit to your complicity just beyond these moments of solidarity with a brotha, and you knew this, just as you knew why many of those 125th Street Negroes all over America sell copies of *Mein Kampf* and *The Protocols of the Elders of Zion* to young minds as easily as they might the Bible. You thought James Baldwin got it right when he wrote about the special disappointment you've reserved for the Jews, ex-slaves, who would be white without a blink— that's where your complicity ended. You knew Jewish people didn't cause more black problems than other whites. You remembered the preacher's story of the mother and her lemon tree, our collective selfhood—this was the real story and it actually had very little to do with Jews, per se. You remembered and you comforted yourself by saying so, but suddenly you felt the urge to spit something out.

Dan and I roomed together during our junior and senior years at Yale. We became close friends even though we competed a lot over grades and once over a woman (who had her own intentions)—we have grown very close in spite of our history because we love each other like brothers since we are. Our kinship is not simple. There is the difference in class: Dan's from Wisconsin and his mother is a judge and his father a geneticist; I am from the Bronx and my parents are social workers. While Dan is a serious cyclist and hiker, I am the sort who watches movies and reads. We don't even have the same sort of friends. Also, differences lurk within our similarities. I was one of a very small number of black people at a school of Jews; Dan in high school was a Jew among many Christians. I'm not a nationalist, cultural or otherwise, and Dan is not religious, and he's not turning religious. But alienation has had radically differing effects on our lives. While I find more to despise about America each day, Dan's outsider status hasn't affected his love of America. He believes in this place—he is a lawyer—there are many lines between us, and they are real. But our bond is also very real. Since today no one believes in "magic" except as a religious promise or a literary device, I will not use that word to describe our connection—no, it is real, an *actual* kinship—which surely, and paradoxically, must be held in wonder.

Just as surely there are explanations for our thang, somewhere—though the mental library is dark and the looking is scary, I will try, gentle reader, for you. And look: I see shelves and shelves of reasons, some handed down by my parents, beautiful and terrible family tales, stories about our "tribes" and others; look: they're running and rerunning in the mind's private studio—I see shelves of secret ethnic memories, playing like a record or a tragedy or a comic romance on the most distant stages of my consciousness.

How they underwrite every human connection I've made. How frightening it is to bring these tales to the light, really, to face your ethnic stuff. As I've said, my high school was nearly all white. They were almost all Jewish. Or all Jewish. Because there was a sense I haven't yet told you about in which we all were the same, talking the same and wearing the same clothes and listening to the same music and laughing at Woody Allen movies for this same reason. We shared, without thought, ways of thinking: I was *of* them, one of them, deeply, and still am—attending the school from third grade on ensured it.

I shared, for instance, my Jewish schoolmates' dislike of WASPs even though I hadn't met many. The WASPs mainly went to Collegiate and places outside the city like Hotchkiss or Andover, and only the dumbest of their children came to Riverdale. The school's chief administrators were of Anglo heritage, and this was a problem for many of the Jewish parents. My peers followed their parents' lead. I remember them saying that the goyim "ruled the country," then saying "You're such a Jew" during a dispute about money; or fawning over Nordic facial features, making fun of the ones with "Jewish" noses. This perspective resembled the distaste for whites expressed around my neighborhood, a blend of vocal contempt and private admiration.

Our parents didn't particularly care for whites, but they weren't hostile in an active way—no one would have acted funny or said anything to any of the block's remaining few. We were Baptist and Catholic and we were almost all black; we were certainly not wealthy but we weren't terribly poor either. There were almost no Jewish landlords or union managers or storekeepers or neighbors or friends around to complain about—Jews and Italians used to live in the neighborhood in the fifties and early sixties, but by the seventies they'd mostly moved to Long Island or Westchester or Jersey or farther away. Mostly you heard talk about Jamaicans or the islanders we derisively called 'Ricans; the whites usually discussed were the Italians, who still had some shops in the area. They were reputedly Mafia and were to be avoided if possible, though they were admired for their sense of family and their piety.

But there wasn't must talk of Jews. It seems odd to me now but in my church the Jewishness was assiduously ignored. I remember a Catholic friend saying they were the ones who betrayed Christ, and it made sense: we had all learned that Jews were the ones who'd inhabited the long dark before the coming of the Lord. But no preacher or Sunday school teacher ever said anything directly against Jewish people when I was around, except that we were oppressed, like the blood of Abraham.

When our parents talked directly about Jews they would sometimes discuss the city's first Jewish mayor, Abe Beame, and the vague sense of dread of Jewish political might that his election brought. But usually the initial topic was commerce: you might be able to go to Delancey Street and "Jew down" a shopkeeper, it was said, but you'd probably fail, because they're too smart with money. The Jew doesn't care about anybody but himself—the Jew keeps money and power inside the Jewish community: if you hire a Jewish accountant he's going to recommend a Jewish lawyer. Believe me. *Black people,* our parents emphasized, *need to learn how to stick together like the Jews do*.

But my easy jangle of attitudes, I think, hardened over time at school, where I encountered Jewish people every day. No matter how Jewish I felt, I could not completely ignore my difference. Lines between black people and Jews were partly hidden, but they were ever present. I remember an outraged conversation about the Holocaust among some of the older children on the bus ride back to our side of town. One of the Jewish students had the nerve to argue that the Holocaust was far worse than slavery; and everyone agreed the kid was *arrogant*. From then on I used this word often, inside—I began to record all events that proved it. There was the pity in the voices of otherwise lovely people when the subject of black America came up; there were the patronizing parents who *wanted* their daughter to date me because "Why should it matter?"; there was the outright racism of certain vicious classmates. In ninth grade Scott W. told me in the library that I should be glad I'm not still in Africa—if it weren't for Europe you would still be chucking spears. I remember his crooked teeth and his curly black dirty hair; he was stronger than me and my black strength so I did not try to bust his ass the way I wanted to. What a perfect time to pull out my sharp tongue—but all I could do was stutter and mumble. *That arrogant bastard*. There must be something these books could say to him but where do I begin? Now he was showing more of his crooked teeth as if I'd said something funny. Scott left the library as proud of himself as could be.

I felt two words: arrogant and Jew. Which I would use again and again to myself, silencing the *Jew,* even to myself, but tasting the shadowy words like candy between the lines of the books assigned to us. Our instructors taught about the fabled Jewish merchants, salesmen clever as Lucifer, and they told us the Jews were hated back then, and during the Inquisition, and in Weimar Germany, and forever, and I could sense the central complaint had always been the same, and the words crossed and crossed and crossed my mind. Another time: Eric, Ronny, and I were members of the G-squad, a general athletics class assigned to uncoordinated or unmotivated students. Eric was one of my best friends in school. Ronny and I were academic competitors; he was the class's science genius, and he was generally disliked, mostly because he was obese. The three of us were in the gym one afternoon toying with the weight machine. Ronny said that black people seem to be better athletes, Joe, don't you agree?

I said, Ronny, let's not limit it to sports. Let's talk about music, too. We gave America its best music and athletes. Plus we built the fucking country.

Ronny smiled and Eric looked amused.

Most Jews got here too late for slavery, he replied.

You're saying you missed all the fun?

He laughed.

How many of our athletes ever played professional sports, Joe? Ronny asked. I don't think we're good at that.

Eric stood there with his arms folded, quiet as a judge. He did not look disturbed. Ronny answered his own question.

But how many black brain surgeons are there? Maybe you know. I know that three Jewish men determined thinking in the twentieth century. Freud and Einstein and Marx.

Ronny smiled, then he laughed, fatly, and I mumbled something about black culture and then I could find no words to speak. And Eric said nothing or maybe he added someone to the list, but since I am close to him I've blocked this memory out completely.

For a long time I wondered whether the Jews were really chosen by God, before anyone else, as Ronny suggested. The argument seemed watertight: wherever Jews have been given the chance they have shown themselves to be smarter than anyone else. *Look at how well we've done in America and everywhere else we've gone. Look at the Jews. Look.* I didn't have to look. Nothing could convince me the *individuals* around me were superior, but then again, no one was saying they were. What Ronny had claimed was a *group* supremacy over other groups. It justified group arrogance. *We have reason to be proud.* Breathing convinced me—all anyone had to do was inhale around school and such logic commandeered the brain.

Which is not to say that Jews were considered by everyone superior in every category. There was, for instance, the tension I've mentioned between Jews and our tiny delegation of black students. Yet our school did have a governing spirit. African-Americans were allowed physical supremacy, and WASPs were considered a sort of ethereal aristocracy, somehow more graceful than anyone else. Folks also knew there were other groups to consider, of course—Japanese, Greek-Americans, sundry Europeans were all enrolled in small numbers, so the actual complexity of the world beyond campus did have some trace effects on our thinking. The brightest among us even thought to ask why Jews seemed to be doing very well in America.

But thinking is hard and most of the time we didn't try, and who can think all the time, especially when the unofficial story is as easy as a swallow to swallow? The unofficial story was simple: There exists a WASP-Jewish-black hierarchy, and it is the real ordering structure of the world. It explains our school: the paltry numbers of African-Americans, the predominance of Jewish students, the continuing dominance of WASP administrators. Everything we saw seemed natural; the blacks were undiscussed untermenschen, the Jews the electorate, the WASPs democracy's vanishing counsel. Each group seemed chosen for its role by nature and God.

In my heart I always knew this stuff was small-minded and wrong. I would love to be a good child and credit my good sense to my parents' pride in blackness, and their belief in human equality, but I also know it has everything to do with the simple fact that each day I returned home the unofficial story shifted; and the ethnic hierarchy I used to order my world there made me suspicious of the line at school.

Still, there was common ground between school and neighborhood on the intelligence and pride of Jews. Since I felt partially Jewish, my inability to dismiss these ideas could, with a stretch, be considered an act of self-love. But at bottom I felt more black than anything else, and I knew Jewish supremacism didn't flatter me. I looked for hammers to use on the idea. On entering Yale I studied my Jewish peers, and kept a firm eye on the school's pretensions to Oxford and Cambridge, its Anglophile yearnings, the way students were asked to call resident advisers "Master," as if slavery never happened. Yale was, to say the least, a problematic institution for African-American students, a cold place that required all sorts of submission, but it was also difficult for Jewish students, and to a degree I hadn't expected.

What I saw dispersed any accumulated belief I had in Jewish chosenness. For the first time in my life since third grade I found myself in a school where Jews were simply one smart group of many; and though reality on the block (and common sense) had already challenged the claims of Jewish intellectual supremacy, seeing *directly* was believing. Many of the smart people I met were African-Americans who had grown up like me in the rarefied precincts of middle-class whiteness. Black students from cities with high concentrations of Jewish people were familiar with the anxieties about "old" wealth and sundry other WASP virtues, and we also considered anti-Semitism a very bad thing. It is fair, however, to say that most of us felt a decidedly grudging admiration for Jewish people. Certainly, my ideas about Jewish supremacy remained a mix of anger and belief until I witnessed directly what Jews really thought of the notion themselves.

I guess I had never had the secret stake my Jewish high school classmates had in admiring WASPs, not really, not beyond recognizing their very real grip on America. How greedily I inhaled the revelation when it became plain: at Yale, Jewish chosenness took a backseat to WASPy chosenness. Many letters I wrote about this but never sent home: I remember a certain Texan saying something bad about the Jews as we stood in the kitchen of his party house, with the Eurofucks convened over the latest in chile peppers and some fine cocaine. There was a pause and then someone said "C'mon" and the lights were turned on and I was determined not to leave the room because I wanted to try the drugs and I knew who the next target was.

I left later with a wet nose and I never hung with those people again, but Nancy did. Nancy was a beautiful woman from one of New York's leading private schools and she was tight with the chic crowd. I remember greeting her once and she refusing to answer to her given surname, responding only when I used the Anglicized version, freshly lifted from a famous English bishop. I remember my buddy Jon from Chicago—who insisted he never really felt Jewish—telling me once over our usual beer and cigarettes how his family had recently been turned down for an apartment they wanted on New York's Upper East Side because of their ethnicity. Jon's circle of male friends in college was almost entirely Jewish—this was not, I think, a consciously designed response, but it wasn't without meaning either.

I was glad the Jews were learning. I remember thinking they are more like blacks now, maybe they will understand. This was not in the main a democratic sentiment, I know, but underneath there was a sympathetic impulse, for I could see my Jewish peers were afraid of being who they were, and were ashamed, and I felt sorry for them, and I thought I knew how that shame felt, and I brought this feeling to my friendships with Jewish people, including Dan.

Sophomore and part of junior year Dan had a black girl-friend, and I met him through her. As I was becoming more and more black conscious, and because I was a masculinist young boy, and because I liked the woman, I was careful with Dan—I wanted to see how he treated her. Soon I came to respect him and to feel shame for having eyed him at all. Her blackness didn't determine his love or eventual contempt—though it may have played some role, it wasn't the main fascination. You could see this in Dan's eyes. He is made of steady material; his body was lean and strong with exercise, settled as an old house. Dan lives in there in dark and generous solitude. Not long after we first met he told me he grew up something of an outsider in Wisconsin—to what extent his Jewishness accounts for the alienation is Dan's call. I won't put words in his mouth except to say the essence of what I know: only a fool would say being Jewish has had no effect on his life, or on his views of himself and others, including blacks. One look at the long tradition of Jewish participation in the African-American struggle for civil rights reveals a Jewish response to blackness quite opposite of that of Podhoretz, but just as prevalent. Dan's parents, I should report, raised him squarely in the progressive Jewish tradition.

The summer after junior year he went to South Africa to monitor what the government called trials. I remember him working on the application at my desk; I remember looking for my parents' old lives down South in the photographs he brought back; I still hang a print he gave me of black and white figures tearing down a great house of cards, "Rise and Destruction of Power." Dan took humanism to South Africa and he brought me back a distant blackness, as he did when he gave me Miles or Billie Holiday records to check out. There is a passage in John Edgar Wideman's *Brothers and Keepers* where the author describes wanting to beat down a white boy for knowing more about the blues than he; I understand his rage but I hardly felt it. I hesitate to admit this in today's climate but it is the truth. Mostly I loved learning about what I didn't know, sometimes covering up how much I was learning, sometimes questioning my friend's authority or authenticity, but always in the main feeling thankful. I believe it is the same mix of sensations Dan or Jon felt for me when I talked. I had, after all, grown up among lots of Jewish people and neither of them really had. Their parents had moved from my city to the Midwest; the references I brought from New York contained a curious and appealing atavism: I was a strange native informant reporting on their ancestral homes, and they were alien natives of mine.

If Dan and Jon were "black" in any way, they were in precisely the same way that I was a "Jew." Our lives were shaped by cross-cultural consumption and the force of political sympathies—neither of which, in the end, makes you a real group member, necessarily. Jewish guys who like black culture—it's a common enough phenomenon, I suppose, as were black kids in the old ghettos who grew up knowing a little Yiddish. Still, our ethnic "guest appearances" counted for something, since they did help make up who we were. Dan and I and Jon and I had chosen each other, after all, in part because we thought we understood.

III.

I've got my pad and pen out, and she's laughing at my officialness. So, Mom, not *how*, but *why* did you become Hettie Jones?

"After the breakup of my marriage," she explains, "people asked me why I didn't change my name, why I didn't, quote, 'go back to the Jews.' There was no going back to something that denied you."

And why is it important to you that we be black and not "biracial"?

"I was not about to delude you guys into thinking you could be anything different in this country. And, frankly, I didn't think that being anything other than black would be any more desirable."

—Lisa Jones interviewing Hettie Jones,
in "Mama's White"

One night early in our acquaintance Jon and I were at a party and he said something about some big black man being scary. Jon is a small guy with a gentle, laughing voice. From his easy, familiar tone I knew he was used to saying such things, but this was going to be the last time he did it in front

of me. I threw Jon to the ground with my skinny weak self and
he thought I was kidding. "Racist?" Jon was laughing out loud
but you should have seen the look on his face.

I meant it. Why was this white boy using the words "big
and scary"? By now, gentle reader, you know I had decided
the answer. I considered Jon a friend, but "big and scary"? I
imagined someone like my father, a bearish man, and I knew I
might look like this someday. Soon my torso would spread
and I would frighten people like Jon even more. I had no use
for that sort of blackness any longer. And so I threw a tackle at
him and in the second it took our bodies to fall to the dark
grass I felt my focus switch. *You're a Jew and you're calling some
black man scary?*

We hit the ground.

"You're calling *me* a racist?"

You're a Negro.

You're a Jew.

So most of the time Jon wasn't like this, and Dan never is.
Dan is someone I love and that's why I came to visit him here
in Seattle, this white place, a place to bicycle and to read. It is
as quiet here as a ghost or a canyon with no wind. The window
is always open and there is almost no news in these green and
flowery gardens about Jews and blacks and how we like to
fight, no, it is only Dan and me and my thoughts and the
blather of the TV set and the smell of fruit blossoms wafting
from the green and flowery outside, in the dark, and it is my
friend Dan. He is still watching *L.A. Law* as he was when I
began this journey by remembering the room where I first read
Podhoretz in that yellow light on my bed and the pages and
pages over me like bandages on my brown body. Still my glass
is turning and turning and the xeroxed pages lay near.

In a minute the show will be over. Dan turns up the set and
suddenly I realize the smell of New York is gone. I make a note
to get my friend to spit out the story of how he came to be
Dan Abrahamson, my brother. First thing will be to talk about
how his experience with black people shaped his end of our

brotherhood. Brother: the word slips through the mind like an eel; every minute it means something else. As with the word "immigrant," which in New York and all over urban America no longer means Jews or Italians so much as Dominicans and Haitians and certain Mexicans and certain Southeast Asians: how swiftly words change significance. Who is a "real" immigrant today, and who is an alien? Who deserves to become a member of the American tribe? I think: There is an emerging line, a neoconservative "political correctness," on these questions. Richard Cohen of the *Washington Post,* for example, had this to say about a recent boycott of an Asian store owner accused of hitting a black woman: "[W]hat a diversion all this picketing and boycotting is. And what a tragedy to boot. In New York, Washington and other cities, certain blacks talk about Asians as if they were involved in a conspiracy against them: Where do they get the money to buy these stores? Certain black leaders curse Asians or, just for good measure, Jews. They are constantly on the lookout for scapegoats. They have so thoroughly accepted the ethic of victimization that they blame others for a situation that they themselves can rectify: open some stores." I think: the president of a Korean grocers' group was more to the point when he told *The New York Times:* "We are no different than the Jews, Italians, or other Europeans."

The television babbles on and my mind keeps wandering. Family is made of the people family says is family; folks like Cohen and the store owner are clearly trying to embrace each other, and leave Negroes outside. Consider the gauzy memories they use, language lifted straight from the blacks-versus-Jews debate—how their memories disguise the contemporary facts of this country! They say, Look at those hardworking Jewish immigrants and sullen, menacing Negroes and remember: Put your Dominicans and Haitians and Mexicans here on the problem side, away, and let in your huddled Koreans and Eastern Europeans and (white) Cubans and maybe a few of the hardworking Mexicans. The good ones—they are most like the model immigrants who came here early in the century. They deserve to be American. They should be family. It was becoming clear now, at Dan's table, in Seattle's perfumed air: if family is made of the people family says is family, and if "family" and "immigrant" do not include people who are deemed problematic, collective responsibility for complaints such as crime, segregated housing, the failure of public education—all of which get blamed on blacks routinely—disappears in a few flicks of the tongue.

The show is over. Dan turns and starts telling me about how all of his law school friends are getting married. Soon they will have babies. I see worry in his dark eyes. Dan doesn't want to settle for just anyone but he is sick and tired of being alone, and he's reminding me of how worried I am, too. One of his friends, a Jew, settled on a partner because she's nice enough and she's all he had energy to find. "And she's Jewish," Dan said, almost approvingly. I turn my eyes from him. For a split second I feel betrayed—I'm not sure why, exactly. I grew up thinking I'd rather marry a black woman than not and I still feel this desire somewhere—I reason and decide not to raise the issue. I will keep focus instead on the ethnic origins of our brotherhood, and how to put our *whole* story into contemporary political discourse. I take a sip of water and turn my eyes to my friend. I point to the photocopy. Read this Podhoretz piece, man, and would you take a look at this thing when I'm finished?

I am pretty sure I know what Dan will say. Once in a while he and I get to talking about pooling our talents to elect him senator from Wisconsin or something. It would make sense because our politics are more same than not; we want more people to get a better deal here, especially the most despised, so often black people. Neither of us takes after Norman Podhoretz—somewhere along the way after facing our many parents we chose to work honestly through the monumental confusion of their stories. We are trying—we are children trying to know our families. Thus far our research has helped usher Dan, the progressive Jew, and me, the progressive black, into the same camp.

But I need to tell you something, gentle reader—I don't mean to mislead you about my thinking. Politics and the other crossings of our heritages are only part of what Dan and I share. I too see the endless shelves of reasons for our kinship in the deep beyond. The heart beats and beats and beats like a dumb unreasonable animal, but it can conjure any feeling. By a secret process it is courageous or fearful or mean or loving and moral or immoral and all of these at once. Even an infant knows that much. Dan and I remember the facts like a mantra: our brotherhood is made of ethnic sympathies but it also has nothing to do with our being black or Jewish or any of that, and I love Dan not because he's Jewish or, in some sense, black, and not because I am black or, in some sense, Jewish—while our tribes, and their memories, and their stories, did make us, they also have nothing to do with it.

This is not what we were told as children. When we were little our parents whispered words about History in our ears and we silenced some of the much we knew in our hearts, what we were born with, the much, but each day we grew and grew and then we saw the stuck pages and the words stuck to our bodies like old bandages and Dan and I looked. We pulled away those leaves and smelled the sharp bitter scent of our selves and then we eyed the terrible naked shivering fruit and now we knew we'd been quickened with light and spit. Our loving families could never tell the secret, gentle reader: the heart is raised on a mess of stories and then it writes its own.

HISTORICAL
AND
POLITICAL
REFLECTIONS

Clayborne Carson

The Politics of Relations between African-Americans and Jews

Clayborne Carson is a professor of history at Stanford University, the director and senior editor of the Martin Luther King, Jr. Papers Project, and the author of In Struggle: SNCC and the Black Awakening of the 1960s.

■ The troubled relationship between African-Americans and Jews survives in part through the pretense that relations were once better. Like married couples who habitually quarrel in public, members of the two groups remain in a relationship that survives for reasons that many observers find inexplicable. More than fifty years ago, Ralph Bunche, then a political scientist at Howard University, commented ruefully: "It is common knowledge that many members of the Negro and Jewish communities of the country share mutual dislike, scorn, and mistrust."* A 1961 article in *Commentary* lamented a revival of anti-Semitism among blacks and concluded that the black-Jewish coalition faced "disruption" and

---

*Bunch, Foreword to Wedlock Lunabelle, *The Reaction of Negro Publications and Organizations to German Anti-Semitism* (Washington, D.C.: Howard University Press, 1942), quoted in Robert G. Weisbord and Arthur Stein, *Bittersweet Encounter: The Afro-American and the American Jew* (New York: Schocken Books, 1970), p. 59.

"dissolution."★ In 1988, journalist Jonathan Kaufman entitled his treatment of black-Jewish relations *Broken Alliance: The Turbulent Times between Blacks and Jews in America.*†

The existence of the so-called black-Jewish alliance is difficult to explain, therefore, given the reoccurring public disputes and the persistent pessimism about future ties. Why do articulate members of each group so readily seek out opportunities for publicly airing intergroup grievances? Why are they so willing to combine conciliatory appeals for good relations with attributions of blame for bad? Why do some in each group even talk to one another when they have nothing nice to say? The literature on black-Jewish relations mixes spiteful polemics and self-serving analysis, manifesting the reasons for intergroup conflicts even while diagnosing them. Yet, while recognizing the folly of speaking out, it is difficult for those of us who are black or Jewish to resist doing so when others speak for us or about us. I find myself wanting black-Jewish dissension to stop—after I have the last word.

Historical perspective tells me that these quarrels will continue, for they have become ritualistic. A typical controversy begins with a controversial statement or action by a black person, which is then publicly condemned by Jewish leaders as a sign of increasing black anti-Semitism. The initial stimuli for past crises in black-Jewish relations have often been statements by obscure individuals; yet the understandable desire of Jewish leaders to expose black anti-Semitism has the effect of transforming obscurity into notoriety. The 1967 anti-Israeli statement of a few individuals in the Student Nonviolent Coordinating Committee (SNCC) was published in an irregular newsletter sent to a few hundred supporters; most people, including those of us close to SNCC, first learned of it in our morning newspapers. In 1968 a high school student's anti-Semitic poem was heard by few listeners of a public radio program before it was widely publicized by New York teachers'

★Tom Brooks, "Negro Militants, Jewish Liberals, and the Unions," *Commentary,* September 1961, p. 209.

†(New York: Charles Scribner's Sons, 1988).

union officials who were embattled with black community control advocates. Farrakhan's anti-Semitic rantings at Nation of Islam rallies made him a nationally known figure while also damaging Jesse Jackson's 1984 presidential campaign. In 1993, a speech delivered to students at Kean College of New Jersey by Khalid Muhammad, a previously little-known minister of the Nation of Islam, was reprinted in *The New York Times,* thereby stimulating a controversy that remained in the news for months afterward. For many Jewish commentators, these events were used as evidence that some black leaders harbored anti-Semitic feelings and that others were unreliable friends who were reluctant to stand up to the black anti-Semites. For many African-Americans, the events suggested that Jewish leaders were overbearing in their insistence that black leaders publicly repudiate isolated expressions of anti-Semitism over which the leaders had no control.

The rituals associated with these recurring crises in black-Jewish relations have usually involved Jewish leaders and intellectuals turning to their black counterparts for assurances that never seem to be adequate. No significant African-American leader has ever admitted to being anti-Semitic, but some leaders with negligible followings, recognizing the benefits of notoriety among alienated blacks, do not fear the label. Jewish concerns are rarely allayed by the attempts of friendly black leaders and intellectuals to distance themselves from anti-Semites. Combining defensiveness and militancy, black assurances of goodwill are usually given reluctantly, often with hints that black anti-Semitism is not high on the list of black concerns. Worried Jews invite black representatives to symposia that are intended to lessen intergroup tensions but sometimes exacerbate them. Outpourings of public statements by national African-American and Jewish leaders never resolve the festering resentments and suspicions in each community.

Scholarly discussions of black-Jewish relations have been more successful in identifying the reasons why members of both groups work together on behalf of civil rights reform than in explaining why this cooperation is continually disrupted.

Similarities in the historical experiences of the two groups—
common experiences of slavery, collective oppression, and
minority status in predominantly white, Christian societies—
are usually cited to explain the close ties between black and
Jewish civil rights advocates. A less noted but related similarity
is that some members of both groups have responded to
minority status in American society by identifying with the
universalistic, egalitarian ideals of the Western liberal tradition.
Although, during the past two centuries, blacks and Jews have
wavered between integrationism and separatism as strategies
for group advancement, the spread of democratic ideas in
Europe and the Americas strengthened the former orientation.
Because African-Americans and American Jews have seen
themselves as at least potential members of the modern, democratic societies, they have been particularly drawn to progressive
political movements that have expanded conceptions of citizenship rights and lessened social inequality. Moreover, in the
United States, the two groups have been among the most
consistent supporters of twentieth-century labor movements
and of the liberal wing of the Democratic party.

In addition, small minorities within each group played
crucial roles in the development of a tradition of leftist social
activism centered in the Communist party of the United States.
I have suggested elsewhere that some of the most committed
black and Jewish activists in the southern black freedom struggle were products of this leftist tradition of political dissent,
despite the fact that it was severely weakened by cold war
repression.* One of the ironies of the dispute over SNCC's
pro-Palestinian stand in 1967 was that Stokely Carmichael
and several other outspoken black critics of Israel had been
influenced by black-Jewish Left culture, as were other black
firebrands such as Maulana Karenga and LeRoi Jones/Amiri
Baraka.

These historical factors help to explain the durability of

*Carson, "Blacks and Jews in the Civil Rights Movement," in Joseph R. Washing-
ton, Jr., *Jews in Black Perspectives: A Dialogue* (Rutherford, N.J.: Fairleigh Dickinson
University Press, 1984), pp. 113–131.

black-Jewish political ties during the period after the founding of the NAACP in 1909, but other historical factors explain the repeated disruptions of those ties. Because they recur regularly, black-Jewish conflicts and controversies cannot be understood merely as responses to particular events but as reflections of underlying social, political, and psychological realities that are different for members of each group. Indeed, African-Americans and Jews often react angrily to suggestions that their oppression is not unique. For example, during a 1979 visit to the Yad Vashem Holocaust Museum, Jesse Jackson once incurred the wrath of many Jews when he used the phrase "one of the great human tragedies of all times" instead of "unique" to describe what he had seen commemorated.★ African-Americans are similarly disturbed by any equation of their oppression in the United States with that of Jewish Americans. As James Baldwin once commented: "One does not wish, in short, to be told by an American Jew that his suffering is as great as the American Negro's suffering. It isn't, and one knows that it isn't from the very tone in which he assures you that it is."†

A common identity as oppressed people is less important in explaining black-Jewish conflicts than the differences in the historical experiences of African-Americans and Jews and the divisions within each group. Jews and African-Americans have followed different strategies of group advancement and remain internally divided over the extent to which their own interests coincide with those of the other group. In a broad sense, most blacks and Jews supported efforts to eliminate racism and bigotry, but only a small minority in each group have been civil rights activists. Civil rights activists and, more generally, political activists who participate in black-Jewish political alliances have faced challenges from leaders who question not only the tactics and goals of the civil rights movement but the importance of civil rights as a means of group advancement.

Moreover, African-American and Jewish civil rights activ-

★The incident is described in Kaufman, *Broken Alliance*, pp. 253–254.
†James Baldwin, "Negroes Are Anti-Semitic Because They're Anti-White," *The New York Times Magazine*, April 9, 1967, p. 136.

ists have often been distinguished from other members of their group because of their class and educational backgrounds or their assimilationist outlooks. Such activists are vulnerable to the charge that they have lost touch with their communities. Although among Jews, religious values encouraged a generalized pro–civil rights sentiment, active involvement in the twentieth-century civil rights efforts has continued to be more common among secular Jews than among those with strong religious commitments. As historian David Lewis has pointed out, black and Jewish civil rights activists of the pre–World War II period were distinctively assimilationist. Early Jewish NAACP supporters, he found, not only constituted an elite—affluent individuals, usually from German-Jewish backgrounds—but also exhibited ambivalent and sometimes antagonistic attitudes toward the rapidly expanding population of Eastern European Jews and toward Judaism as a religion.* More generally, the widespread involvement of Jews in liberal and radical political movements was a byproduct of the nineteenth-century movement of European-American Jews away from Jewish traditions.†

African-American civil rights activists have also tended to be assimilationist, although this was less often the case as the southern black freedom struggle expanded in scale during the 1950s and 1960s. Responding to pressures from grass-roots leaders and from black nationalists such as Malcolm X, civil rights activism became increasingly tied to group goals rather than the ideal of an interracial "beloved community." For black Americans achieving equal citizenship rights was not simply an idealistic goal but also a strategy for group advancement.

Although civil rights reform has not been the sole objective of black politics, it has been far more central to the aspirations of African-Americans than to those of Jewish Americans. Both

---

*David Levering Lewis, "Parallels and Divergences: Assimilationist Strategies of Afro-American and Jewish Elites from 1910 to the Early 1930s," *Journal of American History* 71 (December 1984): 543–564.

†Sara Bershtel and Allen Graubard, "The Mystique of the Progressive Jew," *Working Papers*, March–April 1983, pp. 19–25.

blacks and Jews have experienced discrimination, but the former have been far more adversely affected by such discrimination than the latter. Although European pogroms and the Holocaust of World War II shaped modern Jewish-American identity, African-Americans have been more directly affected by a tradition of overt and often terroristic racism in the United States. Lynching of black people remained a vivid reminder of inferior status long after the lynching of Leo Frank.

The anti-Jewish sentiments held by many Americans are quite different from antiblack ones. The former included stereotypes of group achievement and influence, the latter featured stereotypes of group inadequacy and impotence. The impact of anti-Jewish sentiment on American Jews has never been comparable to the institutionalized discrimination encountered by black Americans. Jews in America have never been forced to depend upon special governmental protections of their citizenship rights; there has been, therefore, no American Jewish movement comparable to the African-American civil rights movement. Not only have Jews refrained from mobilizing mass movements of Jews to secure better treatment, they have seen such movements as counterproductive, given their ability to use their economic power and influence to protect their group interests. Until recent decades, there has been little inclination on the part of Jews to use federal legislation as a direct weapon against anti-Semitism, which rarely affects the life chances of individual Jews and has no appreciable effect on national policies affecting Jews as a group. Only in 1967 and afterward when the question of support for Israel became a major element in Jewish politics did it become conceivable that African American attitudes might potentially affect the group interests of Jews.

African-Americans and Jewish Americans worked closely together in these civil rights efforts, but the success of these efforts affected the lives of black people more than they did the lives of Jewish Americans. Yet, despite the centrality of civil rights in African-American politics, the success or failure of civil rights reform efforts is dependent upon the support of nonblacks. In addition, given the small amount of support for civil rights reform among non-Jewish whites, Jewish support for civil rights efforts has been a matter of considerable importance to black civil rights leaders. During the past quarter century, moreover, Jewish attitudes regarding an issue such as affirmative action could affect national policies regarding the life chances of individual blacks and, more important, national racial policies.

As the civil rights movement expanded and became increasingly militant after 1955, however, both black and Jewish civil rights activists faced new pressures from members of their own race who disagreed with the direction of the movement. This was particularly the case after the resurgence of black nationalism during the mid-1960s, when Malcolm X and the Nation of Islam gained a following as a result of their strong criticisms of the civil rights movement and its integrationist leadership. Even before the rise of the black power movement of the period after 1965, many black activists accepted the notion that their struggle sought more than civil rights reform. Some Jewish civil rights activists agreed with this conception of the struggle, but the growing emphasis on economic and political goals exposed differences between black and Jewish leaders over the ultimate purpose of the civil rights movement. By the late 1960s, some Jews who were former supporters of the civil rights movement had become convinced that black militancy was going too far and questioned the ability of the minority of pro–black power Jews to speak for their community.

The increasing frequency of black-Jewish conflict after 1966 reflected the resurgence in both groups of insular perspectives and of leaders who sought to demonstrate their loyalty to group interests by attacking those involved in intergroup political alliances. While some blacks and some Jews continued to work together to eliminate racial discrimination and bigotry, other blacks and other Jews focused their energies on the achievement of more narrowly conceived group interests and goals. The latter trend was part of a general reassertion of ethnicity as a positive value and valuable commodity. This trend was encouraged by the black power movement, but it was not caused by it. In 1964, for example, Nathan Glazer presaged the black power arguments of Stokely Carmichael when he affirmed the notion of a "group pattern of American life" which would allow groups to maintain "exclusiveness" and areas "restricted to their own kind."*

The upsurge of black self-interest politics during the last of the 1960s revived well-established nationalist and separatist traditions that had never completely disappeared. Some of the black community leaders who placed less emphasis on civil rights goals than on economic and political goals were themselves products of civil rights ferment. Black power politics of the post-1965 period was often portrayed as a decisive break with the previous period of black activism, but the black struggles of the early 1960s were catalysts for the emergence of local black leadership who challenged established civil rights leaders.

While the NAACP brought a small minority of blacks and Jews into a usually close and supportive relationship with each other, black nationalists such as Elijah Muhammad and Louis Farrakhan, black evangelists Daddy Grace and Father Divine, and numerous local black political leaders built substantial grass-roots movements that involved little black-Jewish interaction. Black leadership at the local level has often expressed resentment of Jewish economic and political power, especially when that power manifested itself in black communities. This resentment has been expressed in anti-Semitic harangues by generations of Harlem street corner agitators and exploded in anti-Jewish vandalism during New York race riots in 1935, 1943, and 1964.†

*Nathan Glazer, "Negroes and Jews: the New Challenge to Pluralism," *Commentary*, December 1964, p. 34. Glazer writes: "The force of present-day Negro demands is that the sub-community, because it either protects privileges or creates inequalities, *has no right to exist*. That is why these demands pose a quite new challenge to the Jewish community, or to any sub-community."

†See Isabel Bolko Price, "Black Response to Anti-Semitism: Negroes and Jews in New York, 1880 to World War II" (Ph.D. dissertation, University of New Mexico, 1973); Robert G. Weisbord and Arthur Stein, *Bittersweet Encounter: The Afro-American and the American Jew* (New York: Schocken Books, 1970).

Rather than seeing contemporary tensions in black-Jewish relations as exceptional, therefore, it is more accurate to see them as recurring manifestations of the basic tension between integrationist civil rights activity and ever-present group-interest politics. Particularly during the years since 1966, black and Jewish civil rights advocates have often been compelled to defend their activities against the charge that they are not serving the interests of their own groups. Some Jewish civil rights leaders found it increasingly difficult to support black militancy as it moved beyond the ideological boundaries of earlier civil rights efforts. As Nathan Glazer wrote: "Intending in 1964 to create a color-blind America, we discovered to our surprise in the 1970s that we were creating an increasingly color-conscious society." Glazer, like other Jews, questioned whether the movement for assimilation had become "something different—cultural pluralism, rights distributed by group, group consciousness maintained and enhanced?"* For neoconservative Jews, a civil rights movement had been supplanted by another movement which was unworthy of Jewish support, because it pursued black rather than Jewish interests. For black militants, these changes meant that the civil rights movement had evolved into a liberation movement that was more worthy of black support.

Jewish support for black advancement efforts declined after 1967 not only because blacks moved toward racial separatism but also because Jews moved toward increasingly group consciousness after the 1967 Arab-Israeli war. As a narrowly conceived movement against racial discrimination and bigotry, the civil rights movement had attracted substantial Jewish support, but black power militants correctly charged that that conception of the movement was as much a Jewish creation as it was a black one. Jews such as Henry Moskowitz and Joel Spingarn shaped the early policies of the NAACP more than did W.E.B. Du Bois, who was the only black officer for

*Nathan Glazer, *Ethnic Dilemmas, 1964–1982* (Cambridge: Harvard University Press, 1983), pp. 1, 5.

many years. During the 1930s and 1940s, Jews spearheaded the national campaign for antidiscrimination legislation. As American Jewish Congress leader Will Maslow once commented, slightly overstating the case, "many of these laws were actually written in the offices of Jewish agencies, by Jewish staff people, introduced by Jewish legislators and pressured into being by Jewish voters. In addition, literally hundreds of court actions were taken by Jewish attorneys on behalf of Negro plaintiffs."*

Black nationalists from the era of Marcus Garvey to the present have sought to displace black civil rights leaders by calling attention to the subordinate role these leaders play in black-Jewish alliances. They also attract black support by exploiting other vulnerabilities of many civil rights leaders— namely their assimilationist outlook, middle-class status, and their unwillingness to alienate nonblack allies. The rise of Malcolm X during the late 1950s demonstrated that a spokesman for a tiny religious group could revive the moribund black nationalist tradition and attract a large following among discontented blacks by being more rhetorically militant than the established national black leaders. During his years as a minister of Elijah Muhammad's Nation of Islam, Malcolm X perfected the art of expressing the anger and frustration felt by many blacks who watched civil rights protesters using nonviolent tactics against brutal white segregationists. Without ever engaging in militant political action, Malcolm convinced many blacks that he was nevertheless more militant than civil rights leaders through a mixture of antiwhite rhetoric, fervent affirmation of racial pride, and sardonic criticisms of the nonviolent tactics. During his period as a minister of the Nation of Islam, Malcolm made criticisms of the racial loyalty of the established black leaders that set a model for the black nationalists who came later.

Despite the efforts of the early Malcolm X and these

---

*Quoted in Lenora E. Berson, *The Negroes and the Jews* (New York: Random House, 1971), p. 97.

nationalist successors, substantial numbers of blacks and Jews have continued to join forces to oppose bigotry and racial discrimination. They will do this not because they are impelled to do so by the black or Jewish masses, but because black and Jewish civil rights activists perceive that their best chance to gain influence in their respective communities and in national politics is through political activities that makes their assimilationism an asset rather than a liability. Nevertheless it has also remained the case that blacks and Jews who advocate group-interest politics have used the issue of black-Jewish relations to promote their own leadership over that of assimilationist leaders advocating legislation against discrimination and bigotry. The claim of black power militants that the established black leadership group was insufficiently loyal to black interests parallels the insistence of Jewish neoconservatives that liberal or leftist Jews are victims of self-hatred and even purveyors of Jewish anti-Semitism.*

Ironically, despite claims by blacks that Jews abandoned the civil rights struggle and by Jews that blacks betrayed the struggle, I would suggest that, with the exception of a brief period in the early 1960s, active black and Jewish support for civil rights efforts has remained basically stable during the period since the New Deal. Such support remains an activity of culturally marginal, racially tolerant individuals. Despite claims of rising black anti-Semitism or Jewish racism, such individuals have consistently maintained close relationships and worked toward common goals.

Nevertheless, the political ties between African-Americans and Jews will remain unstable because they do not reflect the full range of political orientations within each community. It is unlikely that blacks and Jews who support common progressive political goals will ever again gain the political influence they once had, given the rise of competing leaders who challenge the group loyalty of those who join extragroup coali-

---

*See quotes by Norman Podhoretz and Nathan Glazer in *Newsweek*, March 1, 1971, p. 58.

tions. The history of black-Jewish relations suggests that the two groups will remain the most dependable sources of support for social change in the United States even as they remain divided, internally and with one another, over the future direction of those efforts.

Cornel West

On Black-Jewish Relations

Cornel West, a professor at Harvard University, is the author of The American Evasion of Philosophy: A Genealogy of Pragmatism, *and other books, including* Race Matters *(1993), in which "On Black-Jewish Relations" appeared.*

For if there are no waving flags and marching songs at the barricades as Walter marches out with his little battalion, it is not because the battle lacks nobility. On the contrary, he has picked up in his way, still imperfect and wobbly in his small view of human destiny, what I believe Arthur Miller once called "the golden thread of history." He becomes, in spite of those who are too intrigued with despair and hatred of man to see it, King Oedipus refusing to tear out his eyes, but attacking the Oracle instead. He is that last Jewish patriot manning his rifle at Warsaw; he is that young girl who swam into sharks to save a friend a few weeks ago; he is Anne Frank, still believing in people; he is the nine small heroes of Little Rock; he is Michelangelo creating David and Beethoven bursting forth with the Ninth Symphony. He is all those things because he has finally reached out in his tiny moment and caught that sweet essence which is human dignity, and it shines like the old star-touched dream that it is in his eyes.

> —Lorraine Hansberry, "An Author's
> Reflections: Walter Lee Younger,
> Willy Loman and He Who Must Live"

Recent debates on the state of black-Jewish relations have generated more heat than light. Instead of critical dialogue and respectful exchange, we have witnessed several bouts of vulgar name-calling and self-righteous finger pointing. Battles conducted on the editorial pages, like the one between Henry Louis Gates, Jr., the eminent Harvard professor, and John Henrik Clarke, the distinguished pan-African scholar, in *The New York Times* and the *City Sun,* respectively, do not take us very far in understanding black-Jewish relations.

Black anti-Semitism and Jewish antiblack racism are real, and both are as profoundly American as cherry pie. There was no *golden age* in which blacks and Jews were free of tension and friction. Yet there was a *better* age when the common histories of oppression and degradation of both groups served as a springboard for genuine empathy and principled alliances. Since the late sixties, black-Jewish relations have reached a nadir. Why is this so?

In order to account for this sad state of affairs we must begin to unearth the truth behind each group's perceptions of the other (and of itself). For example, few blacks recognize and acknowledge one fundamental fact of Jewish history: a profound hatred of Jews sits at the center of medieval and modern European cultures. Jewish persecutions under the Byzantines, Jewish massacres during the Crusades, Jewish expulsions in England (1290), France (1306), Spain (1492), Portugal (1497), Frankfurt (1614), and Vienna (1670), and Jewish pogroms in the Ukraine (1648, 1768), Odessa (1871), and throughout Russia—especially after 1881 culminating in Kishinev (1903)—constitute the vast historical backdrop to current Jewish preoccupations with self-reliance and the Jewish anxiety of group death. Needless to say, the Nazi attempt at Judeocide in the 1930s and 1940s reinforced this preoccupation and anxiety.

The European hatred of Jews rests on religious and social grounds—Christian myths of Jews as Christ-killers and resentment over the disproportionate presence of Jews in certain commercial occupations. The religious bigotry feeds on stereotypes of Jews as villainous transgressors of the sacred; the social bigotry, on alleged Jewish conspiratorial schemes for power and control. Ironically, the founding of the State of Israel—the

triumph of the quest for modern Jewish self-determination—
came about less from Jewish power and more from the consensus of the two superpowers, the United States and USSR, to
secure a homeland for a despised and degraded people after
Hitler's genocidal attempt.

The history of Jews in America for the most part flies in the
face of this tragic Jewish past. The majority of Jewish immigrants arrived in America around the turn of the century
(1881–1924). They brought a strong heritage that put a premium on what had ensured their survival and identity—
institutional autonomy, rabbinical learning, and business zeal.
Like other European immigrants, Jews for the most part became complicitous with the American racial caste system.
Even in "Christian" America with its formidable anti-Semitic
barriers, and despite a rich progressive tradition that made Jews
more likely than other immigrants to feel compassion for
oppressed blacks, large numbers of Jews tried to procure a
foothold in America by falling in step with the widespread
perpetuation of antiblack stereotypes and the garnering of
white-skin privilege benefits available to nonblack Americans.
It goes without saying that a profound hatred of African people
(as seen in slavery, lynching, segregation, and second-class
citizenship) sits at the center of American civilization.

The period of genuine empathy and principled alliances
between Jews and blacks (1910–67) constitutes a major pillar of
American progressive politics in this century. These supportive
links begin with W.E.B. Du Bois's *The Crisis* and Abraham
Cahan's *Jewish Daily Forward* and are seen clearly between
Jewish leftists and A. Philip Randolph's numerous organizations, between Elliot Cohen's *Commentary* and the early career
of James Baldwin, between prophets like Abraham Joshua
Heschel and Martin Luther King, Jr., or between the disproportionately Jewish Students for a Democratic Society (SDS) and
the Student Nonviolent Coordinating Committee (SNCC).
Presently, this inspiring period of black-Jewish cooperation is
often downplayed by blacks and romanticized by Jews. It is
downplayed by blacks because they focus on the astonishingly

rapid entree of most Jews into the middle and upper middle classes during this brief period—an entree that has spawned both an intense conflict with the more slowly growing black middle class and a social resentment from a quickly growing black impoverished class. Jews, on the other hand, tend to romanticize this period because their present status as upper middle dogs and some top dogs in American society unsettles their historic self-image as progressives with a compassion for the underdog.

In the present era, blacks and Jews are in contention over two major issues. The first is the question of what constitutes the most effective means for black progress in America. With over half of all black professionals and managers being employed in the public sphere, and those in the private sphere often gaining entree owing to regulatory checks by the EEOC, attacks by some Jews on affirmative action are perceived as assaults on black livelihood. And since a disproportionate percentage of poor blacks depend on government support to survive, attempts to dismantle public programs are viewed by blacks as opposition to black survival. Visible Jewish resistance to affirmative action and government spending on social programs pits some Jews against black progress. This opposition, though not as strong as that of other groups in the country, is all the more visible to black people because of past Jewish support for black progress. It also seems to reek of naked group interest, as well as a willingness to abandon compassion for the underdogs of American society.

The second major area of contention concerns the meaning and practice of Zionism as embodied in the State of Israel. Without a sympathetic understanding of the deep historic sources of Jewish fears and anxieties about group survival, blacks will not grasp the visceral attachment of most Jews to Israel. Similarly, without a candid acknowledgment of blacks' status as permanent underdogs in American society, Jews will not comprehend what the symbolic predicament and literal plight of Palestinians in Israel means to blacks. Jews rightly point out that the atrocities of African elites on oppressed

Africans in Kenya, Uganda, and Ethiopia are just as bad or worse than those perpetrated on Palestinians by Israeli elites. Some also point out—rightly—that deals and treaties between Israel and South Africa are not so radically different from those between some black African, Latin American, and Asian countries and South Africa. Still, these and other Jewish charges of black double standards with regard to Israel do not take us to the heart of the matter. Blacks often perceive the Jewish defense of the State of Israel as a second instance of naked group interest, and, again, an abandonment of substantive moral deliberation. At the same time, Jews tend to view black critiques of Israel as black rejection of the Jewish right to group survival, and hence as a betrayal of the precondition for a black-Jewish alliance. What is at stake here is not simply black-Jewish relations, but, more importantly, the *moral content* of Jewish and black identities and of their political consequences.

The ascendance of the conservative Likud party in Israel in 1977 and the visibility of narrow black nationalist voices in the eighties helped solidify this impasse. When mainstream American Jewish organizations supported the inhumane policies of Begin and Shamir, they tipped their hats toward cold-hearted interest-group calculations. When black nationalist spokesmen like Farrakhan and Jeffries excessively targeted Jewish power as subordinating black and brown peoples they played the same mean-spirited game. In turning their heads from the ugly truth of Palestinian subjugation, and in refusing to admit the falsity of the alleged Jewish conspiracies, both sides failed to define the *moral* character of their Jewish and black identities.

The present impasse in black-Jewish relations will be overcome only when self-critical exchanges take place within and across black and Jewish communities not simply about their own group interest but also, and, more importantly, about what being black or Jewish mean in *ethical terms*. This kind of reflection should not be so naive as to ignore group interest, but it should take us to a higher moral ground where serious discussions about democracy and justice determine how we define ourselves and our politics and help us formulate strategies and tactics to sidestep the traps of tribalism and chauvinism.

The vicious murder of Yankel Rosenbaum in Crown Heights in the summer of 1991 bore chilling testimony to a growing black anti-Semitism in this country. Although this particular form of xenophobia from below does not have the same institutional power of those racisms that afflict their victims from above, it certainly deserves the same moral condemnation. Furthermore, the very *ethical* character of the black freedom struggle largely depends on the open condemnation by its spokespersons of *any* racist attitude or action.

In our present moment, when a neo-Nazi like David Duke can win fifty-five percent of the white vote (and sixty-nine percent of the white "born-again" Protestant vote) in Louisiana, it may seem misguided to highlight anti-Semitic behavior of black people—the exemplary targets of racial hatred in America. Yet I suggest that this focus is crucial precisely because we black folk have been in the forefront of the struggle against American racism. If these efforts fall prey to anti-Semitism, then the principled attempt to combat racism forfeits much of its moral credibility—and we all lose. To put it bluntly, if the black freedom struggle becomes simply a power-driven war of all against all that pits xenophobia from below against racism from above, then David Duke's project is the wave of the future—and a racial apocalypse awaits us. Despite Duke's resounding defeat, we witness increasing racial and sexual violence, coupled with growing economic deprivation, that together provide the raw ingredients for such a frightening future.

Black people have searched desperately for allies in the struggle against racism—and have found Jews to be disproportionately represented in the ranks of that struggle. The desperation that sometimes informs the antiracist struggle arises out of two conflicting historical forces: America's historically weak will to racial justice *and* an all-inclusive moral vision of freedom and justice for all. Escalating black anti-Semitism is a symptom of this desperation gone sour; it is the bitter fruit of a profound self-destructive impulse, nurtured on the vines of hopelessness and concealed by empty gestures of black unity. The images of black activists yelling "Where is Hitler when we need him?" and "Heil Hitler," juxtaposed with those of David Duke celebrating Hitler's birthday, seem to feed a single fire of intolerance, burning on both ends of the American candle, that threatens to consume us all.

Black anti-Semitism rests on three basic pillars. First, it is a species of anti-whitism. Jewish complicity in American racism—even though it is less extensive than the complicity of other white Americans—reinforces black perceptions that Jews are identical to any other group benefiting from white-skin privileges in racist America. This view denies the actual history and treatment of Jews. And the particular interactions of Jews and black people in the hierarchies of business and education cast Jews as the public face of oppression for the black community, and thus lend evidence to this mistaken view of Jews as any other white folk.

Second, black anti-Semitism is a result of higher expectations some black folk have of Jews. This perspective holds Jews to a moral standard different from that extended to other white ethnic groups, principally owing to the ugly history of anti-Semitism in the world, especially in Europe and the Middle East. Such double standards assume that Jews and blacks are "natural" allies, since both groups have suffered chronic degradation and oppression at the hands of racial and ethnic majorities. So when Jewish neoconservatism gains a high public profile at a time when black people are more and more vulnerable, the charge of "betrayal" surfaces among black folk who feel let down. Such utterances resonate strongly in a black Protestant culture that has inherited many stock Christian anti-Semitic narratives of Jews as Christ-killers. These infamous narratives historically have had less weight in the black community, in stark contrast to the more obdurate white Christian varieties of anti-Semitism. Yet in moments of desperation in the black community, they tend to reemerge, charged with the rhetoric of Jewish betrayal.

Third, black anti-Semitism is a form of underdog resentment and envy, directed at another underdog who has "made it" in American society. The remarkable upward mobility of American Jews—rooted chiefly in a history and culture that places a premium on higher education and self-organization—easily lends itself to myths of Jewish unity and homogeneity that have gained currency among other groups, especially among relatively unorganized groups like black Americans. The high visibility of Jews in the upper reaches of the academy, journalism, the entertainment industry, and the professions—though less so percentagewise in corporate America and national political office—is viewed less as a result of hard work and success fairly won, and more as a matter of favoritism and nepotism among Jews. Ironically, calls for black solidarity and achievement are often modeled on myths of Jewish unity—as both groups respond to American xenophobia and racism. But in times such as these, some blacks view Jews as obstacles rather than allies in the struggle for racial justice.

These three elements of black anti-Semitism—which also characterize the outlooks of some other ethnic groups in America—have a long history among black people. Yet the recent upsurge of black anti-Semitism exploits two other prominent features of the political landscape identified with the American Jewish establishment: the military status of Israel in the Middle East (especially in its enforcement of the occupation of the West Bank and Gaza); and the visible *conservative* Jewish opposition to what is perceived to be a major means of black progress, namely, affirmative action. Of course, principled critiques of U.S. foreign policy in the Middle East, of Israeli denigration of Palestinians, or attacks on affirmative action *transcend* anti-Semitic sensibilities. Yet vulgar critiques do not—and often are shot through with such sensibilities, in white and black America alike. These vulgar critiques—usually based on sheer ignorance and a misinformed thirst for vengeance—add an aggressive edge to black anti-Semitism. And in the rhetoric of a Louis Farrakhan or a Leonard Jeffries, whose audiences rightly hunger for black self-respect and oppose black degradation, these critiques misdirect progressive black energies arrayed against unaccountable corporate power and antiblack racism, steering them instead *toward* Jewish elites and antiblack conspiracies in Jewish America. This displacement is disturbing not only because it is analytically and morally wrong; it also discourages any effective alliances across races.

The rhetoric of Farrakhan and Jeffries feeds on an undeniable history of black denigration at the hands of Americans of every ethnic and religious group. The delicate issues of black self-love and black self-contempt are then viewed in terms of white put-down and Jewish conspiracy. The precious quest for black self-esteem is reduced to immature and cathartic gestures that bespeak an excessive obsession with whites and Jews. There can be no healthy conception of black humanity based on such obsessions. The best of black culture, as manifested, for example, in jazz or the prophetic black church, refuses to put whites or Jews on a pedestal or in the gutter. Rather, black humanity is affirmed alongside that of others, even when those others have at times dehumanized blacks. To put it bluntly, when black humanity is taken for granted and not made to prove itself in white culture, whites, Jews, and others are not that important; they are simply human beings, just like black people. If the best of black culture wanes in the face of black anti-Semitism, black people will become even more isolated as a community and the black freedom struggle will be tarred with the brush of immorality.

For example, most Americans wrongly believe that the black community has been silent in the face of Yankel Rosenbaum's murder. This perception exists because the moral voices in black America have been either ignored or drowned out by the more sensationalist and xenophobic ones. The major New York City newspapers and periodicals seem to have little interest in making known to the public the moral condemnations voiced by Rev. Gary Simpson of Concord Baptist Church in Brooklyn (with ten thousand black members), Rev. James

Forbes of Riverside Church (with three thousand members), Rev. Carolyn Knight of Philadelphia Baptist Church in Harlem, Rev. Susan Johnson of Mariners Baptist Church in Manhattan, Rev. Mark Taylor of the Church of the Open Door in Brooklyn, Rev. Victor Hall of Calvary Baptist Church in Queens, and many more. Black anti-Semitism is not caused by media hype—yet it does sell more newspapers and turn our attention away from those black prophetic energies that give us some hope.

• • •

My fundamental premise is that the black freedom struggle is the major buffer between the David Dukes of America and the hope for a future in which we can begin to take justice and freedom for all seriously. Black anti-Semitism—along with its concomitant xenophobias, such as patriarchal and homophobic prejudices—weakens this buffer. In the process, it plays into the hands of the old-style racists, who appeal to the worst of our fellow citizens amid the silent depression that plagues the majority of Americans. Without some redistribution of wealth and power, downward mobility and debilitating poverty will continue to drive people into desperate channels. And without principled opposition to xenophobias from above *and* below, these desperate channels will produce a coldhearted and mean-spirited America no longer worth fighting for or living in.

Andrew Hacker

Jewish Racism, Black Anti-Semitism

Andrew Hacker teaches political science at Queens College in New York City. He is the author of Two Nations: Black and White, Separate, Hostile, Unequal. *This essay appeared in a slightly different form in* Reconstruction, *Vol. 1, No. 3, 1991.*

■ **B**lack Americans who hold less than friendly feelings toward Jews have respectable company. After all, similar sentiments are common in all-white country clubs. As it happens, no one really knows if blacks and whites differ markedly in their feelings about Jews. (Such surveys as we have offer little reliable information.) What we do know is that if a black public figure makes any kind of statement that could be construed as anti-Semitic, it becomes a subject for widespread concern and discussion.

But, first, what is the meaning of anti-Semitism, at least in the context we are considering? At one level, the phrase simply suggests a distaste for some attributes deemed to be "Jewish." This was probably behind Jesse Jackson's description of New York City as "Hymietown," as well as in Spike Lee's depiction of two nightclub owners in his film *Mo' Better Blues*. Or as expressed in Leonard Jeffries's preoccupation with Jewish influence and power. Anti-Semitism can also have a theological resonance, as when Louis Farrakhan chose to call Judaism a "gutter religion." Or when Imamu Amiri Baraka (then LeRoi Jones) wrote, "the empty Jew betrays us, as he does hanging stupidly from a cross." Opposition to Israel, whether its very existence or its policies, may also carry anti-Semitic overtones. And then there is the wish to rid the world of all Jewish people. That Adolf Hitler also gassed infants made that objective clear. However, this extreme view has never gained much of a following within the United States.

Musing about Jews remains a conversational staple in many quarters. Since Jews are still seen as outsiders, even if not as exotic as in the past, commenting on them gives others an insider status. For black Americans, making critical remarks about Jews is a way of locating oneself within the national mainstream, indeed of establishing an affinity with whites. These tendencies are not new; they go back a long way. In *The Souls of Black Folk,* published in 1903, W.E.B. Du Bois took his readers on a tour of the Black Belt region of Georgia. "The Jew is heir to the slave-baron," he wrote. As a matter of fact, few Jews owned plantations either before or after the Civil War, a fact Du Bois well knew. Yet he somehow felt compelled to specify their presence. Later, speaking of hard economic times, he added that "only a Yankee or a Jew could squeeze more blood from debt-cursed tenants." So the mindset that led to Jesse Jackson's remark about New York can find antecedents in black America's most distinguished scholar.

As black Americans moved to northern cities, especially from the 1920s through the 1960s, they found themselves having more direct contact with Jews. Until a generation ago, Jews were often visible as merchants and landlords in black neighborhoods. Here is how James Baldwin remembered it:

> When we were growing up in Harlem, our demoralizing series of landlords were Jews, and we hated them. We hated them because they were terrible landlords and did not take care of the buildings.
> The grocer was a Jew, and being in debt to him was very

much like being in debt to the company store. The butcher was a Jew and, yes, we certainly paid more for bad cuts of meat than other New York citizens.

In addition, many middle-class Jewish families employed black women as domestic servants. Whether as servants or tenants or shoppers, blacks had few choices and little bargaining power. They saw themselves as being exploited, which was an accurate assessment: they were being overcharged and underpaid. Needless to say, they would have been treated no differently had their contact been with Christian employers and merchants and landlords. Indeed, during slavery in the South, it was Christian owners who bought and sold and punished them, just as it was Christians who lynched them in the postslavery period. In the North, Christian women hired white servants because they didn't want blacks in their houses, just as the stores and apartments Christians owned were likely to be in areas where blacks were not welcome. Yet it is instructive that one hardly ever encounters antipathy expressed explicitly toward white Christians.

The reason Jews bought real estate and set up businesses in black neighborhoods was because, at that time, they themselves faced barriers in the more established sectors of the city. And if many Jewish families appeared to prefer employing black women as their maids and laundresses, it may simply be that black help was cheaper. Indeed, when Jews grew wealthier, they tended to shift to white servants.

Starting in the 1920s, Jews began to play a prominent role in city services, where they often ended up administering rules affecting the lives of black citizens. (It should also be recalled that they gained these positions by passing competitive examinations, which gave them an interest in preserving what they regarded as an objective merit system.) They were also becoming teachers and administrators in the public schools, with a crucial authority over growing numbers of black children. In these settings, Jews often had more direct relationships with blacks than did other white Americans. (One exception was the police.)

As has been suggested, most Jews did not place themselves in proximity to blacks as a matter of choice. Indeed, fewer would do so when better business and professional opportunities opened up to them. Still, there was a lag, since some were tied to civil service careers. The issue came to a head in New York City some twenty-five years ago, in a section of Brooklyn then called Ocean Hill–Brownsville. A group of black parents charged that their children were falling behind educationally because of the lack of concern on the part of Jewish teachers and principals, who at that time still held most of the positions. As a result, there came a call for giving control of the schools to neighborhood boards, with the central aim of replacing existing personnel, especially at supervisory levels. A bitter strike followed, and its fallout is still being felt. While fewer New York City teachers today are Jewish, black disaffection from the schools persists.

It hardly needs recounting that Jews make a vivid target, much easier to identify than, say, Methodists or Presbyterians. For example, the lending policies of commercial banks have played a central role in maintaining residential segregation and blocking the development of black businesses. Moreover, hardly any of the nation's major corporations have made more than a token effort to promote black employees to executive positions. And the great majority of these institutions are owned and managed by Christians. Indeed, by any proportionate measure, Christian Americans have done far more than Jews to keep blacks down and back. In recent years, blacks sought to confront the higher citadels of power. If anti-Semitic utterances have a political purpose—a way of addressing one's real adversaries—it is a rather sad response. Even if no Jews at all lived in the United States, blacks would face the very same conditions they confront today. Much the same can be said of campaigns directed against Korean merchants in New York and Middle Eastern store owners in Detroit.

Finally, there is a more recent source of anti-Semitism. The last decade or so has seen among American blacks a resurgence of fellow feeling, not only for African nations and movements, but Islamic aspirations as well. Needless to say, the presence of Israel in the Middle East is seen as thwarting the rightful status of people of color. Israel is seen essentially as a white and European power, supported from the outside, and occupying space that rightfully belongs to the original inhabitants of Palestine. Nor can it be denied that Israel has been a military power, with its armaments aimed at darker people. That it is also a Jewish state allows anti-Israeli sentiment to meld into anti-Semitism. (The fact that Arabs are also members of the Semitic group is irrelevant here; in current parlance, "anti-Semitism" simply means animus toward Jews.)

In the eyes of many people, not all of them black, many Jews in the United States have a strong loyalty to Israel, almost a second citizenship. Some seem reflexively to defend all its policies, on the ground that anything less than full support could jeopardize the survival of that homeland. In response, some black Americans had identified with more radical Islamic movements. What others may see as terrorism, they perceive as a proud Third World awakening.

A further impetus to anti-Semitic rhetoric comes from blacks' awareness that Jews respond so readily to those onslaughts. When Leonard Jeffries included Italian-Americans in his indictment of Hollywood, they chose to ignore him as an insignificant nuisance. Indeed, it often seems that Jews are the only group who actually react to black attacks. Not the least reason why student groups invite anti-Semitic speakers is the knowledge that a minor campus event will evoke op-ed articles and full-page advertisements. Not least, blacks know that Jews are especially sensitive to accusations of racism, indeed more so than many other groups. To put the matter plainly, speakers like Jeffries and Farrakhan have been shrewd in deciding which buttons to push.

Many Jews will claim that they have—or once had—a distinct relationship with black Americans. If some Jews simply took their profits from ghetto shops and tenements, others devoted themselves to improving social conditions and relations between the races. Julius Rosenwald gave millions to Negro education, as it was then called, while Joel and Arthur Spingarn helped to found and sustain the NAACP. In the 1960s, northern Jews were prominent among those taking part in voter registration drives. Andrew Goodman and Michael Schwerner, on whom more will be said, sacrificed their lives for that cause.

Many of these Jews will also say that they have had a special devotion to liberty and justice, and the poor and deprived. In large measure, they may add, this stems from their own people's experience. But much of it is a matter of moral principle, and not simply sympathy. How, then, can such individuals be called racists? A word or two about this term may be appropriate at this time.

Like anti-Semitism, racism can take several forms. At its simplest, it involves stereotyping. Where racism is directed toward blacks, it begins with the presumption that certain traits and tendencies will be frequently found among members of that race. The next step is to ascribe those attributes to black individuals you do not know but happen to encounter. An oft-cited example is the taxicab driver who refuses to stop for a black rider, because he feels the odds are high that that passenger may turn out to be a robber.

There is also institutional racism. The XYZ Corporation, for example, will proclaim that it is an equal opportunity employer and hires and promotes on the basis of objective qualifications. Its executives will tell you what kinds of qualities they look for: attributes like vision, judgment, maturity, and leadership ability. Yet one "qualification" they never mention is that a candidate should look and act "white," so as to present the authority and image the institution wishes to convey. (To be a little more specific, they are looking for a Colin Powell.) Needless to say, it is not always easy for black candidates to satisfy that requirement, especially if they wish to preserve much of their personal identity.

But the most damaging form of racism goes further and deeper. It posits that people of African origin belong to an inferior subspecies, and no matter how hard they work or how much help they get, they can never perform on a par with members of other races. It is this expression of racism that will be considered here.

Whether they admit to it or not, virtually all white people believe that in genetic and evolutionary development, theirs is the preeminent racial stratum among the human species. And now comes a sensitive issue. Given that this expression of racism is common to whites, can it be said that with Jews it takes a special form? It isn't easy to speak with precision here. Much of what I will say on this point relates to liberalism generally, so the attitudes and reactions are not uniquely Jewish. At the same time, person for person, Jews are more likely than Christians to veer in a liberal direction. That said, there can be some peculiarly Jewish responses to racial issues.

What can be said, first, is that more Jews are apt to insist that they do not harbor racist sentiments. Thus unlike many white Christians, they will seldom be heard saying that they believe blacks to be inherently inferior. Or if they will occasionally admit that they have been guilty of reacting in racist ways, they will add that they hope they can exorcise whatever it is that gives rise to those actions and feelings. Hence a willingness to take part in workshops and seminars, to learn and to atone. If this may seem to mix moral superiority with guilt and humility, that is hardly an uncommon combination.

Three black writers have provided thoughtful comments on the racism they see as inherent in many Jewish well-wishers. It should be noted at the outset that these writers are not saying that Jews are the most racist of white Americans. On the contrary, for real racism, one has to go to those Christians who feel free to say that "niggers" are not only thugs and scum, but primates barely out of the trees. For whatever it is worth, far fewer Jews talk this way. (Even the term *schwartze,* which is seldom heard today, never carried the "nigger" connotations.)

Harold Cruse once remarked that what really roused his "enmity toward Jews" was hearing people who are Jewish say, "I know how you feel because I, too, am discriminated against." What concerned him, clearly, was an attempt to proclaim not only fellow feeling, but a bond of experience. To Cruse and many others, this attempt to establish a parity insults the ordeals black Americans have undergone since they were first put on slave ships. The only Jews who can make such a claim are those who were consigned to the Nazi death camps. Those who died, and they were the vast majority, suffered in the same hideous way as did the percentage of blacks who were expected to perish while crossing the Atlantic. (In fact, the highest death rates—and they were horrendous—were in West Indian plantations.) Yet the few Jews who survived the camps were, on their release, again accepted as members of the white race. In the years since 1945, none of them has known what it is like to be black.

It is revealing that whites who traveled south in 1964 referred to that sojourn as their "Mississippi Summer." It is as if all the efforts of local blacks for voter registration and the desegregation of public facilities had not even existed until white help arrived. Moreover, many of those who came were Jewish. And, as Nathan Wright observed at the time, at least some seemed to feel that their organizational experience and skills entitled them to take charge of the drives. Of course, this was done with benign intentions. The problem was not a lack of fellow feeling, but the condescending tone. One only had to look in on meetings to hear the new arrivals doing most of the talking. As Wright noted, they seemed to style themselves as "patrons" or "parents," with blacks consigned to the role of "children." Needless to say, serving as patron has been a common expression of racism: the belief that black people need white "help" because they lack the capacity to organize activities on their own.

For Jewish liberals, the great memory of that summer has been the deaths of Andrew Goodman and Michael Schwerner and—almost as an afterthought—James Chaney. Indeed, Cha-

ney's name always comes last—he was in the back seat of the
car—as if the life he lost was worth only three fifths of the
others'. And it was the fact that two whites were murdered that
brought media attention and FBI intervention. Even the more
recent movie, *Mississippi Burning,* cast local blacks as totally
dependent on white heroism.

Some sharper comments have come from Julius Lester.
A radio statement he once made deserves to be quoted at
some length.

> Jews tend to be a little self-righteous about their liberal record,
> always jumping to point out that they have been in the forefront
> of the fight for racial equality. . . .
>
> When they remind us continually of this role, then we realize
> that they were pitying us and wanted our gratitude, not the
> realization of the principles of justice and humanity. . . . Jews
> consider themselves liberals. Blacks consider them paternalistic.
>
> Black people have destroyed the previous relationship which
> they had with the Jewish community, in which we were the
> victims of a kind of paternalism, which is only a benevolent
> racism.

This is a serious indictment, for it suggests that Jewish
involvement in racial matters has been essentially an ego trip.
It could be argued that help is help, and one shouldn't worry
about the motives that impel it. Still, as Lester suggests, Jews
gave their support on their own terms. At best, blacks were
junior partners, who were expected to accept not only the pace
and goals deemed suitable by whites, but also to assume a
demeanor which made whites feel at ease. Thus there was the
presumption that black recipients would express gratitude,
with frequent expressions of thanks for white aid and support.

By the mid-1960s, however, such shows of appreciation
were less in evidence, leading many Jews and other liberals to
look for other causes. Indeed, there was widespread feeling
that black ingratitude was what first started the fraying of
the interracial compact. So Lester's association of "benevolent

racism" with Jews is especially important. It raises the question of whether the well-meant motives underlying a Jewish racism put it on a different level from biases that are obviously less sympathetic.

Julius Lester

The Lives People Live

Julius Lester has played a role in relations between blacks and Jews for almost three decades: from the reading of an anti-Semitic poem on his New York radio show in 1968 to his 1979 Village Voice *essay attacking black anti-Semitism to his 1982 conversion to Judaism to his 1985* New Republic *essay on Minister Farrakhan's appearance at Madison Square Garden. He is the author of many books, including* Lovesong: Becoming a Jew, *an autobiographical account of his spiritual odyssey to Judaism. He is a professor at the University of Massachusetts at Amherst and teaches in the Judaic studies, English, and history departments.*

To talk about blacks and Jews is to talk not about politics but the lives people live. After all, it is the lives we live that determine what we call our politics. Unless those lives are respected, there is no possibility of understanding the words we say to one another.

In recent years Jews and blacks have disagreed often over each other's words. Neither has understood sufficiently that in so doing, they are disagreeing with each other's lives. Thus, blacks have hurt Jews and Jews have hurt blacks.

Lives are not philosophical premises with which one is allowed to disagree, or over which one can have an argument. Lives are sacred. They are God's attempt to create prayers of bone and flesh. All too often Jews and blacks regard each other as merely issues to be analyzed and debated. When human beings reduce each other to abstractions, enmity must follow. Who should know this better than Jews and blacks?

First, let us acknowledge that blacks and Jews have real and serious differences, differences that may not be resolved by the most well-meaning of dialogues. That is okay. Agreement is not a prerequisite for alliance. Understanding and respect are.

A major difference is how each views black-Jewish relations. Jews are convinced that they have much in common with blacks, because the two groups share histories of oppression and suffering.

The Jewish version of black-Jewish relations is not shared by many blacks. Indeed, many blacks feel they have nothing in common with Jews. An examination of the historical record indicates that both groups are right, and both are also wrong.

What do blacks and Jews have in common?

(1) The histories of both begin in slavery.

(2) Throughout Western history blacks and Jews have been subjected to stereotyping by the white majority, and, often, the same stereotypes have been applied to both peoples. Jews and blacks have been equated with the devil and considered to have horns and tails. Europeans stereotyped both groups as being sexually licentious.

(3) Both people have been physically segregated from the majority. The word *ghetto* was first used to describe the section of Venice where Jews were segregated from gentiles in the sixteenth century. *Getto* is Italian for "iron foundry," and it was next to the iron foundry that the Jews of Venice were forced to live. Then and now, ghettos make their inhabitants feel like things apart from and less than the majority, and ghettos have stultifying effects on the physical and psychological health of their inhabitants.

(4) Jews and blacks suffered forced separation from their homelands and were dispersed throughout the Western world. Many blacks today refer to themselves as living in the Diaspora, not recognizing, perhaps, that they are using a word from the Jewish experience to describe their own.

However, there is a profound difference in the Diaspora experience of Jews and blacks. Jews not only knew that Israel was their home, they kept Israel alive within themselves as a homeland for two thousand years, a remarkable historical feat. For blacks, such a feat was not within the realm of possibility. Being brought to the New World from so many different parts of Africa, blacks had no common language, no common past, no common memories. For blacks the Diaspora is permanent.

(5) Both have been politically subjugated, with laws being passed restricting their movement in society, their choices of occupation, their social relationships.

(6) Both groups have been subjected to heinous violence. The pogroms against Jews in Eastern Europe have a parallel in this country in violent attacks by whites on black communities during the first two decades of this century.

While blacks as a group have not been targeted—as yet—for extermination as were Jews during the Third Reich, the number of Africans who perished during the centuries of the slave trade is staggering. The most conservative historical estimate is 15 million.

I can think of no two peoples who have endured so many of the same experiences throughout Western history. Both Jews and blacks have been condemned by the white majority, not because of anything we may have done but because of who we are. We are condemned for being, and nothing we do can eradicate who we are. We are Jews; we are blacks; therefore we are Other. The dominant society in whatever country we have lived has imposed a negative value on who we are. Jew and black are epithets in the vocabulary of the ruling majority. To use Max Weber's word, we are "pariahs."

Another similarity, then, is in how we have responded to being "pariahs." It is understandable, though not commendable, that many blacks and Jews have responded by attempting to assimilate. Some Jews have shortened or changed their names while others have shortened or changed their noses. Some have intermarried and disappeared as Jews. While a change of names would not help a black person, black magazines and newspapers still carry ads for creams to lighten the skin color and greases to straighten the hair. Some Jews take pride in being told that they "don't look Jewish." There are blacks who take pride in being told, "Well, you're different. You're not like those others."

Unless one removes himself or herself completely from the dominant society, as do ultra-Orthodox Jews and some black nationalists, it is impossible not to internalize some of the oppressor's value system. Blacks and Jews share much in how they resist and fight back against an oppressive value structure and preserve a sense of self and peoplehood independent of the pariah status. For example, look at comedy in America. Is it an accident that many of the most original and creative comedians in America are either Jewish or black? Lenny Bruce and Richard Pryor could have been brothers. Without Jews and blacks, I wonder if there would be laughter in America.

In their broad histories, Jews and blacks have many similarities, both in historical experiences and their responses to those experiences. So similar are some of the experiences, blacks use words from Jewish history to describe their own.

These similarities are important and neither blacks nor Jews are enough aware of them. I would like to believe that if we know and love what we share, it will be easier to talk about and accept the differences.

However, the differences are profound. The similarities I have just described, while true, are also misleading. They are misleading because these similarities are not, for the most part, the experiences of American Jews and American blacks but those of European Jews and American blacks. In other words, in the broad context of Western history, Jewish and black history have many similarities. However, in the specific context of American history, profound differences stand next to the historical similarities.

While similarity of experience is important, a similarity of experience is not the same as *shared* experience. That is the crucial difference of which many blacks are keenly aware and many Jews are not. Jews and blacks have parallel historical experiences in the broad context of Western civilization. They do not share experiences common to both people in the same time and the same place. This difference affects not only black-Jewish relations but the Jewish response to black anti-Semitism.

All too often Jews assume that black anti-Semitic expression is identical to that expressed throughout European history. This is not always so. Some black anti-Semitic expression stems from the volatile and unstable socioeconomic environment in America today. Although the words are anti-Semitic, the content may not be. This may be difficult for many Jews to understand, given the realities of Jewish history. But making this distinction will enable American Jewry to modify its approaches to black anti-Semitism and black-Jewish relations.

Making this distinction will enable us to pay closer attention to the particularities of American history and culture, which is radically different, in some ways, than that of Europe.

Today, America is undergoing the most profound cultural changes since the Emancipation Proclamation. These changes are confronting all of us with the challenge of redefining what it means to be an American as nonwhite ethnic groups demand that school curricula be reconceptualized and rewritten. Under the guise of a principle of inclusion called multiculturalism, the demand is for revolutionary change in which the centrality of Western culture and civilization in the curriculum will be replaced by an African-centered curriculum, or one in which the cultures of the so-called "peoples of color" will be dominant.

Regardless of how one critiques Afrocentrism and multiculturalism, there are enormous demographic changes taking place today, changes that cannot be ignored. Within the first two decades of the next century, demographers predict that, in the aggregate, African-Americans, Hispanics, and Asians will outnumber whites. America will have to reconceptualize itself from the white Anglo-Saxon Protestant image in which it was created. For the first time in the nation's history, whites will be in a minority. Norman Rockwell images as representative of America will truly become the anachronisms they always were.

On the one hand, we have a tremendous opportunity. America could become the first genuinely heterogeneous nation in the history of humanity, bringing together people from every country on the globe, and creating a new whole. There is a danger, however, that America could disintegrate into ethnic enclaves as much of Eastern Europe is doing. Instead of engaging in actual war, the American one would set groups against groups in a psychological cold war in which each group defends its psychic turf while proclaiming self-righteously that no one can understand them who is not of the group.

More and more, ethnic identity is becoming a substitute for personal identity. For many American blacks, the declaration that "I am an African-American" is an article of faith resonating to the very depths of the soul. Such a declaration bestows upon the individual a positive collective identity as a counterweight to the negative onus being black has had in the West.

However, one should not be deceived that the aggressive articulation of a positive collective identity has done much to dispel the demons of racial self-hatred in the black psyche. On the surface, Afrocentrism may sound like a necessary historical corrective to the centuries of Eurocentrism. Afrocentrism posits that Africa and Africans (and by implication, African-Americans) are the matrix from which all civilization came, that the ancient Egyptians were black, that the concept of monotheism originated in Egypt, that Moses was a black man and, therefore, Judaism was a black religion stolen from Africans and perverted by whites.

One is tempted, of course, to leap to the library shelves and prepare refutations. To do so would miss the deeper reality of despair and hopelessness about who and what one is that makes it necessary to recreate history in his own image.

There is in black America today a nihilism heretofore unknown in American history. It is not a philosophical and political nihilism. It is a nihilism born from the absence of self and the absence of hope. It is a condition without precedent in black American history because even during slavery blacks had hope because they believed in a merciful deity and redemptive suffering. Today, God is dead and suffering is for fools.

This nihilism is one of the factors underlying the thrust to Afrocentrism and anti-Semitism. The issue is no longer one of tensions between blacks and Jews. Jews are merely the lightning rod making visible a loss of self and a consequent violent desperation that we ignore at our peril.

Such an analysis is not meant to exculpate those who lack the moral sensibility to know that public anti-Semitic expression is as unacceptable as antiblack racist expression. But there is a moral double standard that tolerates anti-Semitic expression while condemning speech that is antiblack. Too many black leaders fail to understand that tolerance of anti-Semitic expression helps create an environment in which antiblack racist expression becomes even more acceptable. If blacks are serious in wanting to end racism (and I'm not certain that is a practical goal), then it is in the black self-interest to be in the forefront of those speaking out against black anti-Semitism.

It is in the Jewish self-interest to see black anti-Semitism, not from a European context, but within the complexities of American life today. Not only are we in the midst of an ethnic upheaval, but the American black community finds itself in the position of being economically surpassed, generation after generation, by successive waves of immigrants—Indians, Pakistanis, Arabs, Koreans, Vietnamese, Cambodians.

The immigrant success story is the quintessential American paradigm, and it is a story in which black Americans have had their noses rubbed for all too long. The lesson of the story is simple: "My ancestors came here; they had nothing; they couldn't even speak English. They made it. If you people haven't made it, it's your own fault."

To cite the immigrant experience as the paradigm is to ignore the legacy of slavery. Part of that legacy is a record of black achievement that is absolutely stunning when we consider that blacks of my generation are only three generations from slavery. But we who have achieved are not the whole story. The fact that seventy-five percent of all black infants are born to unwed mothers, half of whom are teenagers, is, in part, a legacy of slavery. This has dire social consequences for our nation in the twenty-first century.

To cite the immigrant experience as the paradigm is also to be blind to the seeming intractability of color prejudice in American society. In a 1988 study of racial attitudes conducted by the National Research Council, the conclusion was reached that the "status of blacks relative to whites has stagnated or regressed since the early 1970s," that "the ideals of equal opportunity and equal treatment for blacks were not endorsed by whites 'when they would result in close, frequent or prolonged contact.'"

Much of black anti-Semitic expression is a desperate attempt to be heard by people who do not have a language. If they hurl epithets at white people, white America doesn't listen. Say something anti-Semitic, however, and Jews will hear.

Black anti-Semitic expression draws attention to the speaker. It does not matter if that attention is negative. Negative attention is better than none at all. Under the glare of disapprobation, one becomes visible.

Perhaps nothing has made blacks more visible recently than the 1992 Los Angeles riots. We are fortunate it was not Jewish stores that were looted and burned. If they had been, Jews would have called the riots a "pogrom" and that would have been a mistake. Over the past few years there have been protests against Korean store owners in Los Angeles and New York, and protests against Indians, Pakistanis, and Arabs in other locales, and sometimes the language of the black protesters has been racist. It is obvious, however, that these protests, like the L.A. riots, are the "have-nots" striking out at the "haves," or, at those who appear to have.

The violence of the L.A. riots could have been averted if America had not been so callously indifferent to the cold statistics which tell us that the largest causes of death for young black men are either murder or suicide. A significant part of black America has been killing itself for two decades. Yet these facts do not produce anything remotely like the outcry that comes when some black utters anti-Semitic obscenities.

Much of black anti-Semitic expression is the ugly and desperate agony of those who cannot hope because they cannot dream because to hope and dream one must feel secure about his and her place on the earth. Without existential security one either becomes free or goes mad. I would suggest that in black America today there are pockets of collective madness which threaten to extinguish the tiny flicker of that flame we call freedom.

I wonder if we have not reached that point in time when an emphasis on black-Jewish relations is not misplaced. We can no longer afford to be nostalgic for the golden days of black-Jewish harmony and cooperation which were not as harmonious as hindsight would have us believe. The political challenge for all of us is to create a broad-based coalition across the ethnic spectrum. None of us want to see antiblack racist or anti-Semitic expression coming in a generation or two from the descendants of today's Hispanic and Asian immigrants.

American Jewry can only participate in a new coalition building if it understands that it is no longer an offshoot of German or East European Jewry. American Jewry is its own entity now, one unlike any Jewry that has ever been.

In Europe Jews had a distinct identity as Jews and were seen as a minority. In America the distinctiveness of that identity has been moderated because there is another group whose distinctiveness is more marked, namely, blacks. In America Jews became white because there existed a people called blacks. Regardless of the extent to which an individual may regard herself or himself a Jew, when walking down the street, that person blends in with the majority. White-skinned Jews look white in a crowd.

Because Jews partake of and share in the majority identity as whites, they have benefited economically. In Europe Jews were victims; in America Jews are a success story. Understandably, the very success makes many Jews nervous because the Jews of Weimar Germany were also a success story and we know what happened to them in less historical time than it takes to blink an eye. There are not many Jews sanguine enough to think that the same could not happen here.

From a black perspective, however, there is something jarring in hearing white-skinned Jews talk about suffering. No black denies that Jews suffered in Europe, but the Jewish experience in America has not been characterized by such suffering. The black experience has.

Many blacks feel that Jews borrow suffering from history to give themselves an identity and status as victims, and then use this vicarious suffering as the credentials to give themselves the right to express empathy with blacks.

Thus, what often comes out as black anti-Semitism is an attempt to express resentment toward Jews for assuming a relationship of shared suffering. As far as many young blacks are concerned, none exists. Blacks resent the Jewish assumption of shared oppression and use the language of anti-Semitism to make that resentment clear.

There are many statistics that could be cited to demonstrate the absence of shared suffering. I'll cite just two of the most chilling: (1) Blacks comprise twelve percent of the population but account for forty-five percent of all deaths by fire; (2) forty-seven percent of all black seventeen-year-olds are functionally illiterate.

I want you to imagine a black woman living in Crown Heights, the South Bronx, East New York, or in the innards of any major American city. I want you to imagine her living in a tenement that is a veritable firetrap. I want you to imagine her with her children and the rats and the roaches, subsisting on welfare with no hope or prospect of ever being employed or ever being able to change her condition. I want you to imagine her trying to understand why she is in this situation. I want you to imagine her trying to explain to her children why they will never be a part of the middle-class world depicted on the

TV screen. And she doesn't know why. There is no explanation that makes any sense whatsoever. Then along comes a black demagogue. He knows who is to blame—the Jew!

If we are dismayed that so many blacks listen to demagogues it is because only the demagogues are speaking to the despair and hopelessness of those trapped in poverty and ignorance. Unfortunately, too often Jews unwittingly enhance the status of such black anti-Semites. One could almost say that if you are black and want to be considered a leader in certain parts of black America today, say something anti-Semitic and get attacked by Jews.

It is time to stop assisting black anti-Semites in their thirst for attention. Denunciations of black anti-Semitism are in danger of being counterproductive. Equally, I wonder if it is useful any longer to speak of black-Jewish tensions. Yes, they exist, but are they the problem? Isn't the problem that a significant number of American citizens, namely, blacks, believe in nothing and no one and are incapable of becoming productive members of the society because they lack even the rudimentary skill of literacy?

Perhaps it is time we stopped speaking of a black problem and began talking about an American problem, because blacks are American citizens, to state an obvious fact that America has not grasped. The alienation, anger, resentment, despair, and hopelessness significant numbers of blacks feels finds expression in the vileness of anti-Semitism. Denunciations of black anti-Semitism are not enough, because anti-Semitism is not the whole problem.

The time has come when the plight of black America must be moved to a place of high priority on the national agenda. This time, however, it will not be done from any sense of liberal do-goodism, nor from any misplaced feelings of empathy or sympathy. This time we must act from our self-interest as Americans. The quality of our lives as Americans is threatened because there are all too many Americans who are not economically viable. Can you imagine the hatred that must be felt by one who knows that he or she is of absolutely no use socially, economically, politically? Can you imagine the rage in one who knows that his or her existence simply does not matter?

This is the context of today's black anti-Semitism. We should not be surprised or dismayed that so many blacks hate Jews. They hate themselves far, far more.

Self-hatred and despair are not justifications for black anti-Semitism, however. Unfortunately, all too many black intellectuals, artists, political and business leaders have been silent in the face of black anti-Semitic expression. All too often they have sought to justify it by saying such things as "Oppressed people can't be racist," or "We are not anti-Semitic because Arabs are Semites." Such statements would be laughable if they were not so obscenely immoral.

Black leaders have failed when they have not spoken out and said that anti-Semitism damages the black soul as surely as antiblack racism damages the white soul, that, in the words of James Baldwin, "It is a terrible, an inexorable, law that one cannot deny the humanity of another without diminishing one's own: in the face of one's victim, one sees oneself. . . . It is so simple a fact and one that is so hard, apparently, to grasp: *Whoever debases others is debasing himself.*"

Today, black America is living in an economic depression that can only get worse. This depression is further complicated by racism and by national and systemic problems. I see only one meaning in the never-ending statistics about life in black America: America does not care about black life. America does not care how black people live; it does not care if black people live. This is the black reality, and to speak of black-Jewish relations without addressing the concrete despair of blacks is to indulge in nostalgia for a time that never was. Poverty does not ennoble; it embitters. It embitters until people are left with no power except that of hatred and destruction.

If there is to be any kind of new black-Jewish coalition it must first put aside sentimental notions that there is some kind of God-ordained bond shared by blacks and Jews. The notion that blacks and Jews should be friends is romanticism at its worst.

There is a hopelessness and despair in black America today which is indescribable. It is shortsighted for white America, including American Jewry, to think that black poverty is a black problem. It is not. It is a national problem. It is a problem of such scope that it has the potential to endanger the very life of the nation. Those black gangs that are now killing blacks will, one day in the near future, start randomly killing whites. It is in the self-interest of blacks and Jews to come together and seriously address the issues of black poverty, unemployment, education, et cetera. If blacks and Jews do not come together and do this, then are we not betraying something of what it means to be a black or a Jew?

Let me close by suggesting the following as a possible course of action:

(1) The economic problems of black America must be taken seriously, even at a time when the nation as a whole is in an economic crisis. What is a crisis in the nation is unmitigated catastrophe in black America.

The nation must be awakened to the danger within its gates. The annual reports put out by the NAACP and Urban League on the state of black America are worthy of study and of being taken seriously.

The first step, then, is educating America to the realities and the implications for the nation as a whole. This could be done through a "Call to Conscience and Responsibility" issued by the major denominations of Christianity and the four branches of Judaism. Such a statement would be read from pulpits and bimahs with follow-up workshops and study sessions.

(2) The second step would be identifying possible areas of common interest that can be worked on at the local level. I reiterate that this would not be the return of sixties liberal paternalism. It is in the self-interest of white and Jewish Americans that the cities be clean

and safe. It is in the self-interest of white and Jewish Americans that drug use be reduced. It is in the self-interest of white and Jewish Americans that all citizens be literate.

What needs to be done is that we save ourselves.

It cannot be done in a year, a decade, or even a generation. But unless the kind of activity I am suggesting is begun, the nihilism swallowing ever larger portions of black America will eventually swallow us all.

Sometimes, we become so focused on our lives as blacks or Jews, we forget that these particulars are not the totality of who we are. What we share and what we must acknowledge that we share is a common humanity and common aspirations for life, liberty, and the pursuit of happiness.

Perhaps it is time, then, that we enlarge our visions beyond our particular pains. Perhaps it is time we came together to address ourselves to the pain of our nation.

Shelby Steele

Breaking Our Bond
of Shame

*Shelby Steele is a professor of English at San Jose State
University and the author of* The Content of Our Character.
This essay originally appeared in a slightly different form in
New York Newsday, *January 4, 1989.*

■ **G**rowing up black in the fifties, I always
knew that Jews were different from other whites. I knew we
had something in common with them. When, at age ten, I
joined an all-white swim team, it was the parents of the only
Jewish boy on the team who made a point of inviting me to
their home in a well-to-do suburb for lunch and a swim in their
pool. There was a striking determination in their kindness that
embarrassed me a little. Clearly my color held a significance
for them. I had a good time and stayed on my best manners,
but I was never altogether comfortable. We couldn't seem to
find much in common.

Unlike the other white families, this very nice Jewish family
could not so easily ignore my outsider's vulnerability in this
situation since they, too, had intimate knowledge of it. And so
their invitation amounted to a recognition of kinship, a kinship
based on the mark of outsidedness. This is the underlying

kinship that blacks and Jews in America have always shared. And though it once inspired a fruitful cooperation, I believe it is now the source of much bitterness between us.

The problem with kinships of any kind is that they are fated rather than chosen. We don't pick our kin. And it was the hard fate that made blacks and Jews the scapegoats of others that also gave them their kinship. Fate, not choice, created our commonality.

And this is a very problematic kind of connection because it gives the impression of more commonality than really exists. Differences between two groups are never more obvious and troublesome than when they chafe against a presumed commonality. I'm sure this is why the media is so fascinated with black-Jewish bickering. It has the fundamental irony that always makes for a good story, the same irony that seduces us to eavesdropping on family spats—the irony of there being conflict where we presume there should be harmony.

But it is not only the media that presumes more commonality than there is. Blacks and Jews, themselves, have too often assumed that their self-interests would be supported by the other because of their kinship. Blacks have felt that Jews, of all people, should understand how their oppression entitles them to affirmative action. And Jews have felt that blacks, of all people, should understand how their long history of suffering and dispersion entitles them to support Israel against all Arab claims.

It is our underlying kinship that makes these differences *personal* rather than impersonal. Kinship creates a context in which disagreement amounts to betrayal. And once each group feels sufficiently betrayed by the other, communication becomes recrimination. Neither group takes it so personally when they find themselves at odds with Polish, Irish, or even Hispanic-Americans.

There is another and, I think, deeper problem with this kinship that is rarely discussed. Because it is a kinship grounded in the common experience of rejection, it has always carried an undercurrent of shame. But shame is an intolerable feeling. We always distance ourselves from it, deny it, or project it onto others. I think Jews and blacks today distance themselves from each other and their kinship as a way of distancing from the shame implied in that kinship. An example of this happened in the New York Democratic presidential primary of 1988, when Mayor Koch made flagrant and provocative attacks on Jesse Jackson, who came into the primary facing considerable Jewish hostility. Just as Mayor Koch was eager to show disdain for Jackson, Jackson himself made a dramatic show of hanging tough against Jewish pressure to apologize for anti-Semitic remarks he had made four years earlier. Both men seemed determined to show the world that the old kinship was dead. They seemed to be fighting the presumption by the larger society that they had a kinship, as much as fighting each other. In this presumption was the shame of both groups, and each man declared his freedom from the other as if from the shame itself.

The unseen problem between blacks and Jews—the third party to their hostilities—is this presumption by the larger society that we make up a brotherhood of outsidedness. This presumption shames us and makes us invisible. And we fight against each other to prove it wrong, to show that we have no such brotherhood. Koch hoped all Americans were listening when he attacked Jackson so they would see that he was aligned with them and not blacks. Jackson hoped the same thing when he granted no special status to Israel.

But this strategy won't work. Neither group can escape its fate at the other's expense. And when we try to, we miss the obvious—that our real struggle remains with ourselves and with the larger society.

SEVERAL
CONTROVERSIES

Ellen Willis

The Myth of the Powerful Jew

Ellen Willis, an associate professor of journalism at New York University, is the author of Beginning to See the Light: Sex, Hope, and Rock-and-Roll *and* No More Nice Girls: Countercultural Essays. *"The Myth of the Powerful Jew" originally appeared in* The Village Voice, *September 2, 1979.*

PROLOGUE (1994)

In the summer of 1979 it came to light that Andrew Young, at the time Jimmy Carter's ambassador to the UN, had met secretly with his counterpart in the PLO. Young was forced to resign, touching off yet another crisis in black-Jewish relations. During the intense debate that followed, *The Village Voice* published an article by a black writer, Joel Dreyfuss, attacking Jews in terms that had by then become all too familiar: Jewish power and Jewish racism, he argued, were the source of black anti-Jewish sentiment. "The Myth of the Powerful Jew," which also appeared in the *Voice,* was my answer not only to Dreyfuss but to the proliferation of black voices that justified hostility to Jews as a rational response to black oppression.

Nearly fifteen years later, anger at "Jewish power" is still a potent emotional current within black communities, finding expression in call-in programs on black radio stations, in the rhetoric of a Farrakhan or a Jeffries, in suggestions that Jews conspired to frame Lemrick Nelson or absolve the driver who hit Gavin Cato. The denial of anti-Semitism—what I call in my essay its "subterranean character"—remains pervasive. Yet if the deep structures of anti-Semitism continue to affect black-Jewish relations—as, of course, do equally entrenched patterns of white racism—the political context of those relations has changed a great deal. For the urban black poor, the legacy of the Reagan-Bush era and its scorched-earth policy toward the cities has been accelerating rage, demoralization, and political impotence. No mainstream organization or politician, Jesse Jackson included, can lay serious claim to mobilizing poor blacks; nor do the remnants of the white left, hopelessly fragmented into single-issue movements, offer any concrete prospects of interracial coalition. What has mostly passed for grass-roots black activism is the crudest form of neonationalism, which during this period has been less a movement than an emotional outlet, venting fury and frustration on Jews, Koreans, feminists, inventing public psychodramas like the Tawana Brawley case.

At the same time, however, the black middle class expanded, producing a sizable new generation of intellectuals just as the disarray of black politics was weakening pressures toward ideological unity. As a result, public debate among blacks is far livelier and further-ranging today than it was at the end of the seventies. While black conservatives have gotten the most attention, in the long run it may be more significant that increasing numbers of black radicals and feminists have rejected nationalism and separatism, challenged many of the conventional assumptions of identity politics, and begun to explore race as part of a larger complex of social and cultural formations. This new brand of radicalism is, if not universalist in the old imperial sense, nevertheless cosmopolitan—and correspondingly allergic to anti-Semitism.

Similar conflicting patterns arose among different groups of Jews in the eighties. In cities like New York, working-class and lower-middle-class Jews generally, and Orthodox Jews in particular, tended to drift rightward: their cultural conservatism and support for Israeli militance resonated with Reaganite themes, while fear of crime and worry about affirmative action hampering Jewish mobility fueled racist resentment. Among middle-class Jews, passionate debates broke out. As the neoconservatives moved further to the right, a self-consciously Jewish left struggled to carve out a distinctive political space: it aimed to publicly confront neoconservatism (and the widespread, erroneous perception that most Jews had thrown their lot in with the right); to oppose the policies of an increasingly hard-right Israeli government while firmly defending Israel's right to exist and pointing out the covert anti-Semitism in much anti-Israel polemic; and to criticize left and populist anti-Semitism, including the black variety, from a standpoint that was clearly democratic and anti-racist.

While this project was already getting started before Reagan's election, he proved to be its most effective organizer. The administration's ruinous antiurbanism, its contempt for the poor, minorities, and anyone marginal or different, its open alliance with the Christian right all pushed Jewish liberal buttons. And unlike Carter, who had aroused Jewish anxiety and defensiveness with his evident desire to shift American Middle East policy in a pro-Arab direction, Reagan and his fundamentalist pals enthusiastically embraced the Likud's rejectionism; as a result many Jews felt freer to acknowledge their own qualms about the marriage of the right's revisionist Zionism and religious fanaticism that threatened Israel's flawed, but still vital, liberal-democratic and secular underpinnings. Public arguments about Israel, no longer taboo, became part of the fabric of intra-Jewish conversation.

All this suggests that black-Jewish relations are by no means of a piece. On one level, it seems, the people most affected by the deterioration of urban life face each other through intractable prisms of ethnic nationalism, of mutually aggravating racism and anti-Semitism, that allow for little hope of resolution; yet on the level of ideas there are encouraging signs of convergence, as skepticism toward nationalist and particularist dogmas has gained currency in both Jewish and black circles. While it's easy to dismiss these signs as coming from a small elite, I'd argue that ideas do matter: just as racism and anti-Semitism are, among other things, ideas that give concrete focus to people's anger and fear, so a renaissance of cosmopolitan thinking might be a catalyst for people's buried hopes and desires for connection beyond their own beleaguered group.

My own perspective has also shifted. When I wrote this essay, I took for granted certain basic propositions of identity politics, including the axiom that national self-determination is a good thing. There followed certain unacknowledged contradictions in my piece: between my analysis of anti-Semitism as embedded in the patriarchal unconscious and my presentation of racism as simply a matter of black oppression versus white power; my acceptance of a national liberationist argument for a Jewish state and my implicit personal commitment to the Diaspora; my call for a just compromise between nationalisms and my recognition that inevitable irredentism would keep any compromise forever unstable and, for Israelis, fundamentally insecure. The last contradiction is of course the toughest—though I'm rooting for the peace agreement as much as anyone, I'd argue that Israel's basic dilemma remains—and how to resolve it is still unclear. What is clear, though, is that the language of nationalism—and more broadly of particularist identity—has become an obstacle to thought. Since the start of the eighties I've been involved, as a feminist, in an intense battle against the repressive version of female cultural nationalism embodied in the antipornography movement. I've had to recognize the inadequacy of separate discourses of black and female liberation that make black women, in effect, disappear. I've witnessed the frightening resurgence of right-wing nationalism in Europe and its apotheosis in the genocidal destruction of Bosnia. As for the Israeli-Palestinian conflict, I can no longer imagine that the terms of this grim zero-sum game have to do with liberation, in any meaningful sense, for either side.

What does all this have to do with blacks and Jews, or anti-Semitism and racism? A lot, it seems to me. More, arguably, than any other group, Jews have had an "excuse" for nationalism: at a fateful historical moment it was the only conceivable way to fight back against relentless, death-dealing isolation. Post-Holocaust Zionism represented in distilled form the urge to jam that isolation in the teeth of one's enemies that is somewhere at the heart of every nationalist response to oppression. Yet by now it should be evident that Israel can neither solve the problem of anti-Semitism nor represent Jews or Jewishness in general. For those of us who continue, spiritually as well as physically, to choose the Diaspora, Israel may have great emotional and political significance, but it is not the touchstone of our identity. And if the Jewish national moment has in some sense been surpassed—even as the danger that produced it is by no means gone!—this surely signifies something profound about the untenability of nationalist solutions. Indeed it calls into question any particularism organized around nationalist metaphors.

I'm suggesting, in other words, that concepts of national liberation no longer speak to the needs of either blacks or Jews. As global capital increasingly supersedes the nation state as the source of authority and power, the hysterical proliferation of new nation states, like fascism in the 1930s, is a rear-guard action against inexorable modernity. What remains, however, is the underlying authoritarian-patriarchal structure in whose cultural psychology the figures of black and Jew play their indispensable roles. The part of my essay that comes out of this understanding is, I think, the part that holds up best.

THE MYTH OF THE POWERFUL JEW (1979)

Anti-Semitism is the socialism of fools.

—August Bebel, German Socialist
and leader of the Social Democrats in
the late nineteenth century

Obviously, the fury of black people at Andy Young's departure reflects a decade or more of increasing tensions between blacks and Jews. What is perhaps less obvious is how much the entire

incident reflects deteriorating relations between Jews and non-
Jews generally. Any useful discussion of black-Jewish conflict
must begin by acknowledging two basic realities. One is that
American Jews are white* and predominantly middle-class and
so tend to have a white middle-class perspective on racial issues.
The other is that blacks are part of the gentile majority and so
tend to share the misconceptions about Jews and the overt or
unconscious anti-Jewish attitudes that permeate our culture.
Unfortunately, neither group has been eager to accept its share
of responsibility for the conflict. If Jews have often minimized
their privileges and denied or rationalized their racism, blacks
have regularly dismissed Jewish protest against anti-Semitism
in the black community as at best oversensitivity, at worst
racist paranoia. And in the end, guess who benefits from all
the bitterness? Hint: The answer isn't blacks or Jews.

Blacks have repeatedly argued that black hostility toward
Jews is simply the logical result of Jews' behavior, either as
landlords, teachers, and other representatives of white authority in black neighborhoods or as political opponents of black
goals. As a Jew who stands considerably left of the mainstream
Jewish organizations, let alone neoconservative intellectuals—
and as a feminist who supports affirmative action for women
as well as minorities—I don't think it's that simple. To attack a
rip-off landlord with standard anti-Semitic rhetoric about
greedy, exploitative Jews is to imply that the problem is the

---

*To be more precise, white Americans have generally classified Ashkenazim—Jews
of European origin—as white, Jews have benefited from white privilege (though we
have suffered from ethnic discrimination as non–Anglo Saxons), and it is probably
accurate to say that most American Jews think of themselves as white. But as a number
of readers—both Jewish and black—pointed out, the definition is questionable. Jews
are a multiracial people and, as one correspondent put it, even among Ashkenazim
"there are those of us who cannot fit the racial designation as white." (He described
himself as dark-skinned and stereotypically Jewish looking.) Several people suggested
that while many Jews can pass as white, identifying with white people has been a way
of internalizing our oppression, and that to be authentically Jewish we must embrace
a nonwhite identity. I would say rather that since Jewishness is not a racial category—
since, on the contrary, the definition of the Jews as one people is an offense to the
very idea of pure races—to identify fully as Jews is to refuse to define ourselves in
racial terms, to repudiate race as a way of categorizing people, and to oppose all
institutions and practices that perpetuate racial hierarchies.

iniquity of Jews rather than the race and class of white land-lords. (When blacks protest the behavior of white cops, who are rarely Jewish, they don't feel compelled to mention the officers' ethnic backgrounds.) Black criticism of Jewish politics invites the same objection. At worst Jews have been no more hostile to black power than the rest of the white population, though most people couldn't withdraw from the civil rights movement since they hadn't been involved in it in the first place. While the resistance of Jewish organizations to affirma-tive action has been to some extent based on fear of maximum quotas for Jews—and on the (illusory) hope that achievement and material security will protect us from anti-Semitism—it has more to do with the fact that most Jewish men share with most other white men the belief that affirmative action is illegitimate "reverse discrimination." In fighting community control, the Ocean Hill–Brownsville teachers were acting not as Jews but as white people whose livelihood was threatened. Besides, on all these issues a significant number of Jewish liberals and radicals has supported blacks and opposed the Jewish establishment. In general, though segments of the Jew-ish community have drifted to the right along with the rest of the country, Jews remain the most liberal group in the white population, far to the left of non-Jews in comparable economic and social circumstances. So why have blacks made such a point of singling out Jews for criticism?

As Joel Dreyfuss noted in last week's *Voice,* disillusionment is a factor; Jews have talked a better line and had a better record on race than other whites, and groups with a history of oppression are always supposed to be more sensitive to each other's aspirations, although, as James Baldwin put it, "if people did learn from history, history would be very different." The disillusionment is compounded when Jews invoke their status as an oppressed people to avoid confronting their racism (though blacks have committed the same evasion in reverse). It is also convenient and tempting to vent one's anger at a visible and relatively vulnerable minority. But the main impetus to black resentment of Jews *as Jews* seems to be that black people do not perceive Jews as vulnerable. Dreyfuss argues that the issue for blacks is Jewish power; he claims that "American Jews exert an economic, political, and intellectual influence on this country far out of proportion to their numbers" and repeats the familiar allegation that Jews dominate the media.

I would guess that this view is shared by a great many, if not most, non-Jewish whites as well as blacks. I think it is profoundly wrong. Jewish privilege is real; Jews certainly exert intellectual influence; but actual power is another matter. As business people, professionals, journalists, academics, Jews are in a position to further whatever interests they share (or think they share) with the rest of the white middle class or with the ruling elite. But the real test of power is whether Jews can protect specifically Jewish interests when they diverge from—or conflict with—the interests of non-Jews. If the United States government decides it is in America's economic and military interest to abandon Israel, do Jews have the power to prevent a change in policy? If there is a resurgence of anti-Semitism in this country, do Jews have the power to quell it and insure their survival? These questions are not hypothetical; America's Middle East policy is certainly changing, to the dismay of most Jews, and I experience more anti-Semitism (mostly from white people) than I did ten years ago.

If Jews have power, its sources are mysterious. Jews may own newspapers and movie studios, but the truly powerful own banks, factories, and oil. Jews have been virtually excluded from America's corporate and financial elite. There are few Jews at the highest levels of government or the military. As a tiny minority—3 percent of the population—Jews do not have the political clout of sheer numbers, except in a few heavily Jewish areas like New York. With the decline of the cities, Jewish influence has decreased; power to set national policy is now centered in the Southwest, hardly a Jewish stronghold, and the widespread anti–New York, antiurban sentiment that has fed the conservative backlash is aimed at Jews as well as blacks.

If Jews are "overrepresented" in certain privileged occupations, it is equally true that Jews' awareness of their vulnerable position and their identification with other oppressed groups have led them to get involved in liberal and radical movements "far out of proportion to their numbers." Yet Dreyfuss, so sensitive to Jewish influence in other areas, not only neglects to mention Jewish leftism but tries to write it out of history. In a bizarre attempt to blame the Jews for Roy Wilkins's and Whitney Young's break with Martin Luther King over the latter's opposition to the Vietnam War, Dreyfuss alleges that the rift "reflected [Wilkins's and Young's] dependence on Jewish support, since Jews strongly supported the U.S. presence in Vietnam." This charge is too absurd to deserve a response, but for the all too easily "forgotten" record, from the start Jews and Jewish organizations were virtually unanimous in their opposition to the war. Jews played a major role in the antiwar movement and the new left generally, and while George McGovern suffered the worst defeat in American electoral history, Jews voted for him 2 to 1. Such politics hardly reflect an uncritical identification with power. Nor do our increasingly conservative rulers share Dreyfuss's incognizance of Jews' leftist tendencies, though they are inclined to encode their distaste in euphemistic references to New Yorkers or intellectuals. Attacked from the left for being too well-off and from the right for being too left-wing, Jews lack even the contingent power of dependable political allies.

Jews are relatively well organized and vocal politically, but as with other well-organized minorities, their effectiveness has depended on the absence of any strong counterforce. It is ridiculous to imagine, as Dreyfuss apparently does, that the United States's Middle East policy is or ever has been dictated by Jews. Here he displays some confusion, since he also points out that Israel is "viewed in the Third World as a surrogate for Western interests" and faults Jews for once again choosing the wrong side. So which is it? Does America support Israel because of the Jews, or are Jews merely bolstering American imperialism? The reality is that until recently, Jewish pressure on behalf of Israel dovetailed neatly with the American government's political objectives. But Jews' stake in Israel and United States interests in the Middle East are by no means the same. Whatever our differences about the Israeli government, Palestinian rights, or American foreign policy, most Jews agree on the need for a Jewish state. The American government encouraged the establishment of Israel for power-political reasons (and perhaps as a way of dealing with the embarrassing problem of Jewish refugees no country was willing to absorb); it has continued to support Israel as a pro-Western, anti-Soviet ally in a strategically vital region. But in the past few years the U.S. has been reevaluating its stance, in line with changing political realities; as a result, Jewish lobbying has met increasing resistance. Despite supposed Jewish control of the media, coverage of the Middle East and the climate of public opinion have evolved more or less in accordance with government policy, growing steadily less sympathetic to Israel.

In general, the major media—including Jewish-owned institutions like *The New York Times*—reflect establishment politics, whether or not they coincide with Jewish interests or opinion. Evidently, either Jews are less dominant in the media than popular wisdom insists, or Jewish publishers and Hollywood producers put their class loyalties before their Jewishness. Dreyfuss complains that "Jewish dissidents in the Soviet Union enjoy a flood of publicity, but black dissidents in South Africa are ignored until they are killed." Can he seriously believe this bias reflects Jewish influence rather than government and corporate hostility to the USSR and sympathy with the staunchly capitalist South African regime? He contrasts indifference to racism in television with the "uproar" that followed the casting of Vanessa Redgrave as a concentration camp victim. Yet the Jewish protest elicited no serious, thoughtful response, only condescending lectures about the evils of blacklisting and the right to criticize Israel. (I keep waiting for someone to notice that these days dumping on Israel is about as daring as defending the family, but no such luck.)

The danger of getting carried away with fantasies about Jewish power is manifest in Dreyfuss's assertion that "Jews have taken control of [New York City's] political apparatus. In the process of exercising their new powers they have neglected to appease the powerless. . . ." Just a minute. Who is this "they"? It certainly isn't me, or even the American Jewish Committee; it would seem, actually, to be one lone Jew, Ed Koch. (What about poor Abe Beame? He may not have been memorable, but he did exist.) In his zeal to pin blacks' troubles on the Jews, Dreyfuss not only makes a dubious leap from the particular to the general, he totally ignores the context of Koch's administration—draconian fiscal retrenchment imposed on the city from outside. Koch's brushing aside of minority concerns is indefensible (again, his whiteness, not his Jewishness, is the relevant category), but the people who really call the shots on New York are the president, Congress, and a bunch of bankers and realtors. I fail to see what Jews as a group are getting out of this depressing situation.

It is disingenuous of Dreyfuss to argue that "Jewish power in America has always been a difficult subject to address. . . . Their most effective tactic has been to attack any references to the power of Jews as 'anti-Semitic,' immediately blocking further discussion." Talk about blocking discussion! I can only pursue this one honestly if I'm permitted to say what I think, which is that the notion of Jewish power is a classic anti-Semitic myth. There are historical parallels to Jews' present position in America. In pre-Inquisition Spain, in Weimar Germany, Jews were a privileged and seemingly powerful group, a conspicuous cultural force. But their status did not protect them; on the contrary, charges of excessive Jewish power and influence in behalf of their own nefarious ends served as a rationale for persecution. Hence American Jews' feelings of insecurity, which—according to Dreyfuss—blacks find so mystifying.

Discrimination against Jews in America has not been comparable to the systematic, relentless bigotry inflicted on blacks. But in concluding that Jewish oppression can be defined as "exclusion similar in conception but vastly different in degree from the black experience," Dreyfuss makes a common mistake. Though there are obvious parallels between white racism and anti-Semitism—particularly racial anti-Semitism of the Nazi variety—the psychology of anti-Semitism, the way it functions in society, and the nature of the threat to the Jews are in certain respects unique. Unlike racism, anti-Semitism does not necessarily involve straightforward economic subjugation. Historically, Jews' distinctive class and cultural patterns, their visibility as representatives or symbols of authority (from the Harlem storekeeper on up the class ladder, but rarely at the very top), and their reputation as hustlers, achievers, intellectuals, and social activists have been the basis of anti-Semitic stereotypes used to justify attacks on Jews. Jews are simultaneously perceived as insiders and outsiders, capitalists and communists, upholders of high ethical and intellectual standards and shrewd purveyors of poisonous subversive ideas. The common theme of these disparate perceptions is that Jews have enormous power, whether to defend established authority or to undermine it. It is this double-edged myth of Jewish power that has made Jews such a useful all-purpose scapegoat for social discontent. The classic constituency for fascism is the conservative lower middle class, oppressed by the rich, threatened by the rebellious poor (particularly if the poor are foreign or another race); for this group Jews are a perfect target, since they represent the top and the bottom at once. Oppressed classes like the peasants in czarist Russia have traditionally directed their anger at the Jews just above them in the social hierarchy. Politically, the specter of the powerful Jew functions in much the same way as a foreign enemy: it invites warring classes, races, and political groups to submerge their conflicts and enjoy a heady sense of spurious unity.

The advantage to ruling classes of keeping Jews around as surrogate authority figures, outside agitators, and enemies of the people is obvious. But anti-Semitism can't be explained simply as a political tool; it is deeply irrational. The insane obsessiveness of Hitler's determination to wipe out the Jews even at the expense of his war effort was, in my view, not an aberrational form of anti-Semitism but its logical extreme. I think anti-Semitism is bound up with people's anger not only at class oppression but at the whole structure of patriarchal civilization—at the authoritarian family and state, at a morality that exalts the mind, denigrates the body, and represses sexuality. It's no coincidence that a Jew, Sigmund Freud, was first to observe that "civilized" self-denial generates an enormous reservoir of unconscious rage. I believe it is this rage, along with misdirected anger at economic and political oppression, that erupts in the murder of Jews. In one sense, Jews *have* been immensely powerful: they created a potent myth—influential in both Christian and Islamic cultures—that explains patriarchal civilization and includes an elaborate set of rules for right living in it. And Jews themselves play a special role in this myth, as God the Father's chosen people, commanded to carry out an ethical and spiritual mission in behalf of the world—to obey God's laws and by doing so bring the Messiah, who will redeem and liberate us all. As the protagonists of this paradoxical vision, Jews are at once superego figures and symbols of revolution, who evoke all the ambivalent feelings that stem from the contradictions of patriarchy.

Just as the idealization of femininity is inseparable from male resentment of women, anti-Semitism is two-faced. It includes admiration of Jewish achievements, the idea that Jews are morally superior, guilt, and identification with the Jew-as-victim. The complementary attitudes inevitably follow: envy; the conviction that Jews are too powerful; a combination of special outrage and covert gloating whenever Jews are revealed to be, alas, morally imperfect (check out the reaction to any Jew judged guilty of unsaintly behavior, from Bernard Bergman to Menachem Begin); resentment at having to feel guilty about the Jews, it was thirty-five years ago, after all; a mixture of self-congratulation and defensiveness at daring to criticize Jews; anger at Jews who refuse to act like victims. (An article on the Vanessa Redgrave flap pointed to her acceptance of the inmate's role as evidence that anti-Zionism and anti-Semitism are not synonymous. On the contrary, Redgrave exemplifies a mentality that has flourished ever since 1967, when Israel became the prime metaphor for the powerful Jew: she hates Bad Jews—

Zionists—and loves Good Jews—victims, preferably dead.) But the power of Jews as emotional symbols would mean little if they were not hugely outnumbered and so, in reality, powerless. It is the combination that makes anti-Semitism so appealing: to kill a gnat, imagining it's an elephant, is to feel powerful indeed.

I think people's feelings about Jews are largely unconscious, that discrimination and outbreaks of anti-Jewish persecution are only the most obvious symptoms of a chronic social disease that exists mainly under the surface. This is why anti-Semitism flares up so readily in times of social crisis; it is why Jews feel permanently insecure; it accounts for the gap in communication between Jews who feel that gentiles are oblivious of the threat of anti-Semitism and gentiles who think that Jews are always looking for anti-Semites under the bed. Anti-Semitism involves dark impulses that most people would rather not recognize in themselves, impulses connected with our deepest guilts and anxieties. Even people who are sophisticated about the politics of race and sex tend to cling to a simplistic view of anti-Semitism as plain old discrimination, punctuated from time to time with persecution by evil lunatics—in either case, nothing to do with *them*. There is enormous resistance, even among Jews, to analyzing anti-Semitism as a serious, ongoing social force or to recognizing the anti-Jewish subtext in superficially reasonable political arguments. A lot of Jewish alienation has to do with the subterranean character of anti-Semitism. Suppose your friends and colleagues were always having fits of selective amnesia, during which they insisted that what you clearly remembered was your imagination. Eventually you would begin to question your reality: What's going on? Am I crazy? Is she doing this to me on purpose? By means of a similar process, Jewish "paranoia" about anti-Semitism often becomes paranoia in fact.

Black people who scapegoat Jews for white racism and exaggerate Jewish power are collaborating in a familiar and scary game. That black leaders should blame Jews for Andy Young's resignation is not surprising, but the evidence doesn't bear them out. Jews, who can add two and two like anyone else, could not fail to note that Young's meeting with Zehdi Terzi was consistent with the noises the administration has been making for some months. It is Carter's policy Jews care about, not Young—a point Jewish spokespeople have taken care to emphasize. If Carter starts talking to the PLO, Young's dismissal won't gain him any Jewish support; if he doesn't, Young's retention wouldn't have lost him any. (And what about black support? Carter's decision to get rid of Young may well have cost him reelection.) Besides, Jewish organizations are hardly unaware of black-Jewish tensions. As subsequent events have shown, it was not in their interest for Young to resign, and most of them pointedly refrained from suggesting it. Did Carter act to appease the Israeli government? I doubt it—I think the Israelis understand that Carter is their problem, not Young—but if he did, it was in behalf of American diplomacy, not the Jews.

I don't know why Carter let Young resign instead of slapping him on the wrist. Maybe it was just what it looked like—that in arranging to talk with Terzi and then lying about it, Young took his individualism a step too far and convinced the president he couldn't be trusted. Maybe not. The affair still has its loose ends, particularly the question of whether, as Murray Kempton plausibly suggested, Young is taking the rap for a meeting that was actually the State Department's idea. But there is disturbing irony in the fact that (Jewish-dominated media notwithstanding) blacks have succeeded in defining the issue as Jewish power. Given the energy crisis and the general economic malaise, Americans may be more than normally receptive to the idea that Jews have been controlling our foreign policy. If Carter plans to move significantly closer to the PLO (and anyone who thinks such a move would reflect solicitude for the Palestinians, as opposed to solicitude for oil, is less cynical than I), it can't hurt him to have anti-Jewish sentiment floating around.

Behind the furor over Young lurks the larger issue of how relations between Jews and blacks, Jews and gentiles, blacks and whites affect and are affected by the Israeli-Palestinian conflict. Dreyfuss draws clear battle lines: Jews, white racists, and imperialists for Israel; blacks for the Palestinians, as victims of racist colonialism. But he leaves something important out of this picture—or cartoon—and that something is anti-Semitism (a semantically unfortunate term since Arabs are also Semites). Middle East politics would be a lot less confusing and agonizing if anti-Zionism and anti-Semitism were, as so many people want to believe, entirely separate issues. Which is to say that things would be a lot simpler if the Israelis weren't Jews. But if anti-Semitism is, as I have argued, a systemic and pervasive pathology endemic to Christian and Islamic cultures (and, I would imagine, easily communicable to any patriarchy), then anti-Semitism is as much a factor in the Middle East as oil, the military importance of the region, the Palestinians' demand for a homeland, and anti-Arab racism. Anti-Semitism is an actual or potential influence on the conduct of the United States, the Soviet Union, Europe, the United Nations, the Arab countries, and the Palestinians themselves. (Overt anti-Semitism has never been as widespread or severe in the Islamic world as in the Christian West. But since World War II, the Arabs have been using explicitly anti-Jewish propaganda, borrowed from Europe, as a weapon against Israel, and anti-Semitic policies have resulted in a massive exodus of Jewish refugees from Arab countries; "Oriental" Jews, largely from the Middle East and North Africa, are now a majority of the Israeli population.) Fear of genocidal anti-Semitism is a determining influence on Israeli policy, far more decisive, I believe, than expansionism, racism, or the fanaticism of religious nationalists. Without anti-Semitism there would still be a power struggle between the West and the Third World, but the Israeli-Palestinian conflict would not exist, since there would be no political Zionism and no Jewish state.

Anti-Zionism, in the modern political sense, is the argument that a Jewish state in Palestine inherently violates the rights of the Palestinian people. It regards Zionism as a racist, imperialist movement in which the European Jewish bourgeoisie (Jewish power, again) acted in concert with the colonial powers to displace the indigenous Arabs, furthering white Western domination of the Middle East. It assumes that religious belief is the movement's ideological rationale, and so the PLO calls for the abolition of the Israeli state in favor of a "democratic, secular" Palestine. The essential problem with this argument is that it ignores or denies the reality of the Jewish condition. First of all, to get around the fact that the Jews also have historic ties to Palestine, that they are not simply aliens and interlopers, anti-Zionists tend to define Jewishness purely in terms of religion and dismiss as mythology the idea that Jews around the world are one people. Thus Yasir Arafat's insistence that there is no contradiction between defining Palestine as an Arab state and guaranteeing equal rights for "Arabs of the Jewish faith." But Jews have always regarded themselves, and been regarded by others, as an organic entity, in some sense a nation; a traditional excuse for anti-Semitism has been that Jews have divided loyalties. Jews from Arab countries consider themselves Jews, not Arabs of the Jewish faith. Nor is political Zionism basically a religious movement. Orthodox Jews who believe in the biblical prophecies are Zionists by definition, but they did not conceive of Zion in political terms—indeed, many opposed the establishment of a Jewish state as sacrilegious. The movement for statehood came from "emancipated" Jews who believed that Jews would always be oppressed so long as they were homeless and forced into marginality in gentile societies. Zionism is a national liberation movement,* and despite the rise of religious nationalism and a powerful religious establishment that (like the Catholic Church elsewhere) has imposed some religious laws on an unwilling majority, Israel is essentially a secular state.

As for the charge that Zionism is an imperialist plot, it does

---

*This term does not quite fit, though it comes closer than any other; as usual, the Jewish experience confounds standard categories. "National liberation" is generally understood to involve an indigenous people's struggle to free themselves from foreign domination. Zionism, as a movement to gather a dispersed, oppressed people and recreate an independent territorial national entity, had no real historical or conceptual precedent, though it was heavily influenced by European nationalism.

not simply misdefine the Jews but makes them disappear. Imperialism involves migrating or extending one's influence from one's own country to another. But Jews in the nineteenth century had no country; they were aliens everywhere. Though anti-Zionists are fond of referring to Western Jews as "Europeans," the Europeans themselves took a rather different view of the matter. In any case, the relationship between Zionists and the Western nations has always been tense and ambiguous; they have served each other's needs, but their needs are very different. The Zionists ended up having to fight Britain as well as the Arabs. And the Jews who settled in Palestine after World War II were neither ambitious capitalists nor Zionist ideologues; they were traumatized refugees who were unwelcome anywhere else. Some years ago, I asked a woman who supported the PLO if she thought Jews had no right to national aspirations. Not at all, she assured me, so long as their nation wasn't on someone else's land. Which set me to musing about possibilities. The Sahara desert? The Amazon jungle? Imagine what would have happened if the Zionists had accepted Britain's offer of a homeland in Uganda. There is enormous and painful irony in the fact that the only conceivable way for Jews to lay claim to a piece of land was for one group of nations to force us on another. But the aspect of this irony that anti-Zionists consistently refuse to face is what it says about the world's attitude toward Jews. In a way, what the PLO and the Arab nations are demanding is their equal right to treat Jews the way nations have always treated us—that is, to deny us the right to exist on our own terms, rather than on sufferance.

As far as I'm concerned, the only solution to the Israeli-Palestinian impasse that makes moral sense is two independent states. Whatever one's intellectual position on Zionism—that is, the idea that all Jews should settle in Israel—Israel's existence as an alternative has clearly reduced Jewish vulnerability and, I believe, is a psychological deterrent to anti-Semites. The abolition of Israel and the incorporation of a Jewish minority in an Arab-dominated Palestine would at best put all Jews back in a pre-Holocaust situation, and for the Israelis the reality could be far worse. It is questionable whether all Israelis would be allowed to remain as equal citizens; the PLO's charter, which defines as Palestinians only Jews who lived in Palestine before "the Zionist invasion," is not reassuring on this point. And is the mutual hatred of all these years expected to just evaporate? But practically speaking, these questions are irrelevant, because the Israelis will defend their state until they are massacred or driven out. In which case the world will no doubt blame them for being stubborn.

Another difficulty with the idea that anti-Zionism has nothing to do with anti-Semitism is that the great majority of Jews perceive the two issues as inseparable. One might argue, with equal logic, "I'm not a racist, I'm just against forced integration," or "I love women, it's feminists I can't stand." Vanessa Redgrave may think that Zionism is "a brutal racist ideology" and "the opposite of Judaism," but she will find precious few Jews who agree with her. This puts her in the peculiar position of implying that except for an enlightened minority, Jews are brutal racists, and that she knows what Judaism is better than we do. Which is why her ritual tributes to Jews' heroic record of struggle, and so on, are not only empty but obnoxious. As most Jews see it, the Israelis' right to national self-determination would be taken for granted if they weren't Jewish. The Palestinians have the same right, of course. What makes the Middle East situation so excruciating is the spectacle of two displaced, oppressed peoples, each of them victimized by more powerful nations, trying to kill each other. But at this point in history, absolute justice for the Palestinians would mean absolute injustice for the Jews.

My guess is that most *Voice* readers have no quarrel with this last point. Anti-Zionist thinking predominates in most of the world, but here it has been mostly confined to the sectarian left. Nearly everyone agrees, in principle, on Israel's right to exist. Yet I feel that non-Jews in America—particularly my peers, middle-class liberals and radicals, the vanguard of "enlightened" opinion—do their own milder version of making the Jews disappear. In theory, they acknowledge that Jews are oppressed. In practice, they see Israel much as Dreyfuss sees the Jews—as a powerful nation beating up on the have-nots. They assume that Israeli chauvinism, expansionism, and refusal to admit the justice of the Palestinian cause are primarily or entirely to blame for preventing a settlement. But a two-state compromise can work only if the international community supports and enforces it, and the international atmosphere is overwhelmingly hostile to Israel. Most countries endorse the PLO's claim to all of Palestine; if it weren't for the United States, Israel would be long gone. And now American support is eroding.

In this situation the Israelis are damned if they do and damned if they don't. If they resist a Palestinian state, they stand condemned as oppressors and obstructionists and give their only major ally an excuse for withdrawing support. If they agree, the Palestinians with their own state as a base will be in an infinitely better position to pursue their claim to what they deeply believe is theirs, and the Israelis have no good reason to believe that anyone will lift a finger to defend them. Is it any wonder that they resist what has got to look like suicide by installments? Why should they trust the PLO to accept a state as more than a temporary expedient? Why should they trust the United States, when no country has ever proved trustworthy in its dealings with Jews? The American ruling class is profoundly anti-Semitic; it is not going to protect Israel for humanitarian reasons, any more than it was willing to provide a haven for Jewish refugees during World War II or "waste" a few planes to bomb Auschwitz. Under the circumstances the self-righteous, simplistic condemnation of Israel that currently passes as a "balanced view" is, in my opinion, anti-Jewish. Many aspects of Israeli government policy, including its alliances with reactionary regimes, disturb me enough to make me wonder if in its determination to survive Israel will lose its reason for being. But at least I can recognize desperation when I see it; at least I can understand—no, share—the bitterness that says, "To hell with morality and world opinion! World opinion never did a thing for the Jews!"

The Israelis are in the classic Jewish bind. To the Palestinians and the Third World they are white oppressors, but to their fellow white oppressors they are Jews. If they are surrogates for the West, it is largely in having to pay for Western sins. For once, the West may end up paying as well; Dreyfuss is probably right, "History is on the side of the 'have-nots,' here and abroad." But no matter whose side history is on, Jews have always been expendable. And so long as we are expendable, to talk of "Jewish power" is obscene.

Richard Goldstein

The New Anti-Semitism: A *Geshrei*

Richard Goldstein is executive editor of The Village Voice.
*He is a writer on cultural and sexual politics, and the author
of* Reporting the Counterculture. *This essay has been
adapted from an article that appeared in* The Village Voice,
October 1, 1991.

■ **M**y grandmother hid in a bureau drawer
for three days while colorful Christians rampaged through the
shtetl. But that stuff happened in the Old World—we lived in
America, the greatest country in the world. I knew about the
Holocaust, of course, but all my relatives had the luxury of
dying from natural causes. We lived in New York, the greatest
Jewish city in the world. We didn't need the promised land—we
were Yankees, safe at last.

When I was eight, we took a vacation in Pennsylvania, my
first trip out of New York. While we stopped for gas on a
country road, I went to get a Coke. I noticed a group of men
in overalls staring at me, whispering. A boy my age stepped
forward and politely asked if I was Jewish. I realized the Star
of David was dangling out of my tee-shirt, and grabbed it
instinctively. When I nodded yes, he asked, in a strangely
animated voice: "Can we please see your horns?" I shuddered

and backed up toward the car. When I told my mother what had happened, she yanked me into the seat beside her and held me tight while my father paid. Then we sped away.

I stopped wearing the Star of David that summer. I had learned an important lesson about the terms of my liberation in America: The less I look Jewish, the safer I will be. Even as an adult, when I tell jokes in dialect I'm always aware of who I am addressing and what their response will be. And I always feel uncomfortable during the High Holy Days watching people in yarmulkes rushing through the streets, knowing they'll be swaying and moaning something ancient and indecipherable, even to me.

I always wear jeans on Yom Kippur. Not just because I'm a secular humanist, but because, on some level, I want to hide. My mother's terror in Pennsylvania stays with me, along with her unspoken message that history is not over for us. Even in America, we are vulnerable to superstitions and slanders so grotesque that there can be no defense against them. And these fairy tales for fanatics linger just below the surface of ordinary life. As they did in Crown Heights.

What happened there in August of 1991 was the worst outbreak of anti-Semitism in New York during my lifetime. Ideas that had been buried were suddenly exhumed, and I was forced to confront their enduring power. For four days, images that belonged in grainy, Nazi-era documentaries were all too live on TV: people shouting "Heil Hitler"; windows smashed in dozens of Jewish homes; and the ultimate, timeless desecration—a Jewish life lost to a raging mob. Yankel Rosenbaum was the child of concentration camp survivors, and he had come to Brooklyn from his native Australia to study the Holocaust. He didn't know, when he left his house to visit friends, that a West Indian child named Gavin Cato had been accidentally run over by a car carrying the Lubavitcher rebbe; or that rumors had spread through the black community that a Hasidic ambulance service had refused to help the dying boy; or that mobs were roaming the streets, screaming "Get the Jews." To these enraged people, many of them recent immi-

grants from the Caribbean, Yankel Rosenbaum had no person-
ality except for what his Hasidic clothing signified. He had
been reduced to the Eternal Jew, and as a gang of teenagers
closed in on him, he was stabbed four times in the chest and
back. "Cowards," he cried. "Cowards." My grandmother
could have said the same, and if she survived what Yankel
Rosenbaum didn't, it was only because she had lived in such
constant dread that she knew when to hide, while he thought
he was safe at last.

In the days that followed, a suspect in the death of Rosenbaum was arrested. Lemrick Nelson was promptly dubbed
"Jew-Slay Teen" by the indefatigable *New York Post*. It seems
his landlord—a fellow named Klein—had complained to his
father about the noise this seventeen-year-old was making.
"The Jew got me in trouble," he was heard to say. On the
night of the riot, when Rosenbaum stumbled toward him,
baffled and babbling, did this young man see his landlord's
face? "I didn't like his accent," the youth told police when they
arrested him, his clothes still wet with Rosenbaum's blood. It
was not enough to convince a jury that this was the killer, and
since no one else from the mob was arrested, whoever murdered Rosenbaum is still at large. That fact, along with the
memory of police failing to stem the violence for four days,
has resonated with the history of pogroms in politically explosive ways, making it tempting for many Jews to conclude that
the black mayor of New York City was responsible for what
befell the Hasidim of Crown Heights. But the more disturbing
possibility is that what happened there in 1991 could happen
again; next time, perhaps, between Latinos and Hasidim in
nearby Williamsburg, or in several neighborhoods at once. The
Crown Heights riot revealed a simmering anti-Semitism that
no amount of police protection could keep at bay. Not in a
sprawling, seething city like New York.

Consider what occurred several days after the Rosenbaum
murder, and miles away, on a train roaring up the West Side of
Manhattan. An Orthodox Jew was punched by a black man
shouting, "That's for killing children." Perhaps this Jew looked

just like the teacher who dissed him back in high school, or the Jews who called his mother "the *schwartzer*" when she came to clean their house. Bad Jews, good Jews; all Jews are the same. And we all risk punishment for daring to assert our Jewishness.

As a child, I was intensely aware of the old men, stooped and scarred, wandering through the neighborhood with long beards and strange fringes spilling out of their pants. They frightened me—and I still recoil from Hasidim. To me they are no different from Christian fundamentalists—just as nasty, narrow-minded, and contemptuous. I remember a group of Hasidim picketing in Greenwich Village during the early days of the AIDS epidemic. "A gay synagogue is like a whorehouse on Yom Kippur," their handout read. That night, I had a nightmare in which a Hasid wearing a long black coat strode into the hospital room where I lay in a stark white bed. He reached across me and turned the resuscitator off.

These days, when Hasidim cruising the Village in their Mitzvah Mobile ask me, "Are you Jewish?" I reply, "Not if you are." Yet I know my uneasiness in their presence is not just a matter of belief. Sitting across from a Hasid in the subway, I feel that old chill in my shoulders. It's not so different from a closet case eyeing a drag queen. These people are *flaming,* and they remind me of my vulnerability. To the anti-Semite all Jews have horns.

I know that there is racism in Hasidic hearts—and fists. And I'm sure that there have been deals struck with politicians and privileges traded for votes. But the riots that followed the death of Gavin Cato cannot be explained solely in terms of class privilege or racial injustice. During that unholy week, the entire mythology of anti-Semitism was unfurled.

Hovering over the rage at a child's accidental death were centuries of belief that Jews prey on Christian children. You can read in Chaucer, that titan of the Western canon, about a schoolboy abducted and ritually murdered by Jews, though his body miraculously emits a hymn of praise. Jews call this the Blood Libel because it stems from the myth that matzoh must be made with the blood of Christian infants. You can give guided tours of matzoh factories till kingdom come, but this idea persists in the subconscious. It allowed a mob to transform a reckless driver into the emblem of their oppression. As the false rumor spread that a Jewish-run ambulance had refused to treat the child, you could sense the ancient belief that Jews promote only their own interests, not with the solidarity every community exhibits toward its own, but from some deeper tribal drive.

In Crown Heights, there's a black Episcopalian priest named Rev. Heron A. Sam who preaches that Jews have appropriated the term Semite, which rightfully belongs to Africans and Arabs as well as "the Hebrew race." (Although the reverend thinks "the hooked nose popularly associated with Semitic types is actually Hittite.") From this racist obsession, it's easy to assert that "the Jew has managed by consanguinity [interbreeding with Europeans] to affect a skin complexion change that has put him outside the realm of blackness, and so he can appeal to his acquired white brothers and sisters. . . ." This tactic "can only lead such a race of people to become manipulators and anarchists."

Imagine the impact of such a sermon on a seventeen-year-old who is furious at his Jewish landlord. Imagine how easy it would be for that boy to conclude: "The Jew got me in trouble." And once the belief has been implanted that Jews are an ersatz people who abandoned their natural skin tone to gain racial advantage, imagine how logical it is to think of the Hasidim as part of an international conspiracy.

"Diamond merchants," Rev. Al Sharpton called them at Gavin Cato's funeral. "Don't just talk about the jeweler [whose store was burned] on Utica. Talk about how Oppenheimer in South Africa sends diamonds straight to Tel Aviv and deals with the diamond merchants here in Crown Heights." There's a social reality here, but the mob in Crown Heights was invited by its leaders to jack it up with the iconography of anti-Semitism. They were encouraged to see the Hasidim, not as a tight-knit voting bloc with significant political clout, but as an incarnation of the Elders of Zion—that invention of the czarist secret police. Black rage at white power was transformed into anti-Semitism by the myth of the omnipotent Jew.

How could this happen? How could people who have never lived in Europe believe in such quintessentially European legends? The answer doesn't lie in the souls of black folks— they are no more anti-Semitic than whites. It lies in the nature of the prejudice. Fear and loathing of Jews is a pervasive force in Western consciousness, ready to be unleashed whenever the time is right. These periodic outbursts are a safety valve for those unable to overcome their oppression, or even compre- hend its source. That was the scenario for the pogroms my grandmother dreaded, the Holocaust my parents escaped, and the violence in Crown Heights. The conditions of life for African-Americans—the growing indifference to worsening poverty, the declining quality of life in the inner cities, and the genteel racism of the governing elite—are a classic matrix for anti-Semitism. Jews have always been a handy target in tough times.

But it's been clear for some time that, among some seg- ments of the black intelligentsia, anti-Semitism is more openly expressed than anywhere else in American life, apart from the far right. Within this milieu, the most primitive ideas have been given an overlay of reason and righteousness that harks back to the dregs of Western civ. Talk about the return of the repressed: When Leonard Jeffries asserts that Jewish faculty at the City College of New York are organized into a secret cabal that actually calls itself the Kaballah, he is piecing together a cos- mology the czar's henchmen, not to mention Goebbels, would be proud to call their own. Talk about Eurocentrism!

Racist scholarship might seem arcane, if not loony, to most black folks if it weren't tethered to the power and glory of hip- hop. And this exhuming of ancient stereotypes in music and movies has done much more than the ravings of Louis Farra- khan to make anti-Semitism respectable again. When Public Enemy rap about the "so-called chosen" who "got me like Jesus"; when Professor Griff says "Jews are responsible for the majority of wickedness that goes on across the globe"; when Spike Lee creates Joe and Josh Flatbush, cardboard club owners who reduce every human emotion to profiteering—they make the most archaic myths about Jews seem modern and heroic again.

Why do these artists get away with Jew baiting? The answer lies partly in the racially mixed market for their work. Black culture often performs a surrogate role in American society, defining rebellion and delineating the forbidden for a funk-hungry nation. Just as rappers play the sex-outlaw many white youths wish they could be, slamming women and gays with all the bile that must be swallowed in bourgeois society, black anti-Semites act out the bigotry other Americans aren't quite willing to express. And their emergence signals something about American culture as a whole.

For the first time since the Great Depression, Jewish stereotypes are being used to provide a gritty frisson to works of art. *The Death of Klinghoffer* has a libretto that equates Jews with bourgeois banality and Palestinians with proletarian dignity. *Barton Fink* has movie moguls who behave like figments of T. S. Eliot's imagination. ("The rats are underneath the pile/ The Jew is underneath the lot.") The fact that Jews played a role in creating these works is itself a sign of profound anxiety. One way for Jews to deal with the horror of anti-Semitism is to deflect it onto an evil Jewish other. But this strategy only fuels the fire.

Not long after the Crown Heights riot, the Family network announced it was pulling a series of Bible videos to change the features of certain Jewish characters. The Anti-Defamation League had objected to the fact that the moneychangers were hook-nosed and epicene. Network officials were embarrassed; and they stressed that making the Jews look like normal people would cost a pretty penny (everything is money with these evangelicals). But the question remains how anyone in modern America could render Bible characters that so closely resemble the cartoons that once graced *Der Stürmer*. The only answer is that the image of the conniving Jews is so entrenched that it doesn't seem remarkable, except to Jews.

By locating anti-Semitism exclusively in the black community, the *Post–Commentary* alignment hopes to convince Jews that their interests lie in an alliance with other white ethnics, under the neocon umbrella. But this ambition blinds the Jewish right to the extent of anti-Semitism in American life. It may seem to many Jews that the tangible signs of their oppression—such as quotas and restrictive covenants—have been swept away. But it takes a Pat Buchanan (not to mention David Duke) to remind us that anti-Semitism is still a potentially potent force in American politics, especially when combined with racism. The omnipotent Jew and the rapacious black male are twin specters in the Western psyche, always available to be played as an instrument of public policy. As they were when George Bush invoked the image of Willie Horton to win the White House in 1988; as they were when Bush portrayed himself in 1991 as "one lone little guy" held hostage by powerful Israel lobbyists.

Demagogues high and low still feed on the mythology that clings to Jews and blacks alike. Yet both groups have forgotten their precariousness in the rush to judge each other guilty of oppression. Crown Heights has given the bigots a golden opportunity. Now blacks may be held up to Jews as the real anti-Semites, even as Jews are held up to blacks as the real racists. This spectacle shatters an alliance that has been the fulcrum of progressivism for generations. It empowers neither blacks nor Jews, but their common enemies.

What's a liberal to do in the face of such a crisis? Pretend it's something else. For the most part, the media have taken note of Jew-baiting asides in rap music, crypto-Nazi imagery in a colorful jazz musical, as if it were a sour belch to be quickly swallowed. Some critics spoke up loud and clear, but the mainstream was reluctant to risk it. As a result, the anti-Semitism of Public Enemy and Spike Lee was less than resolutely condemned, sending a signal to the audience that it's permissible to act on such ideas. Those who overlooked the obvious, for whatever reasons, helped lay the groundwork for Crown Heights.

By now, there's a consensus that the riot was an act of anti-Semitism. But this judgment wasn't generated by the left. At first, many white progressives focused on the advantages the Hasidim enjoy, as if that entitled the crowd to shout, "Kill the Jews." Only gradually did the left confront the truth. It's painful, indeed, to face the fact that victims of bigotry can be guilty of bigotry—it threatens your image of the oppressed. How much easier to buy the claim that blacks cannot be anti-Semitic, or even to convince yourself that what happened in Crown Heights is part of some larger geopolitical struggle—a hip-hop *intifada*.

I'm convinced that some white leftists were silent because, consciously or not, they share the assumptions of the rioters. It's hip, in certain progressive circles, to speak of Jews as if they've lost their legitimacy. You could glimpse this reflex in the antiwar protesters who cheered when the Scud missiles fell on Israel; and you could see it in the lubricious alliance between the New Alliance Party and Farrakhan. There's nothing contradictory about this pact. Anti-Semitism of the left has firm roots in populism as well as Marxist ideology. (The term itself was coined in the nineteenth century by a liberal mayor of Vienna, who used anti-Semitism, as Ed Koch would later use racism, to secure a populist base.)

David Dinkins called the murder of Yankel Rosenbaum what it was: a lynching. But other black leaders were as prone to euphemism as white progressives. Many reiterated the underlying conditions in Crown Heights and demanded a redress of grievances as the price for peace. None spoke of the deadly myths about Jews that had animated this violence, just as few black leaders condemned the anti-Semitism of Leonard Jeffries. (Rev. Calvin Butts, the city's most influential black minister, said he wanted to hear more from Jeffries before addressing the question; and he never did.) Solidarity makes truth-telling difficult, and the reality of oppression makes it hard for any black leader to condemn an eruption of black rage. But the conflation of Jew-baiting with black empowerment is now so evolved that it seems like Tomming, if not treason, to call anti-Semitism what it is. The sight of a phalanx of black men marching through a white neighborhood has achieved the sanctity of a ritual, and hardly anyone on the left questions the context, or the content, of what is being shouted at whom. The likelihood of black—or white—progressives speaking out against icons of resistance is slim indeed.

The silence of humanists had a sickeningly familiar quality to Jews who remember the world's response to the Nazis; the reluctance to act on, or even acknowledge, the possibility of genocide until it was too late. This sense of abandonment remains an indelible part of Jewish consciousness. It fosters the circled-wagons mentality the world so often reads as Jewish paranoia. It animates the comedy of Jewish assimilation, and the Noh drama of Jewish self-hate—both are strategies to hide the dirty secret that can lead to disgrace and even death. And it creates the illusion that the only safety for a Jew is within the tribe. The last tendency—call it psychic Zionism—is the leading beneficiary of what occurred in Crown Heights. In terms of Jewish history, this was another victory for the spirit of Jabotinsky over Einstein—another triumph of nationalism over humanism.

During the height of the violence, the *New York Post* ran a front-page photo of a twelve-year-old boy sobbing by the fallen frame of his injured father. It raised goose bumps when I saw it, resonating with the image of children in the Warsaw Ghetto, surrendering to armed Nazis against a background of flames. The *Post* was milking my memory of Jewish helplessness, just as Sharpton had milked his constituency by envisioning Gavin Cato sharing "heaven's playroom" with the three girls killed in the 1962 firebombing of a black church in Birmingham. While readers of *The City Sun* were invited to regard Aaron Lopez, an eighteenth-century slave trader, as an emblem of the Jews, I was invited to regard Sonny Carson and his storm troopers as the vanguard of the black community.

"Who speaks for New York's blacks if not the . . . riot inciters?" asked *Post* columnist Eric Breindel. He compared the events in Crown Heights to Kristallnacht, when thousands of Jewish businesses were destroyed and thousands lost their lives—with the cooperation of the German state. "The pretext in Crown Heights," Breindel blithely asserted, "was far thinner [than in Nazi Germany.]"

Long before Kristallnacht, the German Socialist leader August Bebel warned his compatriots against the illusion that bigotry is a source of power. "Anti-Semitism is the socialism of fools," Bebel proclaimed. His words have yet to be heeded, as we saw in Crown Heights. The polarization process that followed in the wake of the rioting is now a fact of urban life. The failure of moderate black ministers such as Calvin Butts and Herbert Daughtry to articulate an alternative to demagoguery gave the media an excuse to ignore the African-American clergy who did speak out and also left the door wide open for Sharpton, who rushed right in. Meanwhile, the inability of white progressives to confront anti-Semitism gave right-wingers an excuse to come out swinging. As the *Post* asked disingenuously, "Who else speaks for the black community?" It's a cry that will surely be echoed in *Commentary* and all the house organs of retrenchment. The new excuse for polite white racism will be Crown Heights.

The realpolitik of black anti-Semitism is that it is all too effective at reviving the most painful memories of persecution. These fears push many Jews into an alliance with other white ethnics, almost always to the benefit of the right. Observing this shift, many blacks conclude that Jewish progressivism is a myth, and not a potential to be nurtured. The net effect is a polarization of urban politics along racial and religious grounds, limiting the prospects for multiracial coalitions that have been crucial to the election of African-American mayors. In New York City, where political power flows from ethnic alliances, Crown Heights has given those who hope to split the white liberal vote from the black community a potent weapon. It has made it easier for conservatives to conflate affirmative action, multicultural education, and even the aspiration of black politicians with savagery. So striking is the damage done to black empowerment by those four days of riot and rampage that it's fair to say the men who spurred on the mob were either government agents or fools.

The only way to take back righteousness from the right is for progressives to call this riot what it was: a wannabe pogrom. The OED defines that word as "an organized massacre . . . chiefly applied to those directly against Jews." No one planned this riot, nor did the City of New York tolerate it. You can argue that the police response was too little too late, but their restraint was standard procedure during a racial disturbance, and nothing directed at Jews. In the end, the system worked to contain the violence, something my grandmother, who lived through a real pogrom, would have found miraculous. But what if the mob had been left to its own devices? Were these people so different from the Jew-haters of other eras? Were the demagogues that spurred them on?

The real lesson of Crown Heights is that Jews must learn to live in a more dangerous world, where hate goes unanswered and primitive passions are stoked as a safety valve for helpless rage. Jewish children in years to come may live much like my parents, with a subtle but consuming sense of dread. America could yet turn out to be not so different from the Old World my grandparents fled. But there's another possibility: that by confronting anti-Semitism and racism, people of goodwill can transcend both—or at least keep them dormant. In Crown Heights, the situation remains volatile, and every week, it seems, brings a mugging, a beating, or a quarrel with potentially explosive overtones. In public, the hate persists. In private, I'm convinced, many blacks and Jews are horrified by what's occurred. That may explain why, in the 1992 City Council primary, the worst hatemongers—C. Vernon Mason, Colin Moore, and Yehuda Levin—all went down to defeat. It may be too much to hope for some grand gesture of reconciliation; in the current climate, you take your hope where you can find it—in small courtesies that signal what still can't be proclaimed.

In Brooklyn, two months after the riot, I forgot where my car was parked. Walking down a dark narrow street, I saw a group of black teenagers hanging out. I felt my body tighten against the desire to draw back. I've spent much of my life struggling against that reflex, so I approached the kids and asked directions. They answered politely and we fell into an oddly formal banter—broad smiles and cordial good-nights. I realized we were acting out an elaborate etiquette of communication in tough times. I wouldn't call it trust, but at least I didn't yell for the police, and they didn't ask to see my horns.

Henry Louis Gates, Jr.

The Uses of Anti-Semitism

Henry Louis Gates, Jr., the W.E.B. Du Bois Professor of the Humanities at Harvard, is the author of Colored People, Figures in Black, The Signifying Monkey, *and* Loose Canons. *"The Uses of Anti-Semitism" originally appeared in a slightly different form in* The New York Times, *July 20, 1992, under the title "Black Demagogues and Pseudo-Scholars."*

Over the past decade, the historic relation between African-Americans and Jewish Americans—a relation that sponsored so many of the concrete advances of the civil rights era—showed another and less attractive face. While anti-Semitism is generally on the wane in this country, it has been on the rise among black Americans. A recent survey finds that blacks are twice as likely as whites to hold anti-Semitic views.

The trend has been deeply disquieting for many black intellectuals. But it's something most of us, as if by unstated agreement, simply choose not to talk about. At a time when black America is beleaguered on all sides, there is a strong temptation simply to ignore the phenomenon or to treat it as something strictly marginal. And yet to do so would be a serious mistake. As the African-American philosopher Cornel West has insisted, attention to black anti-Semitism is crucial, however discomfiting, in no small part because the moral credibility of our struggle against racism hangs in the balance.

We must begin by recognizing what is new about the new anti-Semitism. Make no mistake: this is anti-Semitism from the top down, engineered and promoted by leaders who affect to be speaking for a larger resentment. This "top-down" anti-Semitism, in large part the province of the better-educated classes, can thus be contrasted with the anti-Semitism "from below" common among African-American urban communities in the 1930s and '40s, which followed, in many ways, a familiar pattern of clientelistic hostility toward the neighborhood vendor or landlord. In American cities, hostility of this sort is now commonly directed toward Korean shop owners; but "minority" traders and shopkeepers elsewhere in the world—such as the Indians of East Africa or the Chinese of Southeast Asia—have experienced similar ethnic antagonism.

Unfortunately, the old paradigm will not serve to explain the new bigotry and its role in black America. For one thing, its preferred currency is not the mumbled epithet or curse, but the densely argued treatise; it belongs as much to the repertory of campus lecturers as community activists. And it comes in wildly different packages. A book popular with some in the "Afrocentric" movement, *The Iceman Inheritance: Prehistoric Sources of Western Man's Racism, Sexism, and Aggression* by Michael Bradley, argues that white people are so vicious because they, unlike the rest of mankind, are descended from the brutish Neanderthals. More to the point, it speculates that the Jews may have been the "'purest' and oldest Neanderthal-Caucasoids," the iciest of the ice people: hence (he explains) the singularly odious character of ancient Jewish culture. Crackpot as it sounds, the book has lately been reissued with endorsements from two members of the Africana Studies department of City College, New York, as well as an introduction by a professor emeritus of Hunter College and paterfamilias of the Afrocentric movement.

College speakers and publications have also had a role to play in legitimating the new creed. Last year, UCLA's black newspaper *Nommo* defended the importance of the notorious czarist canard, *The Protocols of the Elders of Zion*. (Those who took issue were rebuked with an article headlined: "Anti-Semitic? Ridiculous—Chill.") Speaking at Harvard University earlier this year, Conrad L. Muhammad, national youth representative of the Nation of Islam, neatly annexed environmentalism to anti-Semitism when he blamed the Jews for despoiling the environment and destroying the ozone layer.

But the bible of the new anti-Semitism is *The Secret Relationship Between Blacks and Jews,* an official publication of the Nation of Islam that boasts 1,275 footnotes in the course of 334 pages. Sober and scholarly looking, it may well be one of the most influential books published in the black community in the last twelve months. It is available in black-oriented shops in cities across the nation, even those that specialize in Kente cloth and beads rather than books. It can also be ordered over the phone, by dialing 1-800-48-TRUTH. Meanwhile, the book's conclusions are, in many circles, increasingly treated as damning historical fact.

The book, one of the most sophisticated instances of hate literature yet compiled, was prepared by the historical research department of the Nation of Islam. It charges that the Jews were in fact "key operatives" in the historic crime of slavery, playing an "inordinate" and "disproportionate" role and "carv-[ing] out for themselves a monumental culpability in slavery— and the black holocaust." And among significant sectors of the black community, this brief has become a credo of a new philosophy of black self-affirmation.

To be sure, the book massively misrepresents the historical record, largely through a process of cunningly selective quotation of often reputable sources. But its authors could be confident that few of its readers would go to the trouble of actually hunting down the works cited. For if readers actually did so, they might discover a rather different picture. They might find out—from the book's own vaunted authorities—that, for example, of all the African slaves imported into the New World, American Jewish merchants accounted for less than 2 percent, a finding sharply at odds with the Nation's claim of Jewish "predominance" in this traffic. They might find out that, in the domestic trade, it appears that all of the Jewish slave traders *combined* bought and sold fewer slaves than the single gentile firm of Franklin and Armfield. In short, they might learn what the historian Harold Brackman has documented at length: that the book's repeated insistence that the Jews dominated the slave trade depends on an unscrupulous distortion of the historic record. But the most ominous words in the book are found on the cover: "volume one." More have been promised, carrying on the saga of Jewish iniquity to the present day.

However shoddy the scholarship of works like *The Secret Relationship,* underlying it is something even more troubling: the tacit conviction that culpability is heritable. For it suggests a doctrine of racial continuity, in which the racial evil of a people is merely manifest (rather than constituted) by their historical misdeeds. The reported misdeeds are thus the *signs* of an essential nature that is evil.

How does this theology of guilt surface in our everyday moral discourse? In New York, earlier this spring, a forum was held at the Church of St. Paul and Andrew to provide an occasion for blacks and Jews to engage in dialogue on such issues as slavery and social injustice. Both Jewish and black panelists found common ground, and common causes. But a tone-setting contingent of blacks in the audience took strong issue with the proceedings. Outraged, they demanded to know why the Jews, those historic malefactors, had not apologized to the "descendants of African kings and queens."

And so the organizer of the event, Melanie Kaye/Kantrowitz, did. "I think I speak for a lot of people in this room," she declared, "when I say 'I'm sorry.' We're ashamed of it, we hate it, and that's why we organized this event."

Should the Ms. Kantrowitzes of the world, whose ancestors survived pogroms and, latterly, the Nazi Holocaust, be the primary object of our wrath? And what is yielded by this hateful sport of victimology, save the conversion of a tragic past into a game of recrimination? Perhaps that was on the mind of another audience member. "I don't want an apology," a dreadlocked woman told her. "I want reparations. Forty acres and a mule, plus interest."*

These are times that try the spirit of liberal outreach. In fact, Minister Farrakhan himself explained the real agenda behind his campaign, speaking before an audience of fifteen thousand at the University of Illinois last fall. The purpose of *The Secret Relationship,* he said, was to "rearrange a relationship" that "has been detrimental to us." "Rearrange" is a curiously elliptical term here: if a relation with another group has been detrimental, it only makes sense to sever it as quickly and unequivocally as possible. In short, by "rearrange," he means to convert a relation of friendship, alliance, and uplift into one of enmity, distrust, and hatred.

But why target the Jews? Using the same historical methodology, after all, the researchers of the book could have produced a damning treatise on the involvement of left-handers in the "black holocaust." The answer requires us to go beyond the usual shibboleths about bigotry and view the matter, from the demagogue's perspective, strategically: as the bid of one black elite to supplant another. It requires me, in short, to see anti-Semitism as a weapon in the raging battle of who will speak for black America: those who have sought common cause with others, or those who preach a barricaded withdrawal into racial authenticity.

The strategy of these apostles of hate, I believe, is best understood as ethnic isolationism—they know that the more isolated black America becomes, the greater their power. And what's the most efficient way to begin to sever black America from its allies? Bash the Jews, these demagogues apparently calculate, and you're halfway there.

Many American Jews are puzzled by the recrudescence of black anti-Semitism, in view of the historic alliance between the two groups. The brutal truth has escaped them: that the

---

*Author's note: Ms. Kaye/Kantrowitz has since informed me that her words were misunderstood: that she was expressing sympathy, not contrition.

new anti-Semitism arises not in spite of the black-Jewish alliance, but because of that alliance. For precisely such trans-ethnic, transracial cooperation—epitomized by the historic partnership between blacks and Jews—is what poses the greatest threat to the isolationist movement. In short, for the tacticians of the new anti-Semitism, the original sin of American Jews was their involvement—truly "inordinate," truly "disproportionate"—not in slavery, but in the front ranks of the civil rights struggle.

For decent and principled reasons, many black intellectuals are loath to criticize "oppositional" black leaders. Yet it has become increasingly apparent that to continue to maintain a comradely silence may be, in effect, to capitulate to the isolationist agenda, to betray our charge and trust. And, to be sure, many black writers, intellectuals, and religious leaders *have* taken an unequivocal stand on this issue. When the Reverend Jesse Jackson, in his impassioned address of July seventh, condemned the sordid history of anti-Semitism, he not only went some distance toward retrieving the once abandoned mantle of Martin Luther King, Jr.'s humane statesmanship, but delivered a stern rebuke—implicit but unmistakable—to those black leaders who have sought to bolster their own strength through division. Mr. Jackson and others have learned that we must not allow these demagogues to turn the wellspring of memory into a renewable resource of enmity everlasting.

Cornel West aptly describes black anti-Semitism as "the bitter fruit of a profound self-destructive impulse, nurtured on the vines of hopelessness and concealed by empty gestures of black unity." After twelve years of conservative indifference, those political figures who acquiesced, by malign neglect, to the deepening crisis of black America should not feign surprise that we should prove so vulnerable to the demagogues' rousing messages of hate, their manipulation of the past and present. Bigotry, as a tragic century has taught us, is an opportunistic infection, attacking most virulently when the body politic is in a weakened state. Yet neither should those who care about black America gloss over what cannot be condoned: that much respect we owe to ourselves. For surely it falls to all of us to recapture the basic insight that Dr. King so insistently expounded. "We are caught in an inescapable network of mutuality," he told us. "Whatever affects one directly affects all indirectly." How easy to forget this—and how vital to remember.

MEMOIRS OF AN ANTI-ANTI-SEMITE

"Memoirs of an Anti-Anti-Semite" appeared in *The Village Voice,*
October 20, 1992.

Why did you do it, brother? It was a question I often faced after *The New York Times* published an excerpt of what originated as a talk I'd given before community groups—a talk on our least favorite subject, black anti-Semitism.

The answers, I'm afraid, will sound mundane. I did it because of what a New York taxi driver said to me as we listened to a WLIB program on the black holocaust. Meeting my eyes in his rearview mirror, he asked me to level with him, as a brother: the Jewish conspiracy was for real, wasn't it? I said no. "It's only us in the car here, brother," he said.

I did it because a black student giving an oral report on the Southern plantocracy punctuated a point about the antebellum slave owners by singling out a Jewish student in the classroom and specifying that it was his ancestors he was speaking about. And because of what a few black kids, good kids, have asked me after class.

I did it because those black intellectuals I most admire—like Cornel West, Patricia Williams, Manning Marable, Marian Wright Edelman, Martin Kilson, bell hooks—insisted, by argument and by their example, that it was important to do so. I did it because they showed that being anti-Semitic is not a way of being problack. And because that homely bit of logic had started to fall out of favor and fashion in some circles I cared about: young blacks who give a damn about the crisis in their communities.

I did it because some fellow academics and intellectuals told me my experiences weren't anomalous, that they were disturbed, too, but didn't feel they could say anything about it. And because one of the very few things no one could accuse me of is being a black-basher, a black intellectual whose main sport is denigrating black achievement or skewering black pride. I'm far more likely to be chided for excessive boosterism.

I did it because anti-Semitism is unlikely to help us in the fight against poverty, disease, violence, AIDS, and injustice.

I did it because, for complicated and subtle and tortuous reasons, it has been much harder for many progressive black intellectuals to criticize our own engineers of bigotry than it is for paleface progressives to criticize their David Dukes—and because I've never quite been able to comprehend those complicated and subtle and tortuous reasons.

I did it, in short, because I didn't know any better.

It wasn't what I had to say that stuck in some people's craw; often they shared these sentiments, even agreed, in whole or in part, with my analysis. But they felt I should have stressed that Jewish people do bad things, too. On the one hand this, on the other hand that. Two sides to every story, right?

So that was one transgression. I had eschewed the time-honored conventions of ethnic "evenhandedness." I did this not because the ritual was familiar to the point of banality, but because it had, to my mind, degenerated into a form of moral kitsch. In its crudest form, this compulsive bilateralism begets Conrad Muhammad's pointed question: "Everyone talks about what Hitler did to the Jews, but what did the Jews do to Hitler?" You tell 'em, Brother Muhammad.

Then there is the "Why are you airing our dirty linen?" argument, and the larger question of audience and access—of who is allowed to participate in the dialogue. For example, some have faulted Cornel West for publishing his critique of black anti-Semitism—and his framing argument, from which I took my lead, about why "a focus on black anti-Semitism is crucial"—in the pages of *Tikkun* magazine, which is not primarily an African-American forum. They fail to realize that

the quality of insight in analyses like West's promote an understanding of interethnic tensions on both sides. But there's
something else his critics fail to realize. Just as the time has
passed in which the conversation about racism can exclude
blacks, so, too, the time may have passed when it is possible to
conduct a conversation about anti-Semitism that excludes Jews.

Sensitive as I am to the "dirty linen" argument—which
suggests that a black writer publicly criticizing black people is
playing into whitey's hands—and to the historic force that this
argument has had in the history of African-American cultural
critique, the greater danger, I suspect, lies elsewhere. It lies in
the temptation of silence.

Now, the most potent aspect of the "dirty linen" line is the
Aid and Comfort anxiety: that what you say will give aid and
comfort to the enemy, to those whose sympathies and interests
are not yours. I don't know any black intellectual who doesn't
worry about this sometimes. The cynical ploy is all too commonplace: When black folks are quoted in the political arena,
it's often to have them say something the speaker doesn't want
to be blamed for saying himself. "I didn't say it, Jesse Jackson
said it." It's the same reason the authors of *The Secret Relationship Between Blacks and Jews* boast that they're hanging the Jews
by their own words! In the end, I think, this may be one of the
hazards of discourse we'll have to live with. Because the cure is
even worse than the disease.

For where the Aid and Comfort argument ultimately leads
is contortion or paralysis: You either shut up, or you lie. And
then your opponents have won anyway. And yes, candid talk
may well have perverse effects. Eric Breindel will take your
critique of the black isolationist agenda to advance his own
isolationist agenda. And yet to face up to the inevitability of
perverse effects is not to say that these effects are necessarily
the preponderant ones. I don't believe they are.

Instead of simply capitulating, by self-censorship, to the
Aid and Comfort anxiety, I suggest we follow Cornel West's
lead and critique its most dangerous presupposition, what he
dubs "the pitfalls of racial reasoning." It's a habit of mind

Clarence Thomas should have cured black folks of. Identity is a guarantee of nuthin'. Spread the news. (Single black mothers for Quayle? Gay Jews for Farrakhan? That earns a big "so what?" in my book.)

All the same, isn't there a difference between saying something in the *Times* and saying it in *The City Sun*? Well, sure. I might note in passing that *The City Sun* has already weighed in on this issue, having published last year a long essay dwelling on Jewish complicity in the slave trade. In general, this newspaper has been antagonistic to the sort of transracial politics that West represents, to the point of publishing a lengthy diatribe against him by Molefi Kete Asante, who directs the country's largest black studies graduate program.

More to the point, however, is the irony that, with a circulation of approximately thirty thousand, the *Sun*'s black readership is far smaller, far more localized, and far less influential than that of the *Times*. For all the rhetoric, romantic or regretful, of "two nations," the fact remains that, at least for now, those who wish to address black intellectuals and leaders of opinion cannot eschew such "crossover" forums.

Careful, he might hear you: we all know that feeling and that fear. And yet the hermetic spaces of racial solitude have not been left intact in a world transfused by mass media and mass communication. (For starters, no one asked my permission to reproduce my op-ed piece as an advertisement.) I'll pass over the irony that those who say you shouldn't criticize other blacks seldom hesitate to criticize those blacks whom they accuse of criticizing other blacks. As Toni Morrison has recently declared, "The time for undiscriminating racial unity has passed." Now, when black intellectuals engage in dialogue in the pages of a "white" weekly like the *Voice,* we can try to disguise and encode our discourse for the elect alone, policing an ethic of secrecy, attempting a "surreptitious speech." But at what cost to ourselves? And at what cost to the larger project—which is one shared and advanced by West, Williams, hooks, Wallace, and so many others—of forging a common discourse of inclusion and alliance?

But back to the matter at hand. How much of a problem is black anti-Semitism really? And whose problem is it? The questions are easier to raise than to settle. I opened with a reference to research by Yankelovich Clancy Shulman indicating that, over the past thirty years, anti-Semitic attitudes have generally declined in this country while anti-Semitic attitudes among blacks have risen. More recent surveys confirm a dramatic disparity in anti-Jewish attitudes among black and white Americans. (In general, blacks are more than twice as likely as whites to assent to anti-Semitic propositions.) These studies may be inaccurate or flawed in design. I would only ask that those who think so make the effort to adduce more than simply impressionistic reasons for arguing that there really is not a problem.

My analysis sought to distinguish what I took to be a more recent development from the old-fashioned patterns of "neighborhood" anti-Semitism. I argued that the former had been engineered by those wishing to discredit the very notion of a transracial politics—in short, that the newer black anti-Semitism is being whipped up by black demagogues in search of power.

There is an older religious tradition, predating this new demagogy, that should not be shunted aside: I have in mind the figure of the ancient Hebrews in the formation of African-American religion. As numerous commentators have noted, a profound identification has linked African-Americans and Jews through the years. Invocations of the Children of Israel and their experience of slavery and oppression, the prophetic tradition of the Old Testament, black spirituals themselves: all speak to a typology constructed between the biblical account of the ancient Hebrews and the enslaved people of the New World. And so a complex dialectic of identification and antagonism, symbolic intimacy and symbolic enmity, is the product of an involuted history.

As Letty Cottin Pogrebin observed, "Maybe Jews and blacks lock horns more than other groups because we are the only ones who take each other seriously, the only minority groups who still seem to believe that our destinies are inter-woven." There are, she notes, "innumerable Jewish-black dialogues, but where are the Italian-black or Irish-black con-claves?" Where indeed?

Still, why should we be so preoccupied by ethnic scapegoat-ing among people who are themselves ethnic scapegoats and relatively disempowered? Whom does it really hurt? Fair ques-tion. The answer: first and foremost, it hurts black people, through the politics of distraction and distortion. Getting the source of our problems wrong is an obstacle to solving them. Objectively speaking, black anti-Semitism isn't primarily a Jewish problem, it's a black problem. In the words of the formidable critic and activist Barbara Smith, "We don't oppose anti-Semitism because we owe something to Jewish people, but because we owe something very basic to ourselves."

bell hooks

Keeping a Legacy
of Shared Struggle

*bell hooks is a feminist theorist and cultural critic and is the
author of, among other books,* Black Looks: Race and
Representation *and* Sisters of the Yam: Black Women in
Self-Recovery. *Her essay "Keeping a Legacy of Shared
Struggle" originally appeared in the September 1992 issue
of* Zeta.

Recently teaching women's studies
courses for two months at a European university, engaging in
intense discussions about race and racism, I found myself
speaking much more about anti-Semitism than I ever did in the
United States. Emphasizing connections between the global
development of anti-Semitism and antiblack racism, I often
referred to Ronald Sanders's book *Lost Tribes and Promised
Lands: The Origins of American Racism* Within the European
context to talk of white supremacy one must necessarily look
at the history of Jews (white and nonwhite in the world) and
make sense of that history in relationship to the development
of racist thinking about black people. These discussions led me
to reflect often on the growing antagonism between white
Jewish people and black folks in the United States. [There are
black Jews either by birth or conversion. To respect their
culture and faith throughout this essay when I am speaking

about white Jews that is the term I will use. Usually folks refer solely to the experiences of white Jews (i.e., when scholars and writers talk about the relationship between blacks and Jews).]

I remember heated arguments in classrooms at Oberlin when black students would talk about white people and white culture and Jewish students would speak out and insist that they not be included in this category of whiteness. What these discussions always revealed was that we lacked a complex language to talk about white Jewish identity in the United States and its relationship to blackness and black identity. It was hard and painful for some Jewish students to acknowledge that in a white supremacist society like the United States where race/ethnicity is often defined solely by skin color, the fact of whiteness can subsume allegiance to Jewish identity, religion, et cetera and overdetermine one's actions in daily life, or how one is treated. To some extent these students believe so deeply in the notion of democracy and individual rights that they are convinced that if they choose not to identify as "white" no one will see them that way. Their fierce denial of any allegiance or participation in constructions of whiteness seemed to evoke an equally fierce desire on the part of black students to insist that not only was the fact of whiteness more obvious than Jewishness, but that it was the denial of this reality that made it possible for Jewish students to be complicit with racism and remain unaware of the nature of that participation. When such conflicts arise it is always useful to send students to read *Yours in Struggle: Three Feminist Perspectives on Anti-Semitism and Racism,* especially the sections by Elly Bulkin.

In her section Bulkin asserts that she assumes that "all non-Jews, even those without institutional power, have internalized the norm of anti-Semitism in this culture and are capable of being anti-Semitic, whether through hostility or ignorance." Agreeing with this assumption, I have always deemed it significant that Bulkin chose to highlight that we are all capable of anti-Semitic thought and action, rather than to assert as some folks do, that we are all "naturally" anti-Semitic because we are born into an anti-Semitic culture. By focusing on our "capability," she reminds us that we are able to act in ways that fundamentally resist and oppose anti-Semitism. Growing up in the segregated South the fundamental lesson that I was taught via the black Baptist church was that Jews all over the world had suffered exploitation and oppression, that we identified with them and took their struggle to be our own because of shared experience. Most importantly, we were taught that anti-Semitism and antiblack racism were fundamentally connected. One could not be raised in hard-core Klan country and not be aware of this connection. It was deeply embedded in our consciousness as southern blacks that we had to oppose anti-Semitism—always.

Given these teachings, we knew as children that white Jews born and raised in the South often suffered at the hands of white supremacists. We also knew that in high school it bolstered the image of the "Jew" in the eyes of white supremacists when white Jewish students would make a point of acting in a racist way toward black folks. Like us, many of these young Jews had been taught in the context of home and religious experience to identify with the oppressed, and therefore to recognize their connections with black folks. So early on, we all experienced contradictions in how we thought and how we behaved. Jewish white students who might be the most racist in front of other southern white folks might in a different context act in a nonracist manner. When we "reported" these contradictions in our segregated religious contexts, we were taught that no matter the actions of individual Jews, we were called by our faith and our destiny as a people to stand in solidarity with them.

Perhaps it was solely due to the backwoods provincial nature of my region and upbringing, but it was not until I left the South for college that I first heard black folks make anti-Semitic remarks. These were northern black folks who behaved and acted in ways that were completely alien to me. Indeed, it was those early years of college that shook up my notions of monolithic black identity. I learned that not all black folks thought the same way or shared the same values. And I learned that we did not always think alike on the subject of the relationship between blacks and Jews. I learned that not all black people were Christians. I learned this from the followers of Elijah Muhammad who sold their papers and spread their teachings on campus. And it was there as an undergraduate that I developed deep friendships and political alliances with young white Jews. Then, we did not feel that there was a need to define the nature of our solidarity; we accepted the bonds of history, a continuum of shared struggle. It was only when we began to look beyond our small circles of intimacy and fellow-ship that we had to think critically about the relationship between blacks and white Jews. Within feminist circles we focused our discussions on the relationships between women, not directing them to a larger audience. This may be why folks act as though women thinkers have no worthwhile perspectives to offer on the subject. Usually when relations between "blacks and Jews" are talked about what is really evoked is the relation-ship between black men and white Jewish men.

The discussion of black-Jewish relationships in the United States has mainly been an exchange between male thinkers. It has often been dominated by northern voices. *Yours in Struggle* was published in 1984 and it did not lead to a growth of literature by black women (some of whom are Jewish) and white Jewish women. It was impossible to read Henry Louis Gates's recent *New York Times* editorial "Black Demagogues and Pseudo-Scholars" and not notice that all the critical think-ers mentioned are males. However, I assume that he includes black females when he asserts: "While anti-Semitism is gener-ally on the wane in this country, it has been on the rise among black Americans. A recent survey finds not only that blacks are twice as likely as whites to hold anti-Semitic views but—sig-nificantly—that it is among the younger and more educated blacks that anti-Semitism is most pronounced." This assertion is dangerously provocative. I wanted to know how, when, and who had conducted such a survey. And whether or not this was equally true for blacks in different regions—if there were any differences of opinions based on gender. Unlike Gates, I do not believe that anti-Semitism is on the wane in this country. Anyone who has followed the campaign of David Duke and the rise in white supremacist groups would do well to question such an assertion. Since I see anti-Semitism as connected to antiblack racism, which is on the rise, I can only assume that anti-Semitism is also gaining new ground. From my perspective, it is precisely the rise in conservative thinking that advocates and supports white supremacy that has created a climate where anti-Semitism and racism are both flourishing.

The Gates piece paints a graphically harsh portrait of black anti-Semitism that does not include a concomitant picture of black resistance to anti-Semitism. By so doing he runs the risk of further perpetuating a schism between blacks and Jews. Though his critique of recent black anti-Semitic thought and his citing of specific scholars is useful, his article tends to construct a monolithic black community that can be and is easily duped by outspoken black males (mostly self-appointed leaders) who are pushing anti-Semitic thinking. And even though Gates cites work written by white males as central to the development of anti-Semitic thought among some blacks, he does not identify them as "white" influences, which really does distort the issue. There is a profound link between white fascism in this society and black fascism, white conservatism and black conservatism. Blacks folks who are anti-Semitic are not just under the influence of "crazed" black male leaders, they are also guided by the anti-Semitism that is rampant in the culture as a whole. To refuse to see this as a force that shapes the thinking of conservative black folks, in conjunction with that anti-Semitic teaching that is an aspect of some Afrocentric thought, is to fail to understand the problem. And if we do not accurately name how anti-Semitism is taught to young black minds we will not be able to honestly confront, challenge, and change the situation. Concurrently, if black anti-Semitism is to be eradicated and not merely evoked in ways that pit one group of black folks against another, that make one group of black folks "darlings" among white Jews and another the "enemy," we must create critical spaces for dia-

logue where the aim is not to cast "blame" but to look more
deeply at why two groups who should and must maintain
solidarity are drifting apart.

In my classrooms I can see that one of the primary tensions
between young educated black students (some of whom are
Jewish) and white Jews is engendered by the feeling (whether
rooted in fact or fantasy) on the part of blacks that many Jews
who have class privilege, who are able to use white skin
privilege in a white supremacist society like this one, no
longer identify with the oppressed (if they ever did) and more
importantly often act in a "colonizing" manner in relation to
black experience. As with other black folks in the larger society
who no longer see Jews as allies in struggle, they feel the legacy
of solidarity has been betrayed. Contrary to the Gates piece,
they see Jews as breaking that connection in the interest of
further assimilation into mainstream white culture. Their hostility at this perceived betrayal is often expressed via anti-
Semitic comments. Yet, when probed, I find they do not see
the dangerous connection between making these comments
and complicity with those who would institutionalize exploitation and oppression of Jews globally. Not only do they not
recognize how systems of domination are maintained, they are
ignorant of the ways those of us who are relatively "powerless"
can act as agents upholding forms of oppression inimical to our
own interest.

However wrongheaded, it is not surprising that black
youth, many of whom are from materially privileged backgrounds, who feel their chances of gaining economic success
are continually thwarted by systems of racial injustice, make
the mistake of targeting their rage at white Jews. This is part of
the way racism works—it is easier to "scapegoat" Jews (especially when one has concrete racist encounters) than to target
larger structures of white supremacy. To seriously challenge
this anti-Semitism we must have a better knowledge of institutionalized white supremacy. That includes consciously understanding the way white supremacist culture promotes black
anti-Semitism. For example, from whom do young black folks

get the notion that Jews control Hollywood? This stereotype trickles down from mainstream white culture. It is just one of many. In his *NYT* article, Gates never acknowledges a link between white Christian fundamentalism that perpetuates anti-Semitic thinking and the fundamentalist thinking of narrow black nationalists. It is a distortion of reality to act as though any form of black anti-Semitism, however virulent, exists in isolation from the anti-Semitism that is learned whenever anyone absorbs without question the values of mainstream white culture, values that are taught via mass media, et cetera.

Indeed, if we were to investigate why masses of black youth all over the United States know who Louis Farrakhan is, or Leonard Jeffries, et cetera, we would probably find that a white-dominated mass media has been the educational source, not those black bookstores that Gates writes about. Again I want to strongly state that the anti-Semitism expressed by such leaders in public forums is irrevocably linked to the anti-Semitism of those whites who provide the forums but who are not overtly spreading anti-Semitic thinking. It would be a grave mistake for white Jewish readers of the Gates piece to come away imagining that the group that they must see as enemies and armor themselves against is young educated black folks, or black people in general. It is significant that narrow nationalist black leaders who push anti-Semitic thought tend to also push sexist domination of women. The majority are male unless they are the female followers of Farrakhan. It would have been interesting had the Gates piece raised the question of gender for it is not apparent whether or not black women, young and old, educated or not, are as taken with the black male scholars and leaders he identifies as spreading anti-Semitic thinking as are black males.

The only black woman mentioned in the Gates piece is evoked as a figure of ridicule. Referred to as the "dreadlocked woman" who spoke "angrily" at a dialogue between blacks and white Jews saying to one of the white female organizers: "I don't want an apology. I want reparations. Forty acres and a mule, plus interest." Whether one is speaking in a heated manner to an audience that includes white Jews or not, why is the rage of black folks about white supremacy made to appear ridiculous, even if the direction that rage is targeted at is not an appropriate one? Surprisingly, even though Gates evokes Martin Luther King to emphasize the need for us all to remember that white Jews and black Americans are "caught in an inescapable network of mutuality," this understanding does not lead to the recognition that since both groups are accountable for perpetuating conflict, hostility, and xenophobic/racist thinking about the other, then both groups must work to create the space for dialogue and reconciliation.

Many black folks want white Jews to confront and change their racism. Elly Bulkin writes passionately and honestly about the need for white Jews to confront antiblack racism, acknowledging: ". . . we do not yet know how to raise the issues of Jewish oppression and racism in the best possible way, or, given the history and complexity of both, in ways that will assure us not only that we have done it well, but that we are likely to be heard." The existence of Jewish racism does not justify or excuse black anti-Semitism. However, to honestly name and assume accountability for it does heighten our awareness that not all Jews have been or are friends and allies to black folks. It allows us to face the reality that there are real circumstances in which Jewish racism manifested in daily life encounters leads some black folks to see white Jews as enemies and to imagine that they gain power over this threat by expressing anti-Semitic thought. Gates suggests that "many Jews are puzzled by the recrudescence of black anti-Semitism in view of the historic alliance" but he does not respond to this puzzlement by sharing that it is for some black folks a defense against antiblack racism on the part of Jews.

Solidarity between blacks and white Jews must be mutual. It cannot be based on a notion of black people as needy victims that white Jews "help." It cannot be based on gratitude extended by blacks to white Jews for those historical moments when they have been steadfast comrades in struggle furthering black liberation. It has to be rooted in a recognition on the part of both groups of shared history, shared struggle, and the ways in which our past and future destinies both connect and diverge. It has to be rooted in an ongoing political recognition that white supremacy relies on the maintenance of antiblack racism and anti-Semitism, hence there will never be a time when these two struggles will not be connected. No matter how many or how strong the ties Jewish Americans make with white South Africa, thereby condoning the maintenance of white supremacy, this reality will remain. Wherever there is white supremacy, there will be anti-Semitism and racism.

The failure of blacks and white Jews to engage in critical dialogue that does not reflect prevailing racist hierarchy has meant that it is unclear in what context either group can be critical of the other without being labeled racist or anti-Semitic. Where is the context where blacks can come together with white Jews and talk critically about Jewish appropriation and commodification of black culture? Where is the context where Jews can come together with black non-Jews and talk about the sense of betrayal of a historical legacy of solidarity? What is the context in which black people can be critical of Zionist policies that condone the colonization and exploitation of Palestinians? Where is the context in which Jews can question black folks about our attitudes and opinions about Israel, about Jewish nationalism? Unless these contexts exist we will not be able to create the kind of critical thinking and writing that can challenge and transform black anti-Semitism or white Jewish racism. Targeting our critiques solely at anti-Semitic black leaders (who represent a small fragment of black populations) does not enable masses of blacks and white Jews to understand both the historical and present-day connections between the growth of white supremacy, the development of anti-Semitic thought and practice globally, and the spread of antiblack racism. It is this knowledge that would enable folks from both groups to understand why solidarity between us must be nurtured and sustained.

Black people are not more responsible for eradicating strains of anti-Semitism in black life than in the culture as a whole. However, we must stand against anti-Semitism wherever we encounter it. It is the task facing any of us who work for freedom. To honor our bond of inescapable mutuality, black people and white Jews must share in the collective work of creating theory and practice that can counter the anti-Semitic biases of the culture, in whatever location those biases speak themselves. Working equally to eradicate anti-Semitism, we work to end racism.

Jim Sleeper

The Battle for Enlightenment at City College

Jim Sleeper is a columnist at the New York Daily News *and the author of* The Closest of Strangers: Liberalism and the Politics of Race in New York.

 I.

In the 1930s, Irving Howe and his generation of democratic socialists realized, to their dismay, that they would have to expend their talent not on building a decent socialist society but on defeating Stalinism—that is, on rescuing the very hope of socialism from those who, starting from wholly legitimate grievances and rage, had bloodied its vision virtually beyond recognition. Leftists, from Marx to the Frankfurt school, would brilliantly diagnose capitalism's predisposition to slide, under stress, into the disease of totalitarianism; yet a larger part of the left—the Communists and their many supporters and sympathizers—seemed to lack the antibodies necessary to keep them from contracting the very disease they were committed to defeat.

As Howe and his colleagues tried to develop those antibodies—to fight not only fascism and Aryan racism but also the totalitarian terror stealing over their own camp—their efforts to warn of the peril in their midst seemed at times to put them on the same side of certain disputes as anti-Communists who were racist or right-wing. Not surprisingly, the democratic socialists were anathematized by many on the left as apologists for, or even collaborators with, racist capitalism here and abroad. As if that weren't painful enough, the condemnation came not only from Stalinists but also from seemingly more moderate, honorable Americans who'd chosen, out of elite guilt, naive idealism, or stubborn loyalty to the original Communist vision, to excuse or even celebrate Stalinist brutality.

Every conceivable rationalization was employed against the democratic socialists: that Communist deceit and brutality were figments of their fevered imaginations; that, where abuses did exist on the left, they were inevitable reactions to capitalist oppression, imperatives in the struggle for liberation carried on by any means necessary; that, even at its worst, leftist terror retained the virtue of stark truth because, as the French philosopher Maurice Merleau-Ponty advised, revolutionary terror exposes capitalism's deeper, systemic violence by discrediting liberal institutions and pieties that mask untold exploitation and misery.

How harsh—and how hollow—these rationalizations sound today, when the peoples of the Soviet Union have spoken for themselves and for the millions of corpses and broken spirits the Stalinists left behind! Democratic socialists have been vindicated, even if only morally, belatedly, and within limits dispiriting to contemplate. We can only wonder what the larger left might have accomplished had it found ways to combat oppression and irrationalism without betraying the humanist, Enlightenment alternatives it claimed to embody.

We ought to wonder about that in earnest, for today the tawdriest of the old left's rationalizations are being recycled to defend a collection of new liberationist "struggles," led by black intellectuals, politicians, activists, and their leftist white supporters and enablers. Democratic socialists and liberals can't help but hear frightening echoes of the old left's tragic past when prominent Americans characterize desperate black assaults on Korean shopkeepers and Orthodox Jews as "uprisings" against racist oppression or when members of the Congressional Black Caucus leap to their feet to applaud Minister Louis Farrakhan at their annual convention in Washington.

The demagogues and their wider, more dangerous, circle of apologists contest the legitimacy of such liberal institutions as the criminal justice system, public schools, and electoral politics, and of such Enlightenment legacies as rational analysis, color-blind justice, and individual rights. Since whites have often abused these institutions and ideas to mask racism, the argument goes, there is something inherently racist about the institutions and ideas themselves and about the American civic culture that has grown up around them. According to advocates of what is called "critical race theory," the very idea of a transracial, "American" identity is designed to coopt blacks into white notions of comity, in violation of more authentic, non-Eurocentric ways of thinking and ordering society. The antidote to the "false universalism prevalent in the myth of equal opportunity," as one black champion of critical race theory puts it, is a kind of equality of results, a regime of racial group rights in which the personal and collective "racial narratives" of the oppressed supplant Enlightenment "abstractions" as the fount of discourse and politics.

The profound and dangerous flaws in these arguments force us to take up where Howe's generation of democratic socialists left off. We have to face the prospect—as dismaying, even if more modest, as that faced by democratic socialists in the 1930s of isolating and defeating what has come to pass for "antiracist" politics in America. We have to do that on behalf of a more transformative politics, grounded in a new appreciation of the importance of class and of the transracial, liberal consensus that must temper class as well as race politics to advance economic justice.

That means opposing the practitioners of the so-called identity politics that sustains critical race theory, Afrocentrism, and other pedagogical and political projects that, we knew from experience, will only recapitulate the oppressions they claim to oppose. It means warning that many of today's champions of multiculturalism and antiracism, like well-meaning supporters of Communists in the 1930s, lack essential antibodies against the debilitating tribal resentments, the dehumanizing stereotypes rooted in folkish tales of blood and soil, which they claim to oppose. Instead of advancing a common civic culture strong enough to challenge racism and economic injustice, as the civil rights movement did, the new antiracists are embracing or indulging rank demagoguery and totalitarian impulses, some of them appropriately named "Afrofascism." It is time to stop fooling ourselves about this and to craft a strategy of determined, unrelenting opposition.

II.

Here is an example of the problem, set, ironically, in the exact place where Howe and his circle began their struggle against totalitarianism in the 1930s: City College.

"Leonard Jeffries is a charismatic figure, with an almost cultlike following at City College," the writer James Traub informed readers of *The New Yorker* in a vivid profile of the professor in 1993. "He moves across the campus like a heavyweight champion, trailed by an entourage that often includes bodyguards, gofers, members of 'the community,' . . . The air around Jeffries seems charged with menace."

Traub attended several of Jeffries's classes and described one in detail: "When Jeffries arrived, wearing his trademark dashiki and cap, he gave the class the ancient Egyptian salutation, '*Hautep!*' and the students chanted back, '*Hautep!*' . . ." Taking advantage of Traub's presence to stage a ritualized confrontation with his white critics, Jeffries defiantly recited his credentials, challenging Traub to disparage them. He responded to interruptions from only one student, whose questions served as setups to his monologue.

After the students had responded with applause and snickers at Traub's expense, Jeffries turned to a blackboard covered with his trademark symbols and triangles and began expounding his belief that peoples of African descent have a "humanistic, spiritualistic value system," while European-Americans have values that are "egotistic, individualistic, and exploitative." As he warmed to his subject, he became angry, and

wheeled from the blackboard to face the class directly. "In Brazil," he said, "black youths are being killed like dogs in the street." The students shuddered. Jeffries was talking faster and faster, pacing back and forth across the room. Interruption was unthinkable. He talked about Hollywood, and the old racial stereotypes. He said, "This is the institutionalization of racism that the Jewish community is largely responsible for!" Now, for the first time, Jeffries was shouting. He talked more about sun people and ice people. And then he came back to the Jews—the Jews who had run City College and had opposed the call for "open admissions" during the great struggle of 1969. "We've never been given anything by the Jews!" Jeffries shouted.

Finally, Jeffries reached his great, consuming obsession—the involvement of Jews in the slave trade. He was speaking rapidly, almost automatically. . . . And now he was rattling off dates, and stray facts, and titles and authors. "Don't just listen to Dr. J.," he said. "It's in the books. It's all there. But I've talked about the Jews, so the whole power structure, the whole Jewish-controlled media, has set out to destroy me. . . . On this altar . . . I'm being slaughtered, my family is being slaughtered, a whole community is being slaughtered!" he cried. "But we won't bow down. We won't give up. *La luta continua!* The struggle continues!" Jeffries turned away to look out the window, and the class burst into applause.

Jeffries had been conducting his classes in this way for years, yet he did not become infamous outside the City University of New York until 1991, when he delivered a harangue laced with anti-Semitism at a black arts festival in Albany. There he charged that Jews and mafiosi had conspired to perpetuate negative stereotypes of blacks in Hollywood films and that champions of multicultural education were under "systemic, unrelenting" attack by "the Jewish community," especially George Bush's under secretary of education, Diane Ravitch, whom Jeffries called "a Texas Jew" and "debonair racist."

The speech, well received by its audience of several hundred black educators, artists, and activists, was videotaped and broadcast a few weeks later on a state-funded cable television channel, which *New York Post* reporter Fred Dicker happened to see. It is instructive that controversy erupted only after the *Post*'s account appeared. Under pressure from an outraged Governor Mario Cuomo and other prominent politicians, CUNY found reasons to deny Jeffries an expected three-year renewal of his nineteen-year black-studies department chairmanship, which had already been approved by the members of Jeffries's hand-picked department colleagues and was awaiting ratification by CUNY's trustees.

Although Jeffries's removal as chairman did not deprive him of his tenure, salary, students, or office space, he instantly became a martyr in the black community, and he sued CUNY in federal court, charging that his freedom of speech had been violated and demanding reinstatement as chairman and $25 million in punitive damages. Judge Kenneth Conboy imposed minor damages on the university and ordered Jeffries's reinstatement in September, 1993.

That Jeffries had been vindicated by the "white justice" he'd always derided was an irony lost on few of his detractors at City. But that the college hadn't moved against him years earlier for more substantive and legally defensible reasons reflects a perverse mix of white liberal fear and racism that for decades has enabled black demagogues to damage liberal institutions. The college had long known of Jeffries's intimidating behavior toward students and colleagues and his characterizations of whites as "ice people" who spread "the three D's—domination, destruction, and death." Yet he had been quietly accommodated ever since 1972, when college president Robert Marshak, shaken by black demands for a separate school

of black studies, had promised full-professor status and tenure
to a qualified candidate to head a new black studies department.

Jeffries was then a newly minted Ph.D. from Columbia, an
Africanist with an unpublished dissertation on politics in the
Ivory Coast—clearly unqualified for the post. But Moyibi
Amoda, the new department's interim chairman and head of
the search team, told Traub he'd found Jeffries "prodigiously
qualified—by real standards." To this assessment, Marshak
had mysteriously acceded; Amoda denies reports that black
students and activists had threatened major disruptions if he
didn't.

Professor Leonard Kriegel suggests more precisely how
the sense of menace around Jeffries arose from City's own
abrogation of academic standards. "In order to advance from
assistant to associate to full professor," Kriegel wrote in the
black journal *Reconstruction,* "I had to perform tasks academics
are expected to perform." Jeffries was exempted from all that
because "he had been hired to serve as a spiritual force, a priest
of blackness. . . . In hiring him as it did, CCNY itself issued
an invitation to intellectual fraud."

Over the next twenty years, Jeffries rewarded the white
liberal condescension implicit in his hiring with contempt for
all academic and administrative demands. He never published;
he overspent his budget; students and faculty reported that he
intimidated them; he failed to meet his classes; and, when he
did show up, he regaled his awestruck charges, as Traub describes, with the fantastical theories, incantations, mnemonic
devices, and withering denunciations of the liberal Jews who'd
given him his platform. Jeffries "should have been removed in
1975, but they were afraid of him," I was told by a former
City College dean who had fielded student complaints against
Jeffries and witnessed his intimidating diatribes against colleagues. His Albany speech only "made public what we'd kept
as a family secret. I left because I wanted to be where academics
aren't so intimidated by politics," the dean added.

"Jeffries is an extremist," Traub observes, "but he lives in a
world sympathetic to extremism—or, at any rate, unwilling to

repudiate it." In 1989, Jeffries was hired as a consultant to a state panel developing a "curriculum of inclusion" for all New York schools. He wrote the African-American section of the commission's report, hawking notions about black learning styles and family structures that would have confirmed the misapprehensions of a diehard white segregationist. Only after the historian Arthur Schlesinger, Jr. and others mounted a vigorous dissent did state education commissioner Thomas Sobol reassess the wisdom of the report. He convened another panel, whose work continues.

Yet Jeffries continues to be accommodated and defended by black academics like a senior professor in the humanities at City whom I interviewed "off the record" for my column in the *Daily News*. Active in campus governance and well regarded by white and black colleagues, the professor said he thinks it important that all who care about black studies rally around Jeffries, for it is really the field, not the man, that is under attack.

"But isn't that precisely why you need to make clear that Jeffries isn't representative of the field?" I asked. "Wouldn't its reputation be enhanced if its serious scholars disowned Jeffries's nonsense?"

"Well, you may say it's nonsense, and I may disagree with a lot of what Len says," the professor replied, "but his is a valid, if controversial, mode of study. He is celebratory, while others of us are more positivist in our approach."

A black dean at a college in New Jersey said much the same thing, only more conspiratorially: "These attacks on Jeffries are really just designed to put us Africanists in our place, to show us where the limits are," he told me. "We can't simply knuckle under to that."

Whether the line taken by Jeffries's defenders and apologists is rooted in fear of him or in a sublimated hostility to "white" liberalism, or in some deeper intellectual confusion, it seems to influence CUNY's administration. In 1993, a committee appointed by Chancellor W. Ann Reynolds proposed a reorganization that would have ended City's philosophy major on the grounds that only a few hundred students were taking upper-level courses in that department; yet the reorganization would have expanded ethnic-studies programs whose enrollments were no larger. It was as if CUNY were thinking, "Give 'em ethnic playpens and they won't notice us shortchanging students who hunger for philosophy's introduction to a larger world." Only strong faculty protests—buttressed by community fears that racist condescension was indeed involved in the proposal to drop philosophy and other majors—stopped the plan, at least temporarily.

III.

Jeffries's story hints at a tragedy of incalculable dimensions. Now, more than at any time since the thirties, progressive politics should be striving to build coalitions strong enough to reverse federal and state abandonment of cities and the poor (including, notably, the severe underfunding of institutions like CUNY); destructive economic practices hypocritically justified as inherent in the workings of free markets; and, amid the devastation caused by these forces, racial and ethnic hostilities that blight lives and foreclose coalition politics. Precisely because racism, economic injustice, and right-wing politics are such powerful undertows, leaders groping for alternatives cannot afford fantasies of racial destiny that fracture coalitions for social change.

We must learn to distinguish group psychodramas, which do have their place in communal theaters, churches, and literature, from the interracial discourse and organizing, based on transracial truths, that are needed in pluralist academies, workplaces, courts, and elections. Progressive politics simply can't make headway in a diverse society without nourishing the Enlightenment legacies I've mentioned. The commitment to rational analysis posits the primacy of admittedly evolving public truths and a common civic language over mythic, communal truths enshrouded in racial narratives. The defense of individual over group rights, in a context of civic and moral obligation to propel across race lines, undergirds the right to dissent and even to depart from one's own ethnic or religious community, whether to protest an injustice within the community itself or to affirm and deepen one's membership in a larger civic culture.

Yet, as the Jeffries story illustrates, it has become increasingly difficult for liberals, black as well as white, to appeal to these legacies in confronting ethnocentrist demagogues who suppress dissent, dehumanize real and putative adversaries, vilify innocent parties, and elevate lies to the status of "different truths." To delegitimize a Farrakhan or a Jeffries—or, for that matter, a Meier Kahane or a David Duke—we must first challenge a phalanx of apparently more benign enablers. Just as democratic socialists had to struggle not only against Stalinists but also against Stalinism's fashionable, sometimes eloquent, apologists, we will find ourselves challenging blacks and whites whose often naive deference to the misplaced agendas of identity politics empowers the demagogues.

Doing that may entail being called racists or Uncle Toms, and no wonder. Just as democratic socialists who attacked American Stalinists and their fellow travelers risked playing into the hands of right-wing anti-Communists who later imposed McCarthyist terror, our vigorous criticism of racialist demagoguery risks abetting the formation of an antiblack alliance. Ironically, though, black demagogues and their apologists have already burned so many bridges to liberal Jews, feminists, Asian-Americans, and Hispanics that any antiblack alliance is likely to be multiracial, and all the more tragic for that. The lesson of such developments, both in the thirties and today, is to redouble our efforts, not abandon them.

We also need to confront straightforwardly the notion that skin color is a kind of proxy for political wisdom. Racism and oppression are terrible precisely because they blight and maim; their victims are at least as likely to oppress others as they are to become the bearers of great insights. Liberation is always advanced by people of all colors and class backgrounds who somehow find footholds in the interstices between the oppressor and the oppressed, bringing moral imagination to bear upon their experience, and, in so doing, transcending their own parochial pains. Mere membership in a subjugated minority is no guarantor of such moral imagination or the courage to transcend. It certainly is no substitute for submitting one's ideas to peer review in an evolving, transracial discourse, as Jeffries has declined to do by publishing nothing during his twenty-one years at City College.

Liberal Jews are especially sensitive to the dangers of using racial or religious identity as a proxy for a serious critique of oppression, because we have a strong commitment to the Enlightenment universalism and rational analysis that identity politics and critical race theory disdain. That may explain the anti-Semitic cast or coloration of some of the pronouncements by ethnocentrists who perceive, quite accurately, that Jews have been foremost among universalism's interpreters and defenders. As critical race theorists such as Derrick Bell insist that Enlightenment nostrums are inherently racist, or, at best, parochially Eurocentric, they indulge critics of universalism such as Farrakhan and Jeffries, who single out Jews as insidiously effective accomplices in the hegemony of Enlightenment ideas.

Jeffries's tendency to exaggerate the role of Jews in the slave trade illustrates the complexity of the problem. International slavery was actually an ecumenical business, the commodity market of its day. It was invented largely by Arab Muslims; instituted in the West by European Christians; catered to by Africans who sold blacks from other tribes; and bankrolled and managed to a very limited extent by a small number of Sephardic Jews who owned some plantations using slave labor in Brazil and invested in the sugar processing industry, which brought black slaves to the West Indies. To understand Jeffries's exaggeration of Jewish complicity, imagine a white racist or black nationalist historian of the future, looking back on the New York of the 1990s, seeing a black mayor, a black Ford Foundation president, a few black CEOs, and scores of black corporate vice presidents for community affairs—and concluding that blacks had driven the urban capitalist agenda.

Jeffries singles out Jews for purposes closer to home and to his own personal experience (which, in keeping with the premises of identity politics, he conflates with a larger racial truth). First, he was succored, tutored, and advanced by Jews, who he now seems to believe were manipulating him for their own ends. Second, Jeffries understands that Jews, out of their peculiar mix of idealism and insecurity, born of a dependency on Enlightenment ideas and the institutions that embody them, are the first to take alarm at black rage. Baiting them ensures a reaction from at least a portion of the liberal establishment, no small gain for aggrieved blacks to whom no one listens.

Yet Jeffries's mischaracterization of Jews is just the kind of distortion identity politics flirts with all the time, and the mystery is why liberal Jews have been so slow to confront it. Two reasons come to mind, one parochial, the other political. The parochial reason is that most of us have worked so hard and sacrificed so much to embrace—one might almost say, to be worthy of—the universalism of the Enlightenment that we're embarrassed by anything that smacks of self-interested, special pleading on behalf of Jews. (How much the more true this is when the Jews in question are Crown Heights Hasidim, consumed with yearning for the Messiah and linked so tenuously to the Enlightenment that they seem even more tenuously linked to us!)

The political and, to my mind, more important reason for our hesitation to raise our voices is the one I've already alluded to—our almost instinctual fear, born of past struggles, of playing into the hands of right-wing racists. It's disconcerting to find ourselves cast as apologists for the dominant, racist discourse simply for arguing that Enlightenment legacies such as universal human rights, democracy, and class- and color-blind justice are historic if precarious human gains, not masks for privilege. Yet that is precisely what we must find the courage to claim.

We need to acknowledge clearly that while the genocidal

brutalities that went into the building of the United States are roughly on a par with those of every other civilization, the Madisonian constitutional emphasis on checks and balances and the breaking of factions makes ours the first truly multiracial civilization since ancient Rome to nourish the seeds of its own transcendence. People of all colors, believing this, have watered those seeds with their blood, sweat, and tears to make them grow, again and again.

We need to warn that critical race theory, and identity politics generally, have abandoned that struggle in favor of narratives and fantasies for people whose horizons have been tragically constricted by their experiences of oppression. Practitioners of identity politics prattle on about the fact that Thomas Jefferson held slaves and ignored women when he wrote the Declaration of Independence, instead of taking what he wrote as a uniquely precious text awaiting interpretation and fulfillment, as many ordinary women and people of color have done with great courage. They refuse to acknowledge what the recent deluge of immigration by people of color to these shores confirms: Only in the constitutional framework inherited, by an accident of history, from dead white men do women and minorities—and multiculturalism itself—find breathing room and footholds. Feminism and minority rights do not fare well in Africa, the Islamic world, or most of Asia. America, portrayed not so long ago as the center of world imperialism and oppression, turns out to be the best hope.

It's not difficult to imagine why blacks who have experienced such brutal, unrelenting oppression in America greet such truths more with dread than exhilaration. It is a bit harder to understand why blacks whose careers have advanced and whose prospects are brighter now than they could have been even thirty years ago react similarly. We have to encourage the latter to think more clearly about what they risk destroying by continuing to posit an implacable, indissoluble racism. For Jews, making this argument means clarifying, for ourselves as well as for blacks who will listen to us, the distinction we perceive between America and Europe.

In America, we must acknowledge, blacks were indeed robbed of their African culture and identity and forced to endure what even Clarence Thomas called "the totalitarianism of segregation." But blacks were always aware of a "white" world of apparent order and freedom beyond the wall. It was a world they aspired to, imitated when they could, and, in time, appealed to on its own terms, forging alliances with sympathetic whites to make it bend.

What the critical race theorists and demagogues such as Jeffries have not experienced, however, and apparently have not imagined, is an entire society's descent into a regime of universal terror. They act as if the ordered "white" world of liberal institutions will always remain a foil to and justification for even their most irresponsible assaults. They seem to have no idea how deeply their own freedom to denounce white liberalism depends upon its very strength. They seem to have no sense of its fragility; and no idea that they can bring it down. Thus Jeffries feels free to deepen his students' conviction that "white justice" will never serve them, even as it restores him to his chairmanship.

Whether that contradictory, indeed hypocritical, message is delivered in erudite tones by critical race theorists positing an implacable white hostility to hiring blacks at law schools, or in hoarse denunciations of the jury system by street demagogues, it is essentially the same: "Our only duty is to evoke and provoke; it is somebody else's duty"—the grown-ups, perhaps?—"to determine the truth and set matters to rights. We will spin our pain into webs of narrative and metaphor; someone else"—always, someone else—"will translate it into politics and policy."

Such talk stirs Jews' memories of the rise of the Nazis, who similarly abused the liberal institutions of the Weimar Republic. But it stands in heartbreaking contrast to the heroic work blacks themselves have done, sometimes in alliance with Jews, to strengthen American liberal institutions by holding them to the Enlightenment promises upon which they're based. What's perhaps most disconcerting about critical race theorists is their willingness not simply to criticize that history—our history, made out of our personal and collective yearnings and struggles—but to dismiss it, to consign our narratives of those struggles to a void labeled "hegemonic racist discourse."

"Who controls the past, controls the future," wrote George Orwell in *1984,* and we all know that history written by its "winners" works this way. Yet we cannot afford to let bitterness about the abuses of liberal institutions excuse the dismantling of the institutions themselves. What Stalinism ought to have taught us is that the narratives of history's "losers" can be destructive, too—that the oppressed can fight as blindly and brutally as the oppressor. Counterintuitive though it may seem, defenders of liberal institutions must sometimes speak truth to powerlessness, which can become as blind as power itself.

Leon Wieseltier

Taking Yes for an Answer

Leon Wieseltier is the literary editor of The New Republic. *A version of this essay appeared in* Time *magazine, February 28, 1994.*

■ The great disputations between American blacks and American Jews in recent decades—not all American blacks and not all American Jews, certainly, but the disputations are nonetheless real—have not exactly been edifying, at least from the standpoint of a rational politics. Many of the arguments are more roiling than reasoning. They are not free from prejudice, rumor, and demagoguery. In the black community, this has been especially true of what might loosely be called the line of Malcolm, which has flourished in popular culture and, more recently, in the movement of Louis Farrakhan (who, to paraphrase the prophet Elijah's words, killed Malcolm and also took possession). Farrakhan is not exactly a national leader of his people, but he is not exactly an invention of the media, either. And it is beneath the dignity of decent and intelligent men and women to struggle over the superstitions of a figure such as Farrakhan, except that the struggle is really over the definition of dignity. Farrakhan, and more generally the line of Malcolm, represents the view that hatred is an element of dignity, that a proper respect for oneself and one's own is well expressed by a proper disrespect for others.

As a society, we have gone from a hatred of hatred to a fascination with it. Or, to put it differently: the persistence of racism in America notwithstanding, the age of American racism has been succeeded by the age of American racialism. Racism and racialism agree that the color of a person's skin is an essential attribute of the person. For racism, the attribute is a negative one. For racialism, the attribute is a positive one. For a just social order, of course, the attribute is a neutral one. Neutral, not because race is not a fact; neutral, because race is not a value. Many people who do not share Farrakhan's bizarre beliefs share his belief that race is a value, which is why he, like many local urban politicians and many rap singers, has the power to disturb.

Farrakhan is foul, but he is useful insofar as he casts light upon the larger confusion. For this reason, he should not be pressured nor should any black leader be pressured, to recant anything. This lets him, and the present state of race relations in this country, off the hook. It is an invitation to euphemism, as Farrakhan cheerfully showed. We all should know what each of us thinks, and draw our conclusions. The advertisement in which the Anti-Defamation League reprinted the little catalogue of hatreds that was proffered at Kean College by a deputy of Farrakhan was brilliant for its restraint. It was an exercise in clarification. It said to its readers: Here is prejudice, measure yourself by it. If it made some (but hardly all) black leaders trim and squirm, well, that was clarifying, too.

The ADL advertisement was also an uncanny moment in Jewish history. In what other country would Jews themselves have disseminated anti-Semitic propaganda, in the certainty that its dissemination would protect them? The ADL's response to Farrakhan was an expression of the confidence of American Jews in America. I do not expect quite this degree of confidence in America from American blacks; racism, not anti-Semitism, has always been America's ugliness of choice, and the fate of blacks in America was, for whole centuries, obscene. In this century, however, this country has challenged its black citizens precisely as it has challenged its Jewish citizens. The political and philosophical procedures of America have dared both these groups, and not only these groups, to take yes for an answer.

Taking yes for an answer is not as easy as it sounds. It means celebrating individual experience even as you celebrate collective memory; acknowledging the changes of the present in full, learned sight of the unchanging cruelties of the past; rejecting the fatalism that was a perfectly legitimate part, and a perfectly inevitable part, of the tradition that you inherited; believing in politics, and pitting politics against the lachrymosities of culture. For groups that have suffered extremely, as blacks and Jews have suffered, taking yes for an answer may even be experienced as a form of betrayal. And so, in such groups, the improvement of life will be a great opportunity for the mongerers of guilt, and for those who flog their own brethren with ideals of authenticity so as to prevent them from recognizing the reality of progress.

Farrakhan and the other racialists in the black community (again, they are not all figures of the margin) are precisely such mongerers and such floggers. Their chilling thesis is that the similarity between the black past in America and the black present in America is greater than the difference. For the last hundred years or so, the Jews have also had to contend with such a thesis about their own modernity. If they are more secure than they have ever been, in America and (for different reasons) in Israel, it is because they repudiated that thesis, not without bitter internecine battle, and because they made themselves ready, in their own self-interest, for the costs of change. Those costs, inner and outer, were considerable. But they were not so considerable that they made the rest of their wretchedness bearable.

America represented a revolution in Jewish experience, and the Jews wisely assented to the revolution. But there has also occurred another revolution in this country, more recently, in the name of civil rights. Can anybody any longer doubt that America, most comprehensively in the realms of law and politics, has repented of its repulsive treatment of blacks? Indeed, the contemporary troubles of the inner cities are so painful precisely because they are taking place after, and not before, the civil rights revolution. But even those troubles are not great enough to justify a denial of the revolution. Farrakhan and company speak for such a denial. It is grimly amusing to watch black politicians who owe their distinction to the new dispensation flirting with this teacher of the old dispensation, with this peddler of reaction.

These parallels between American blacks and American Jews are not an occasion for sentimentality. There is no law of American history according to which all its minorities will forever be friends. To be sure, some of the conflicts between blacks and Jews have been false; but a false comity is not much better than a false conflict. Not every fight is the result of misunderstanding. There are fights that are the result of understanding. In the wake of the latest Farrakhan flap, but surely not the last, the positions of many black leaders are more clearly understood. In some cases, this is for the worse. In many cases, it is for the better. The new distance between blacks and Jews may have its uses. We do not need to honor each other as brothers. We need to honor each other as citizens.

Derrick Bell

A Semblance
of Safety

Derrick Bell is a scholar in residence at New York University Law School and the author, most recently, of Faces at the Bottom of the Well: The Permanence of Racism. *His essay originally appeared in* New York Newsday, *February 1, 1994.*

■ The pattern is becoming familiar. First, a black professor, politician, or religious leader steps before a microphone and makes hateful statements about whites in general and Jews in particular. Instead of ignoring these patently wrong and irresponsible statements, the media immediately pay them a great deal of attention and, in the process, bestow upon the hate speaker undeserved celebrity.

Second, outraged whites, in addition to castigating the speaker, demand that black leaders step forward and condemn the hate speech and its propagator. Whether or not they have any connection—beyond color—with the hate speaker, whites ask: "Did you hear what that man said about us? What are you going to do about it?"

The reaction is unique to black-white relations. No other ethnic group's leaders are called upon to repudiate and condemn individuals in their groups who do or say outrageous things.

Even so, some black leaders respond to such calls for condemnation. They do so because they view the statements as offensive, and as potentially harmful to the Black Cause. In the hope that their voices will ameliorate the harm, the Reverend Jesse Jackson and others take the risk that political enemies will misinterpret their words as admissions of black moral failure and use them to justify repressive or divisive racial policies.

The Reverend Calvin O. Butts, pastor of the Abyssinian Baptist Church in Harlem, is among those blacks who are unwilling to take that risk. Refusing to respond to Rev. Louis Farrakhan's anti-Semitic remarks a few years ago, he said that, "if in response to Israel's refusal to impose sanctions on South Africa to protest its policies of racial separation, I jumped up and said all Jewish leaders in the United States should denounce Israel, how many Jewish people would join me in that? I don't think many."

What are whites seeking when they insist that blacks condemn other blacks for hateful speech? Let me hazard a guess. Despite the widespread denial that racial discrimination remains a barrier to black progress, I think many whites both know that racism remains oppressive and fear that blacks may unite and retaliate against a society that has repressed them for so long. Thus any black around whom other blacks are willing to rally is deemed a potential leader of this long-feared rebellion. This threat is present even when the leader, like Dr. Martin Luther King, Jr., is committed to nonviolence. When the leader is as charismatic and as unnerving to many whites as Rev. Farrakhan, the sense of threat becomes overwhelming.

The fear that a long-oppressed people will vent their rage against those they believe are their oppressors will not be eased by condemning the speech of Farrakhan or his top aide. Indeed, as has happened with so many outspoken black leaders before him, Rev. Farrakhan could be removed violently from the scene tomorrow, and yet the threat would remain. Indeed, it could become far worse.

When Farrakhan came to New York recently and seventeen thousand black men came out to hear him on short notice, he spoke critically of whites, but he also preached a message of nonviolence and self-help.

Even those who strongly disagree with some of his positions must ask whether the negatives justify total condemnation. As no one needs to be reminded, black men fill the nation's prisons and commit a disproportionately large percentage of violent crime. It is also, as many of us tend to forget, black men and their families who suffer the most from the frustration of unemployment and the rage resulting from racial bias in the job market. The usual responses to these bitter facts—ignoring the soul-killing desperation afflicting our inner cities, and building more prisons to house those convicted of crimes—provide the same semblance of safety that whites enjoy when we "responsible blacks" criticize those blacks who make hateful comments.

I do not expect this Plantation Mentality to change, but meaningful responses to black rage fed by poverty and despair must include providing opportunities for training and employment, measures the nation is reluctant to take in more than token amounts. The alternative, continuing to call on black leaders to condemn other blacks deemed threatening to whites, neither defers nor defuses the racial disaster that threatens to engulf us all.

PHILOSOPHICAL
OBSERVATIONS

Michel Feher

The Schisms of '67: On Certain Restructurings of the American Left, from the Civil Rights Movement to the Multiculturalist Constellation

Michel Feher is a founding editor of Zone Books, the author of the forthcoming Un histoire des arts d'aimer en occident, *and a contributor to* Esprit, *in which this essay originally appeared in December 1992. The translation from the French is by Erik Brunar.*

■ 1. The New Left in Crisis

When the National Convention on New Politics met in Chicago's Palmer House, over the 1967 Labor Day weekend, it was the new left's last-ditch attempt to mend its inner divisions and to settle on a single platform for the 1968 presidential election. Many of the civil rights veterans and anti-Vietnam War activists who took part were still hoping the new left would unite behind a Martin Luther King–Benjamin Spock ticket. Instead the events that unfolded signaled the end of an era.

Black power was at its peak. Gathered in a Black Caucus, the black power delegates at the conference demanded fifty percent of the votes although they accounted for less than twenty percent of the activists in attendance. The delegates of the student movement, the radicalized Student Nonviolent

Coordinating Committee (SNCC) and the mostly white members of Students for a Democratic Society (SDS), were particularly intimidated by the "true radicalism" of Malcolm X's political offspring and quickly granted their request. Yet this easy victory for black power did little to alleviate the tension. In fact, sensing the feelings of guilt or even self-hatred that prompted the white students' decision, the black delegates immediately insisted that one of the first acts of the conference be to adopt a resolution condemning "Zionist imperialism" (this was two months after the Six-Day War). Such a motion had little bearing on the purpose of the gathering, but everybody knew that a majority of the student delegates were Jewish. The draft resolution was an open provocation, but the conventioners approved it instantly. As one can imagine, this "conciliatory gesture," far from restoring confidence, only further embittered participants from all factions and convinced them that the coalition that had led the civil rights struggle had simply ceased to exist.

At the same time, stimulated by the initial mood of the proceedings, some of the more radical women, who had recently begun to set their own priorities within the new left, asked to be given fifty-one percent of the votes on the grounds that they, too, were the victims of a specific oppression and represented fifty-one percent of the total population. Their motion wasn't even rejected. The organizers simply refused to put it on the agenda, arguing that the conference had been called to discuss far more serious issues than women's liberation. So in addition to the irreversible split between the more radical black groups and the student movement, the former busy spearheading the ghetto uprisings, the latter completely absorbed in the fight against the Vietnam War, the convention witnessed the secession of women who had grown tired of the all-pervasive male condescension—especially its embodiment within SDS.

In her poignant book on the beginnings of the women's

movement*, Sara Evans interprets the "double schism" of Chicago as a crucial turning point in the genesis of an autonomous feminist movement, whose strategy deliberately followed black power's radical lead. Like black activists, feminists became concerned with setting their own course to emancipation. They felt that it was time to wrestle with the conditions of their own subjection, that they could no longer let anyone else articulate the conditions of their oppression for them. Furthermore, black and feminist militants set out to find their true voices, feeling that these had been silenced and rejected for too long by a dominant culture that was both white and male. Regardless of its historical importance, the 1967 New Politics Convention has an undeniable heuristic value. While it showed the terminal state of disarray of the civil rights movement, it also foreshadowed the emergence of the identity politics that have dominated the American left ever since.

Born of the struggle against racial segregation in the southern states, the civil rights movement was founded on a grass-roots mobilization that consisted largely of blacks and Jews. However, the existence of this alliance became apparent when the alliance was in its death throes. At the time of their common struggle, the men and women who fought for school integration and black voter registration didn't see themselves in terms of their ethnic or religious identity but rather as driven by a shared aversion to all forms of inequality based on race, religion, or nationality.

Martin Luther King came to symbolize this "humanistic" phase of 1960s activism, when the fight for equality had not yet come into conflict with the affirmation of difference. Even the leaders of the student movement, whose opposition to the establishment tended to be radical, shared the Baptist preacher's

*Sara Evans, *Personal Politics; the Roots of Women's Liberation in the Civil Rights Movement and the New Left,* Vintage Books, 1980, pp. 196–200. For a description of the National Conference for New Politics from the point of view of black-Jewish relationships, see Jonathan Kaufman, *Broken Alliance: The Turbulent Times Between Blacks and Jews in America,* Mentor Books, 1989, pp. 198–201.

concern to bridge the gap between communities. The white founders of SDS and the first black leaders of SNCC, the main southern student organization, were motivated by an idealism that was closer to Albert Camus than to Frantz Fanon. The principal aim of SDS's Port Huron manifesto was to forge a social environment in which every human being could live, think, and love freely, in which the right of every individual to attain creative fulfillment would be established. To achieve this goal, SDS activists needed to find the best strategy for defeating the mechanisms of a society that they mainly accused of alienating individuals, i.e., of robbing people of control over their own lives, while bringing them into conflict with one another. In this respect, the student movement appealed to the kind of solidarity that is motivated by a universal thirst for emancipation, rather than to the sense of community that arises from particular roots.

2. The Uprising of the Wretched of the Earth

This unified front would soon start crumbling. C. Wright Mills and Herbert Marcuse were still striving to preserve the old concept of a universal and revolutionary proletariat by substituting a theoretical coalition of young people, women, and marginalized ethnic minorities for a working class that was completely spent and converted to the promises of the welfare state. But the black organizations, inspired by Malcolm X's ideas, resolutely embraced the dual challenge of autonomous revolt and the defense of the cultural identity underpinning their struggle. In other words, the black activists would no longer let whites speak for them or submit their agenda to programs of which they were only coauthors and which didn't exclusively target the black community. Converted to Islam or adopting a Third World "national liberation" agenda, black leaders of the late 1960s broke with the spirit of the civil rights movement in three essential ways.

First, they categorically dismissed any integrationist ideas: not only integration within the current structure of American society, but more profoundly, any form of integration that ignored the different heritage that comes with a different skin color. They saw color-blindness as a disguise for the process of absorbing oppressed minorities, which merely erased their cultural identity definitively. To become integrated, the members of these minorities would have to surrender to the standards of the dominant group, which the latter would complacently accept as a tribute to the universality of its own values.

Second, the black organizations that strove toward political autonomy or even separatism also embarked on a quest for cultural authenticity. A collective identity could be built not only around one's solidarity in the face of oppression, but also around forms of endurance and resistance invented by the oppressed together with the remembrance of traditions crushed by the oppressor. Starting with the famous slogan "black is beautiful," the black community was urged to search for the features of its specific culture and for its African roots. Moreover, insofar as this affirmation of identity was part of a strategy to break away from white America, it stressed the integrity of black culture over interracial mixes and exchanges; hence, it rejected the cosmopolitanism of European and European-influenced intellectuals as an enterprise of appropriation in disguise.

The complete and violent rejection of white society necessarily led to a switch in alliances. Rather than exposing themselves to the pitfalls of integration and the ambiguities of their former partners' bad consciences, the most militant black organizations turned to the national liberation movements that were sprouting in Africa, as well as in Asia and Latin America. From that point on, the perspective of a coalition of the "wretched of the earth" against the political and cultural imperialism of the West—led by the government of the United States and defending the interests of its white population—replaced the new left's wish for a progressive, propeace, and antiracist front.

The focus on national liberation hastened the undoing of

the civil rights movement's central hinge, the alliance between blacks and Jews. Until then, this alliance had remained largely unstated. Although they were much more integrated in American society than their African-American fellow citizens, large numbers of Jewish activists nevertheless joined the most radical wings of the new left. On the other hand, they could never have agreed on an ethnic or separatist definition of the revolution. They could not think of what an ethnic or separatist project would have meant in their case, because they did not make an issue of their Jewishness and displayed instead a cosmopolitan sensibility that made them particularly averse to ideals of national pride or racial authenticity. But even if they had bracketed their doubts about the political merits of national liberation ideology, their former allies would have ruled that they had no place in the anti-Western coalition anyway, because as a people they were associated with the State of Israel.

As the Chicago conference shows, supporting the Palestinian movement and condemning Zionism fired much of the "anti-imperialist" rhetoric, in particular among the black leaders who had converted to Islam. This singular insistence, which sometimes took the form of blatant anti-Semitism, created an unbearable tension, even though most of the Jewish activists were far from being fervent Zionists. In fact, their cosmopolitanism made them extremely wary of any nationalistic sentiment. However, the denunciation of Israel they were asked to subscribe to wasn't based on the wish to see races unite and borders abolished; it was an expression of the irreducible conflict between Western expansionism and the emancipation of the people it crushed. In terms of this dichotomy, the only plausible place for Jews seemed to be on the side of the oppressors. Therefore, the young Jews of the new left had some difficulty trying to imagine how they could reject a national identity that they had never embraced in the first place, while at the same time remaining in a movement informed by notions of cultural authenticity and national liberation.

3. Identity Politics

In the seventies, the hope—or the fear—of an uprising of the peoples of the Third World against Western imperialism faded, as did the revolutionary aspirations that had fueled the mobilization of the black community in the United States. From the Khmer Rouge to the Iranian revolution, from Cuba to the "progressive" African regimes, disillusionment poured in from abroad; resignation overcame the ghettos and chased black power and the Black Panthers from the political scene. At the same time, the quest for cultural identity and the will for solidarity within the community survived, especially after 1980, when the Republican administration began systematically to dismantle the Great Society of the 1960s.

The new identity politics that emerged from the demise of a global revolutionary perspective rested on the articulation of specific demands and on the defense of cultural difference. Minority groups endeavored to win collective reparations for the social and economic injustices caused by racism, an endeavor typified by their support of affirmative action programs in favor of minorities. They also fought for the right to reshape their own cultural identities, which had been completely skewed by racial stereotypes and erased by the liberal integration model. The proponents of these politics intended to get the white majority to acknowledge the multicultural character of American society. In their multiculturalism they substituted the image of the mosaic for the dented metaphor of the melting pot with which blacks had never been comfortable. This redefinition led to stressing and strengthening alliances among groups on the domestic front. A natural convergence of similarly unintegrated or oppressed ethnic minorities occurred—blacks and Hispanics, and also, to a lesser degree, Asians—while the women's movement became increasingly influential. After a history that in many ways paralleled the evolution of the black organizations, women's liberation had arrived at the juncture of identity politics where affirmative action and the appeal to a common experience meet. One could even say that identity politics found their fullest expression in the work of the most militant strands of feminism.

In the beginning, the radical feminists of the late 1960s picked up on the black radicals' wholesale rejection of the idea of integration into a society of white males. Frustrated by their participation in "mixed" political organizations, these female activists—many of them hailing from the ranks of the new left—decided to take control of their own emancipation. They set out to analyze the mechanisms of domination that America's patriarchal society had devised to perpetuate their submission and sought to define the terms of an authentic female subjectivity freed of the shackles of male oppression. At first they followed the antiauthoritarian movement that was sweeping through the American youth, but the more radical of the feminists quickly picked up the separatist strategies of the black organizations. They put women's solidarity in the resistance struggle before personal emancipation. They even saw the latter as ultimately being just another process of integration into male society, another alienating cooptation. The separatist sentiment soon dominated radical feminism, leading its proponents to cut all the lopsided ties they had with men—the political, emotional, and sexual relationships in which they had subservient roles. This rhetoric of sedition was intended as part of a global uprising against the Western patriarchal order. However, it was aimed at the social construction of male gender rather than at actual men. Separatism was thus presented as a provisional "detoxication" or "severance" motivated solely by the social patterns that ruled relations between men and women at the time.

This tone of bravado—both aggressive and playful— dissipated as the revolutionary wind died down. The collapse of insurrectional national liberation projects and of the black organizations that promoted them helped precipitate the transformation of radical feminism into a very different movement, later called "cultural" feminism, which ultimately led its militants toward identity politics. While radical feminism incited women to invent new ways of relating to themselves and to the world, the advocates of cultural feminism called upon women to discover or rediscover their true identity. Stifled by a civilization that cultivated only male interests, the feminine identity was also repressed by women themselves because for generations they had been forced to meet the expectations of men. The cultural feminists sought to recuperate a repressed but still living female culture. They wanted to recapture the specificity of the feminine experience and the authenticity of women's voices. Both had been suppressed in the supremacy of male stereotyping; both were in danger of being given short shrift in the name of a neutral human identity.

The identity politics of cultural feminists didn't stop at listing the forms of violence, exploitation, and abasement of which women were constantly the victims. Nor did it stop at fighting for special protections for women, for equality of rights, and for compensatory measures. Moreover, cultural feminism was grounded in a belief in intrinsically female values that were either inscribed in nature or were the result of a long history of resistance to servitude, but that had, in any case, always been marginalized by the dominant culture. The affirmation of such distinctive traits or of profound cultural differerences between the sexes led first to a separatism of withdrawal—i.e., a political praxis informed by the dream of a self-sufficient female community—then toward a more realistic contractual model based on negotiated settlements. For women who felt the bond of their specific values and interests, this last approach meant demanding rights and guarantees to ensure that the relations they engaged in with men were free of abuse and faithful to women's own culture.

4. Tensions within the Mosaic

The unbridled neoconservatism of the Republican administrations of the 1980s left the radical opposition isolated and distraught. Within the political left, the decade was also an era of consolidation for the identity politics and for the "confederal" multicultural mosaic scheme. Representatives of the homosexual community joined the black, Hispanic, and feminist groupings in an alliance that found in Jesse Jackson its mouthpiece within the Democratic party—the Rainbow Coalition.

Two external factors boosted the viability of the multiculturalist coalition. On the one hand, the Republican administration, by means of its own policies managed to antagonize an incredibly heterogenous constellation of people. The government's enthusiastic promotion of a two-tiered society and its relentless defense of the "moral majority" that helped it get elected created an atmosphere of solidarity among groups with diverging interests and often incompatible values. On the other hand, the confederation of identity politics benefited from the listlessness of the liberal opposition, i.e., the New Deal and Great Society Democrats whose doctrine called for active state support for both racial integration and the fight against poverty, as well as for scrupulous protection of citizens' privacy.

The liberal call for state activism came under attack from both ends of the political spectrum. While an increasingly conservative middle class opposed budget policies based on the redistribution of wealth, feminists and minority organizations questioned the liberal notion of equality. They accused the liberals of erasing differences in sensibility and denying cultural diversity in the name of a so-called neutral individual, who was merely the conceptualization of the preoccupations of white heterosexual men. Similarly, the liberal commitment to protect privacy also came under attack, both from the conservative guardians of religious principles and "family values" and from the proponents of identity politics.

First, many feminists rejected the right to privacy as a desirable ground for their claims. They saw the private sphere as the main site of the subjection of women and the unconditional respect for privacy as the most powerful instrument of their exploitation. Moreover, a number of cultural feminists specialized in lobbying for a total ban on pornographic material, arguing that pornography promoted the degradation of women. Finally, most multiculturalist groups questioned the traditional interpretation of First Amendment values and pushed for speech codes at universities and workplaces to punish racist and sexist insults. So, with the right accusing liberalism of discouraging private enterprise by raising taxes and letting bureaucracy run out of control, and with the left accusing it of stifling women and minorities, the Kennedy-Johnson school liberals were for the most part forced off the political stage. Thus, the Democrats' 1984 and 1988 presidential campaigns carefully avoided any kind of reference to liberalism. Instead, they adopted an elastic ideology that embraced a newfound monetarism and budgetary austerity—conservative watchwords—and attempted to combine these economic ideas with an array of concessions to the various components of the Rainbow Coalition.

In the hostile environment of the times, but without any serious critical opposition, the multicultural constellation stood on the small but visible ground once occupied by the liberal and radical left. However, the coalition quickly began to experience serious internal tensions, despite the free publicity it got from neoconservative intellectuals in their campaign against the "political correctness" that was supposedly threatening university campuses.

First of all, insofar as the cultural aspect of identity politics hinged on representation, i.e., on a group's control of its own image, its proponents strove to articulate "positive" values and promote exemplary individuals, thereby downplaying the existence of conflicts and abuses of power within their community. On this principle, black or Hispanic women or homosexuals were not supposed to mention the misogyny and the homophobia that were rife in their ethnic minorities if they didn't want to be branded as traitors and abettors of white racism. For this reason, a number of black organizations unconditionally supported Judge Clarence Thomas and the boxer, Mike Tyson, against the black women who accused the former of sexual harassment and the latter of rape. The women accusers and the black feminists who stood by them were violently upbraided for having reinforced racial stereotypes about the sexual aggressiveness of black men, for having applied these stereotypes to well-known men whose professional success set examples for the community, and for having judged their aggressors according to "imported" values and criteria—i.e., the allegedly puritanical feminism that is associated with white women.

Second, in addition to tensions between the different communities, each patch of the multicultural mosaic experienced internal rifts over the content or even the very substance of the identity it sought to promote. For instance, the question of Afrocentrism caused serious controversy among representatives of the black community. Only a fringe of African-American activists and theorists embraced the rereading of universal history in the light of an original supremacy of the peoples of Africa. However, all black intellectuals had to define their attitude toward these historically unfounded notions and their clearly racist implications. Should they firmly denounce them, if only to defuse counterattacks by those who would be all too glad to pit black racism against white racism, as if the two racisms were historically equal? Should they keep silent about Afrocentric theories, or even give them some form of justification in order to spare the African-American community the spectacle of internal division, and in that way be able to concentrate on questioning the dubious intentions of whites who were quick to make accusations about black hegemonism?

Just as crucial for the fate of identity politics, the clashes between "women against pornography" and the feminists who opposed censorship revealed the incompatibility of 1970s-style cultural feminism with the ideals of the previous decade. Indeed, for many militants who were still attached to the initial ideals of radical feminism, protection against symbolic and actual forms of sexual violence against women must not restrict their autonomy as individuals. The essentialist undercurrent of identity politics was also evidenced in the debate over the nature of homosexuality—is it genetic?—within the gay community. Beyond the scientific quarrel, the dispute was really about the political ability of homosexuals to define the conditions of a solidarity as deep and indisputable as that of their neighbors in the mosaic. For some, the inscription of homosexual identity in their brain or in their genes was cause for relief and elation, while others underlined the fact that a similar theory was once used to link homosexuality to degeneracy and led to the most abominable enterprise of extermination of homosexuals.

These controversies bespeak the intense intellectual activity that went on in the multicultural movement. However, none of the questions ever challenged the model of the mosaic. Speakers intervened only on behalf of the community they represented. Their contributions were aimed principally at strengthening the identity of their sisters and/or brothers while respecting the integrity of their allies. There was ample practical justification for such a position. Community solidarity constituted the best reply to all forms of exclusion inflicted by the dominant culture. Collective pride could exorcise self-destructive tendencies generated by materially impoverished lifestyles. The celebration of communitarian real-life experience helped resist the alienating representations of "universality" that actually addressed only the needs of white males. Still, for all the vigor that was shown in denouncing racist and sexist stereotypes and the liberal integration model that was based on the neutralization of difference, the defenders of multiculturalism displayed surprising lapses when it came to noticing the oppressive effects that identity politics could have when the multicultural idea went from describing cultural heritages to prescribing so-called authentic values.

5. The Repression of Cosmopolitanism

Multiculturalism's blind spot does not lie in its understanding of liberalism, which the advocates of identity politics explicitly reject, but in its repression—in a Freudian sense—of cosmopolitanism, which represents a perspective that is erroneously associated with a liberal position. Liberalism calls for transcending racial and sexual difference in the name of the universal rights of human beings. Cosmopolitanism, on the other hand, entertains curiosity about these differences. It is "color-curious" rather than color-blind or color-bound—and thus opposes both liberal and multiculturalist politics when they confuse differences with identities. From the cosmopolitan viewpoint, differences are misrepresented just as badly when they are neutralized as when they are naturalized. In other words, difference is neither meant to define an inviolable territory nor to be reduced to a secondary particularity. It is a source of attraction. Therefore, a cosmopolitan perspective calls for a dynamic of mutual transformation, not for a static respect of the other's integrity or for a pledge to a universal notion of humanity.

Cosmopolitanism criticizes identity politics and liberal universalism both. It accuses the liberal universalists of obliterating the specificity of their own origins and history in order to submit human diversity to the intangible standards of the liberal integration model that they themselves have devised and of which they are the only guardians. Cosmopolitanism views democracy as the art of opening up the field of possibilities. In this respect, the protection of both individual rights and cultural specificity is necessary but not sufficient. Men and women of all backgrounds must also have the liberty to question the way in which society identifies them, and thus to invent their own relations to themselves and to other people. Hence the cosmopolitan abhorrence of any measure intended to affix an identity on anyone—be it the identity of a rational person with universal rights or that of a given community.

During the 1980s, the advocates of the multicultural mosaic tended to view the cosmopolitan thesis as a sort of liberalism in disguise—even though cosmopolitanism's project also envisioned a multicultural society. Given the current state of the balance of power, argued the proponents of identity politics, invitations to mix and to cross perspectives were nothing but the dominant order's strategies to appropriate and control subservient cultures. The multicultural coalition came to concentrate on the struggle against the strangling or the cooptation of community identity. At times the multicultural coalition even gave precedence to this struggle over the fight against segregation and its hierarchies—hierarchies of race, gender, sexual preference, etc.

More precisely, while identity politics activists derived their militant fervor from their resistance to the Republican administrations, they tended to concentrate their ideological attacks on the shortcomings of Democratic liberalism. For one, they claimed that liberal Democratic civil rights programs provided no protection against the two-tiered society bred by neoconservative policies. The multiculturalists accused liberalism of denying its distinctly white and male origin in order to preach its gospel of a color-blind social justice and thus silencing the voices of women and minorities whom identity politics could empower. A number of conservative intellectuals took advantage of this antiliberal overtone of "leftist" discourse to present themselves as the champions of the universalist position. In particular, they warned against the so-called threat of the multiculturalists' "politically correct" relativism to the American educational system. The proponents of identity politics responded to the attack by adopting the strategy known as the "besieged fortress." They accused all their critics of collusion with the right, even those who merely articulated another practice of difference and questioned only the most suspect forms of the rhetoric of cultural or racial authenticity.

The fact that a coalition named after the rainbow could so easily reject cosmopolitanism—or at least fail to recognize its differences with liberalism—is astonishing, especially since the two intellectual movements that had the greatest influence on the academic multiculturalist community were steeped in it. The Frankfurt school balanced its criticism of Enlightenment universalism with warnings against the danger of a return to roots and of looking to roots for justification. As for the various French philosophers labeled as poststructuralists in the United States, the only position they all undeniably shared was precisely their refusal to reduce difference to identity. One can understand the perplexity of the European admirers of Theodor Adorno, Walter Benjamin, Michel Foucault, or Jacques Derrida when they see their intellectual mentors enlisted in the defense of identity politics. These authors have tried to teach their readers to question the hegemony of Western humanism, but also to resist all quests for authenticity—along with their relativist and essentialist undercurrents.

Troubling though it is from a strictly intellectual viewpoint, the rejection of cosmopolitanism sheds a vivid light on the uncomfortable position of Jews with respect to the multicultural mosaic, for Jews were inevitably associated with cosmopolitanism. After their active involvement in the liberal and integrationist civil rights movement and their great presence in the overtly cosmopolitan new left, Jews lost their place in the anti-Western front that was imagined by black power and the Black Panthers. Jews were not only criticized for being completely integrated into America's white society, but also seen as representatives of the people of Israel and thus as affiliates of Western imperialism. In response, many Jewish activists were increasingly drawn toward the political center. More often than not, their movement toward the center brought them into the mainstream of the Democratic party, although some did end up living out their bourgeois respectability by joining the ranks of the new right that carried Ronald Reagan into office. As for the Jews who remained on the left, once the tide of revolutionary national liberation had subsided, the rise of identity politics presented them with a new set of problems.

Among the black community, the demise of the Black Panthers' militant anti-Zionism opened the way for the unencumbered anti-Semitism that was spread by certain Afrocentrist groups and especially by the clearinghouses of Louis Farrakhan's Nation of Islam. The propaganda action of these groups included reprinting *The Protocols of the Elders of Zion* and spreading "new revelations" on the supposedly prominent role of Jews in the slave trade. The propaganda caught on because of the neighborhood tensions between the two communities in some American cities—New York saw the most violent outbreaks—and also due to the social and economic chasm that had separated the two communities from the period even before the breakup of the civil rights movement. The tensions were further amplified by a vicious circle of declarations in bad faith. To justify their growing conservatism and the racist sentiment on the rise in their community, a number of Jewish organizations brandished the threat of black anti-Semitism, while the spokespersons of the African-American minority cited the betrayal of Jews to explain the resentment of some blacks.

Those Jewish militants and intellectuals who resisted polarization along community lines and who remained attached to the idea of a Rainbow Coalition, despite Jesse Jackson's anti-Semitic slip during the 1984 presidential campaign, could not claim their spot in the mosaic without giving up their traditional agnostic cosmopolitanism. While not necessarily converting to the religious aspects of Judaism, they nonetheless entered the realm of identity politics by speaking in the name of their own particular heritage. These veterans of the new left couldn't ignore the irony of the situation: while their initial political engagement was based on the rejection of any conformist attitude (relating to issues of society, family, or community) together with a radical critique of all forms of allegiances (whether religious, cultural, or patriotic), now, in order to find their place in the multicultural constellation, they had to invoke their roots and draw their legitimacy from the suffering of their forebears. Despite their economically privileged status, Jews weren't excluded from the mosaic; but in order to be part of it, they had to articulate grievances that referred to their tragic history and values that stemmed from their cultural heritage. Any hints of cosmopolitanism, of a reluctance to commemorate, or of an aesthetics of uprootedness were total anathema.

• • •

The terms of the multiculturalist acceptance of the Jews were visible in Jesse Jackson's early 1990s strategy to reconcile Jews and blacks. When he addressed the World Jewish Congress in July 1992, Jackson acknowledged that Zionism was a national liberation movement. He called for solidarity between the two communities based on their similar experiences of suffering.* In other words, he appealed to Jews to join the Rainbow Coalition by adopting a tone and a posture previously reserved for the more conservative Jewish factions. There are Jews on the left who have accepted the same terms of what could be called "progressive traditionalism." Its promoters often propose a puzzling new interpretation of what the sixties were about. For instance, they don't associate Jewish participation in the struggles and ideals of the period with Jewish political thinkers and activists like Herbert Marcuse, Todd Gitlin, or Abbie Hoffman, but rather with Rabbi Abraham Joshua Heschel. While the former stood for a secular, socialist, and cosmopolitan project of emancipation, the latter joined the civil rights movement in the name of what he saw as intrinsically "Jewish" values of justice.

From the viewpoint of multiculturalism and its future course, one may wonder whether this "Freudian" repression of cosmopolitanism was a necessary measure or a disastrous turn. The defenders of identity politics haven't let the question bother them, justifying their silence by citing more urgent issues. First, they saw the population of the inner-city ghettos, left to its own devices in a void of government, turning to self-destruction in the form of crack abuse or gang warfare and starting to vent its rage on its own neighborhoods. Then, the reactionary judges of the Supreme Court were threatening women's rights, such as the constitutional freedom to choose an abortion, and restricting the field of civil rights by limiting the application of affirmative action. An arrogant conservative

*See *The New York Times*, July 8, 1992, pp. A1 and A13.

ideology dedicated to the cult of personal success demanded the abandonment of community values as the price of integration, and substituted the "multiculturalist menace" for the extinct Communist conspiracy. Hence, the most urgent task seemed to be to tighten bonds among the communities and to defuse tensions within the various components of the multicultural constellation. In this context, the cosmopolitan critique seemed futile, or at least inadequate. Isn't it fundamentally elitist anyway? Who can afford to split hairs over notions such as identity and difference other than the members of the leisure class? With its potential for demoralizing division, cosmopolitanism could thus be dismissed as either an irresponsible political strategy or indeed as a deliberate maneuver by liberals to coopt the multicultural movement.

However, despite all their intimidating forcefulness, these arguments wither under two objections. The first, informed by modern history, takes note of the danger inherent in any coalition bonded by resentment and group pride. In light of the tragic fate of so many national liberation movements around the world, one is led to question the ethical and political validity of a notion of solidarity based solely on shared suffering, on the identification of a common oppressor, and on the celebration of stifled roots and traditions. The shortcomings of such a coalition are compounded when, in order to avoid clashes, its promoters fail to address relations between the sexes and the races in the multicultural society they envision. Knowing who the enemy is and establishing respectful relations with one's allies aren't enough. The nationalistic exploitation of "authenticity" and the appropriation by new rulers of their people's past oppression—in view of asserting their own power—are sufficiently widespread traits, especially in postcolonial regimes. It is therefore crucial that a multicultural coalition go beyond the question of its members' representativeness in order to clarify the ethical motivation and the sociopolitical aims of their action.

• • •

The second objection to multiculturalism's repression of cosmopolitanism springs from a new urgency. In the political landscape of the 1980s, where the multicultural coalition constituted the only enclave of resistance to a waste-laying neoconservatism, the argument of the besieged fortress might have been detrimental both to the future and the principles of multiculturalism, but under the circumstances, these detrimental aspects were very hard to avoid. However, when conflicting loyalties within the mosaic came to a head with the Thomas and Tyson affairs in 1991, and when Bill Clinton's 1992 campaign renewed the tradition of liberal reformism, the terms of the problem changed drastically.

6. The Return of the Liberals and the Future of Multiculturalism

The Democratic platform adopted at the July 1992 convention hailed interventionist budgetary policies—even if the accepted phrase was no longer "public spending" but "investment in the future"—as well as the liberal vision of racial integration. Often accused of being controlled by special-interest groups such as unions, feminists, and minorities, the Democratic party worked hard to dispel this image and to recapture a humanist discourse reminiscent of the heyday of the civil rights movement. The success of this enterprise targeting white, middle-class forty-somethings was amplified by the terrible figure cut by the Republicans at their own convention in August 1992, which was dominated by the special interests of the religious and all but openly racist far right. On a deeper level, the Democrats' return to "color-blind" and "gender-neutral" integration policies was a response to the frustration of a large number of moderate whites, i.e., the people who felt both suspicious and left out of the multicultural movement, but who refused to be called conservatives and didn't want to ignore the decay of the inner cities or the discrimination still endured by women and minorities.

●　●　●

How are the advocates of identity politics to react to the resurgence of liberal ideology and its embodiment in the policies and especially the rhetoric of the Clinton administration? Should they dismiss this resurgence as they had the universalism professed by right-wing intellectuals during the quarrel over political correctness? Should they lump liberal Democrats and conservative Republicans together under the pretext that they both refuse to take into account the cultural diversity of the communities making up American society? Or are the advocates of identity politics going to accept their differences with the agenda of the new administration and begin to negotiate with the liberals? If they choose the latter strategy, the multiculturalists' discussions with the ruling Democrats will probably range from friendly criticism to constructive opposition. More importantly, the main focus of these discussions may shift from the issue of granting recognition to particular identities, to the possibility of making some differences in the actual organization of society as a whole. Beyond the power struggles around the representation of each community in party policy, the time may thus have come for open debates over the construction of new social relations between men and women, blacks and whites, heterosexuals and homosexuals, and so forth.

This fundamental choice facing the multiculturalist American left should also bring under renewed scrutiny the habit of overlooking the cosmopolitan alternative. Indeed, if the main actors in the multicultural coalition decide to retreat into isolation in the name of the primacy of identity politics, many closet liberals, and above all the "Marranized"* cosmopolites still committed to the mosaic, will quickly come home to the center of the Democratic party. What's more, they will leave their former allies alone with the more frightening fringes of the movement—the cultural feminists, the Afrocentrist ideo-

---

*The Marranos were Spanish Jews who pretended to convert to Christianity while secretly remaining Jewish.

logues, the champions of genetic homosexuality—and will let them cope with the vortex of exclusion and the chimera of authenticity. On the other hand, if the multicultural coalition initiates a necessarily tense and perpetual negotiation with the liberals, despite their differences of sensibility and aspiration, then the multiculturalists could pick up useful arguments from the cosmopolitan critique. First, the latter would help them stand up to liberal accusations by warding off the essentialist tendencies of some identity practices. Second, cosmopolitanism could serve as a powerful ally since it also denounces the dangerous homogenization and the loss of human creativity inherent in the universalism underlying the liberal integration model.

Can the multicultural dynamic and the cosmopolitan critique of both identity politics and liberalism make good bedfellows? A fairly recent event illustrates how difficult it may be to give a clear answer to this question. In July 1992, Henry Louis Gates, Jr., the head of African-American studies at Harvard University, wrote an op-ed piece in *The New York Times* denouncing the rise of anti-Semitism in the black community. He was not the first black intellectual to point out this trend, but his article was unique. First of all, it was highly visible; and secondly it wasn't just a moral indictment of all forms of racism and intolerance. Gates underlined the strategic aspect of the new black anti-Semitism. In the struggle for power within the African-American community, separatist hardliners such as the Nation of Islam and Afrocentrist theorists hit an anti-Semitic note in order to besmirch pluralistic options such as the old cosmopolitan alliance between blacks and Jews.

Gates's article was certainly no bolt from the blue. His colleague Cornel West* had published an essay in a similar vein, and Jesse Jackson had amended his rhetoric to distance himself from the followers of Farrakhan and the Afrocentrist

*Cornel West, "Black Anti-Semitism and the Rhetoric of Resentment" in *Tikkun*, vol. 7, No. 1, January–February 1992, 15–16.

ideologues. Does this mean that the rift that had appeared at the Chicago conference twenty-five years earlier was on its way to being mended? The contrast between the enthusiasm generated by the Gates article among liberal Jews or nostalgic new leftists* and the silent hostility it met within many African-American intellectual circles—many blacks agreed with the thesis but resented the division it laid bare in the "white" press—can also suggest quite the opposite. Threatened by the prospect of a critique that could not be easily labeled racist or conservative, many supporters of identity politics might be tempted to protect themselves by following an essentialist and relativist line. Meanwhile, liberal doctrinaires, back in action after years of self-imposed silence and hence insufferably self-righteous, may not be ready to acknowledge their own failings or the validity of some multiculturalist arguments. It is too early to tell which trend will prevail, but the return to power of the Democratic party and the new luster of liberal humanism—however temporary—have ushered in another era of recomposition within the American left.†

---

*The bad taste of the Anti-Defamation League spoiled that enthusiasm a bit. The ADL bought reproduction rights for Gates's article and paid to have it printed in a periodical serving the African-American community.

†Since November 1992—when this article was written—the new administration has laboriously tried to avoid clashes between its centrist and multiculturalist constituencies by consistently running away from any debate. Rather than assuming the risk of a dissensus and thus of a difficult decision, the so-called New Democrats have either devised unnegotiated and shallow compromises—e.g., the lifting of the ban on gays in the military—or opted for hasty retreat—e.g., the Lani Guinier nomination. Moreover, a new brand of "progressive traditionalism" has emerged as the main framework for a dialogue between liberals and multiculturalists. Rather than promoting a cosmopolitan critique of both identity politics and liberal universalism, influential "progressive traditionalists" like Michael Lerner have attempted to reconcile liberals and multiculturalists by drawing on the clichés of "recovery psychology." According to this rhetoric, each community is invited to celebrate its unique experience of hardship and achievements, but also to empathize with the other communities in the name of the universality of suffering and of a common desire to heal. Consistent with the compromises and the hesitations of the Clinton administration, progressive traditionalism replaces actual debates with formal declarations of care and respect, and thus substitutes the cultivation of self-esteem and empathy for any sort of political project.

Laurence Thomas

Group Autonomy and Narrative Identity: Blacks and Jews

Laurence Thomas is a professor of philosophy, political science, and Judaic studies at Syracuse University and the author of Vessels of Evil: American Slavery and the Holocaust *and* Living Morally: A Psychology of Moral Character. *His essay was written with the assistance of Mariah Bradford, Jonathan Brodsky, and Adam Gerstein.*

Any attempt to compare the suffering of blacks and Jews would seem likely to be felled by the waves of invidious comparisons. That is because any such comparison is likely to be seen, however obliquely, as an endeavor to answer the question: Which group has suffered more—blacks or Jews? And the feeling, of course, is that the suffering of both has been (and is) so heinous that to be concerned with answering that question is to embark upon a most despicable kind of moral enterprise. Be that as it may, there can be instructive comparisons regarding the suffering of Jews and blacks. I shall attempt such a comparison in this essay. At the very end of this essay, I shall speak to why it has seemed so natural to compare Jews and blacks.

I.

My thesis is that *despite* the Holocaust contemporary Jews have group autonomy, whereas *on account of* American slavery contemporary blacks do not. An identifiable group of people has group autonomy when its members are generally regarded by others not belonging to the group as the foremost interpreters of their own historical-cultural traditions. I take it to be obvious that group autonomy, understood in that way, is a moral good of enormous importance. On an individual level the most significant indication that others take us seriously is that they regard us as the foremost interpreters of who we are: our desires, aims, values, beliefs, and so on. Suppose I were to ask a person about her aims and so forth—but only as a matter of courtesy, it being evident that I have already satisfied myself as to what the person is like. If the person has any self-respect at all, she would rightly feel insulted, resentful, and angry. The importance of group autonomy is analogous. Normally, it is only because a group has an extraordinary command of its own history and experiences that it has group autonomy. It is logically possible that a group could have such autonomy and yet lack a command of these things, if the group is regarded as having mastery of its historical-cultural traditions when, in actuality, it does not. On the other hand, it is not sufficient for group autonomy that a group has such mastery, since having the mastery is quite compatible with other groups not acknowledging that it does.

To be sure, it is a consequence of my account that group autonomy is contingent upon being held in a certain regard by others. This is true of self-regarding attitudes in general. Insofar as we respect ourselves as individuals, it is precisely because we have been respected often enough by others. If respect from others has been adequate at the very formative stages of our lives, then it is possible to endure a considerable amount of disrespect from others for a period of time without losing our respect for ourselves, even if our self-respect shows signs of wearing out. And massive displays of respect after the ordeal would be crucial to repairing the damage done—to strengthening the paths of self-respect that had worn thin. Our own self-respect is not thereby diminished because it is anchored in the respect that we receive from others. By parity of reasoning, then, group autonomy is not diminished because it is anchored in the respect that a group receives from other groups.

I maintain that despite the Holocaust contemporary Jews have group autonomy, whereas on account of American slavery contemporary blacks do not. At any rate, blacks have considerably less group autonomy than Jews. What fuels my thinking are the following considerations: 1) Given the evil of the Holocaust for Jews and the evil of slavery for blacks, if any two groups should interact in harmony with one another it is Jews and blacks. 2) It is clear that they do not. And 3) I do not find the prevailing explanation that there is enormous economic disparity between blacks and Jews to be a complete explanation for the disharmony between the two groups. I do not wish to discount the reality of the economic disparity between blacks and Jews as a factor in black-Jewish tensions; rather, I believe that the disharmony between the two groups can be explained in a different and morally more satisfying way.

I suggest that some of the negative feelings toward Jews that are so prevalent among blacks can be attributed to the fact that Jews have considerably more group autonomy than blacks. This difference has given rise to resentment born of envy on the part of blacks toward Jews. At the end of this essay, I shall say something about racism on the part of Jews toward blacks.

Group autonomy is an indisputable moral good. It is understandable that every group should want to have it. Likewise, if a group which has been egregiously wronged should fail to have it, then it is understandable, though in no way justifiable, that the members of that group should be envious of the members of groups which have it, especially the members of groups which have also been egregiously wronged. For envy is a function of the uncomfortably small distance that we find between ourselves and others who possess goods that we prize. It does not require any wrongdoing on anyone's part. As social beings, we inevitably have a comparative conception of ourselves, and sometimes we cannot prevent or blunt the force of a stark comparison between ourselves and those who possess a prized good. It is perfectly understandable, for instance, that a person without legs might experience envy from time to time toward persons with legs. Envy is no less understandable when it can be attributed to a prized good that is moral, as group autonomy certainly is.

When we see the negative feelings that blacks have toward Jews derives, in large part, from the disparity in group autonomy between the two groups rather than from the economic disparity between them, we thereby view those negative feelings from a different part of the moral landscape. Of course, understandable envy is no less envy, and we should do all that we can to dissipate it. But our attitude toward understandable envy should be different from our attitude toward envy born of rapaciousness. And this holds all the more when the envy can be attributed to a failure to possess the prized moral good of group autonomy owing to social victimization. I do not want to deny the existence of anti-Semitism on the part of blacks toward Jews. It is very real indeed. Rather, I have tried to show that not all negative feelings that blacks might have toward Jews are properly characterized as anti-Semitic. I take it to be obvious that resentment on the part of blacks toward Jews owing to the differential between them with respect to group autonomy is far more morally palatable than resentment owing to the economic success of Jews.

Needless to say, I am no more blaming blacks for lacking group autonomy than I am crediting Jews for having it. Neither situation can be construed as a matter of choice.

It is perhaps tempting to suppose that group autonomy comes in the wake of economic success. This temptation should be resisted, however. In *A Certain People* (1906), Charles E. Silberman paints a glowing picture of the success of American Jews. Well, the success of Jews should not blind us to the reality that in general Jews did not arrive in America well-off. On the contrary, many were quite poor when they came here. Yet they had group autonomy.

It was not too long ago that Jews had considerable difficulty getting into so venerable an institution as Harvard University, as Bruce Kuklick has shown in *The Rise of American Philosophy*

(1977). Indeed, the Harvard philosophy department has come a very long way since the days of Harvard University's president, Lawrence Lowell, who wrote that "Cambridge could make a Jew indistinguishable from an Anglo-Saxon; but not even Harvard could make a black man white." But even in those days—when Harvard philosophy professors could write, in a letter on behalf of a Jew, that "he has none of the traits calculated to excite prejudice" (Ralph Perry), and that his Jewishness is "faintly marked and by no means offensive" (James Wood)—the Jews, I submit, still had group autonomy.

On the other hand, it is far from obvious that economically well-off blacks have group autonomy. In the area of sports and entertainment, numerous blacks are making millions upon millions of dollars. All the same, there is no reason to suppose that, collectively or individually, blacks in sports and entertainment have more group autonomy than other blacks. Together, these considerations show that economic good fortune is neither a necessary basis for group autonomy nor a sufficient basis for it. What then is? The answer, I suggest, is a narrative.

II.

By a narrative, I mean a set of stories which defines values and entirely positive goals, which specifies a set of fixed points of historical significance, and which defines a set of ennobling rituals to be regularly performed. A goal is entirely positive only if it is not in any way defined in terms of avoiding some harm. Thus, simply eliminating sexism, or racism, or anti-Semitism does not constitute a positive goal, as important as these objectives are. Learning Swahili, by contrast, can be a positive goal, even if it turns out to help one avoid some harm, since the goal itself can be entirely specified independently of avoiding any harm. A narrative can be understood as a group's conception of its good. The stories which constitute a narrative may very well be true, but they need not be—though perhaps they cannot be blatantly inconsistent with the facts. For example, the Jewish narrative (as well as the Muslim one) holds that

Abraham circumcised himself in his old age, with a stone no less. Can this be true? Well, it simply does not matter at this point. For circumcision has been required of Jewish males down through the ages. What Abraham actually did does not change one iota the fact that this has been an ennobling ritual among Jewish males down through the ages.

Now, given the character of American slavery, it can hardly be surprising that this institution and its racist legacy left blacks bereft of a narrative, and so of group autonomy. The Holocaust did not leave Jews bereft of a narrative, and so of their conception of the good. This is not because the Holocaust was a less nefarious institution than American slavery, but because the Holocaust was a radically different kind of nefarious institution. The telos of American slavery was utter dependence; the telos of the Holocaust was the extermination of the Jews. The former is best achieved by depriving the victims of any sense of their history. As a matter of logic, the latter, of course, is achieved by death. But Hitler did not succeed in exterminating the Jews; and his failure made it possible for the Jewish narrative to survive. Reflection upon the extent to which he almost succeeded, and the means that he employed to achieve that end, leaves any morally decent person numb. But that he did not succeed is an unvarnished truth. The survival of the Jewish narrative owes to that fact. Many will insist that surely blacks have a narrative, as shown by black music and art. I think not, a point to which I shall return in due course (Section III).

Now, I believe that it is impossible for a people to flourish in a society that is hostile toward them without a narrative that is essentially isomorphic with respect to them. A narrative is essentially isomorphic when, taken in its totality, it cannot be shared by others. There are primarily two reasons why a narrative is crucial to the flourishing of a people in a hostile society. One is the obvious truth that genuine cooperation is necessary if a people is to be successful in the face of systematic hostility. The other is that there can be no genuine cooperation among a people in the absence of a narrative, for a narrative provides the basis for trust.

Having a common enemy does not, in and of itself, suffice to ensure cooperating among a people, precisely because it cannot be a basis for trust. If a member of an oppressed group has good reason to believe that she can entirely avoid social hostility without cooperating with others in her group, or that she can avoid as much hostility on her own as she would avoid if she cooperated, then she has no rationally compelling reason to cooperate with others like herself. For if one's only aim is to avoid harm, then it is totally irrelevant whether one does so with one's group or on one's own, since in either case one avoids the harm in question. What is more, there will always be the incentive to avoid the harm on one's own, regardless of what might happen to the group. Naturally, a person could be motivated by altruistic considerations to help others in his group. But the motive of altruism is something distinct from and additional to the motive that stems purely from having a common enemy.

A common enemy makes for very unstable cooperation, if any at all, among a people. We can trust people when they have given us a good reason to believe that they will do their part, although they could refrain from doing so without bearing any loss whatsoever—that is, they will do their part whether they are being observed by others or not. A common enemy alone does not deliver such a basis for trust.

By contrast, when a people has a narrative, then their self-identity is tied to a set of goals and values that is independent of a common enemy. What is more, there is what I shall call contributory pride. Contributory pride is no more mysterious than pride itself or than the delight we generally take in doing things that reflect well upon our talents. Even when alone, and there is no chance of being heard by someone, a person who can play the piano well will want to do so because she delights in playing up to her level of competence. Likewise, we want our lives to reflect those values and goals which are dear to us, and it is a source of pleasure to us when this is so.

Because a narrative provides a basis for contributory pride, it allows for the possibility of genuine cooperation, in that others who belong to the group—and so identify with the narrative—can be counted on to do their part even if no one is observing their performances. Sometimes, in fact, people can be counted on to do their part even when this is at some cost to them. Such is the power of identification with an ideal. The moral of the story, then, is this. There can be no genuine cooperation among a people who belong to the same group simply on account of their desire to overcome the same hostile social forces, since the existence of the same social forces cannot suffice as a basis for mutual trust. What is needed is a set of positive values and goals which are constitutive of the self-identity of persons who belong to the group. For positive values and goals have their own motivational force, as the case of contributory pride makes abundantly clear.

III.

Let me now apply the account of a narrative, with its implications for group trust, directly to the situation of blacks and Jews. I take it to be obvious that there is an isomorphic narrative for Jews. Even people who do not like Jews are prepared to acknowledge that the Old Testament is primarily about the history of the Jews. What is more, there is a universal set of ennobling rituals which, when practiced, define being a good Jew or, at any rate, are the reference point against which a good Jew is defined, such as keeping kosher and mastering the Torah. These ennobling rituals are defined by the narrative and are entirely independent of the culture in which Jews happen to find themselves (the State of Israel aside). Wearing a yarmulke is an ennobling Jewish ritual. And notice that a non-Jew who outside of a synagogue generally wore what was unmistakably a yarmulke would be showing utter disrespect for Judaism. This speaks to the point that a narrative cannot be readily appropriated by nonmembers of the group.

Do blacks have a narrative, their conception of the good? Clearly, there is no denying the influence of African traditions upon the lives of black Americans. In voice, music, and dance the influence of Africa is unshakably there. Martin Luther King's speech, "I Have a Dream," surely owes some of its majesty to the cadence of voice, with its indelible African influence. It is impossible to listen to black gospel music and preaching without seeing—nay, feeling—the distinctiveness and richness. But form does not a narrative make. I want to say that blacks do not have a narrative—at least not as yet, anyway.

It is important to distinguish between culture and what I am calling a narrative. A narrative can be part of a culture, but it is quite possible to have a culture without a narrative. And even where a narrative is part of a culture, not everything in the culture is part of the narrative. Although bagels are very much identified with Jewish American culture, they are not part of the Jewish narrative. There are various Jewish cultures, but one Jewish narrative—though various disagreements over that narrative. While it is manifestly obvious that there is a black culture in America, that culture is not underwritten or guided by a narrative. Black music and style do not constitute an ennobling ritual. Neither rap music nor braids constitute ennobling rituals, although both are deep aspects of black culture. Things do not change with black gospel music and preaching. The distinctiveness here is indicative of black culture, and not to some ennobling ritual that black gospel music and preaching exemplify. Blacks have no special claim to preaching and gospel music, only to the style of performance.

Let me acknowledge the role of black Christianity in the lives of black Americans and black slaves. It stands to reason that without Christianity both American slavery and racism in general would have taken a much greater toll upon the lives of black people. Some of the great Negro spirituals such as "Swing Low, Sweet Chariot" and "Let My People Go" were surely an emotional balm in a very harsh world. Notwithstanding this moral reality, the truth of the matter is that blacks do not have any isomorphic relationship to Christianity. Christianity is a universal doctrine. Even if Jesus is given a black face, that will not change the fact that Christianity remains a universal doctrine. There are no texts in the Christian writings that blacks can claim as applying specifically to them. Nor have blacks gone on either to produce a reading of Christianity that applies specifically to blacks or to produce a set of ennobling rituals that only black Christians lay claim to performing. No basis for such rituals can be found in the Christian writings themselves.

So, in denying that blacks have a narrative, I do not mean to be taking anything away from the richness of black culture—just as in claiming that Jews do have narrative, I do not mean to be taking anything away from the suffering that Jews have endured. What is more, if it seems reasonable that blacks do not have group autonomy owing to American slavery and its racist legacy, then it should also stand to reason that blacks do not have a narrative, given the nature of slavery and racism. While I have maintained that it is possible to have a culture without a narrative, the converse is not true: a people with a narrative will have a culture. The idea that slavery robbed blacks of a narrative helps us to appreciate just how devastating the effect was that slavery had upon blacks. To be sure, there were whips and chains. There were even deaths. But the real pain of slavery, I suggest, is not to be located here but in the fact that it robbed blacks of a narrative. This makes it clear that I am using the notion of narrative in a very technical sense. The slave narratives—that is, the memoirs written by the slaves themselves—do not constitute what I have called a ritual. These are primarily accounts of the experience of slavery. The slave narratives do not specify ennobling rituals or fixed points of historical reference nor do they define a set of positive goals and values to be achieved by blacks independently of racism. As I have said, I regard the fact that black slaves were robbed of a narrative to be the very essence of the real pain of American slavery.

On the other hand, from just the fact that Hitler failed in his attempt to exterminate the Jews, and the Jewish narrative survived, we can see the hope that can arise out of the utter ashes of despair, and so appreciate all the more Emil Facken-heim's so-called 614th Commandment: Lest Hitler be handed a posthumous victory, every Jew must continue being a Jew in practice.

Jews have both group autonomy and a narrative, whereas blacks have neither—so I have claimed. All the same, the picture is somewhat more complicated than I have allowed. It is not just that Jews have a narrative, but that the Jewish narrative is an indispensable aspect of the Christian narrative, since the Christ story is inextricably tied to the Jewish narrative. The Christian narrative, by its very own account, is conceptually tied to the Jewish narrative (see also Section V). But if the Jewish narrative is an ineliminable part of the Christian narrative, then the Jewish narrative is also an ineliminable part of the narrative of Western culture, because of the place of Christianity in Western culture. Thus, insofar as Christianity takes itself seriously, it is conceptually bound to acknowledge that at the very least Judaism once had an indisputable claim to being meritorious. So, while Christianity may insist that Jews are now quite mistaken about the importance of their rituals and traditions, it must concede the importance of these things at an earlier time. And it must concede that Jews are rightly an authority on those rituals and traditions.

By contrast, neither the Western nor the Christian narrative is conceptually required to take the black experience seriously. Lest there be any misunderstanding, I do not deny that there have been gross distortions of the contributions of blacks to Western thought. But, as I have already observed, truth as such is not the defining feature of a narrative. I am not here debating whether Christianity and Western culture have discounted the accomplishments of blacks. My point, instead, is that as these two narratives, the Christian and the Western, have been formulated, they are not conceptually bound, by their very own formulations, to take blacks seriously at any point in time, in the way that Christianity is required to take Judaism seriously.

From these considerations it might be thought to follow that Western culture has been more racist than anti-Semitic. But not so. While I shall not argue the case here, suffice it to say that having to take a people seriously is perfectly compatible with despising them to the very core. Indeed, one may despise them precisely because one has to take them seriously.

In the next section, I shall look at some of the practical implications of the account of group autonomy and narrative which I have offered.

IV.

Recall the 1967 Six-Day War, when Israel fought Egypt, Syria, and Jordan. Jews of virtually every stripe and persuasion banded together in support of Israel. This was no accident, because in the face of an imminent threat, a narrative—a group's conception of its good—orders priorities. For Orthodox Jews, kashrut laws are extremely important; for Reform Jews, nothing could be further from the truth. But during the 1967 war, a good Jew was most certainly one who supported the State of Israel, regardless of her or his other shortcomings. A common threat can be most galvanizing. But it is a narrative that gives directions that amount to more than avoiding harm.

For just about every Jew, including quite secular Jews, the existence of synagogues and the State of Israel is a good thing. It is regarded as a good thing by just about every Jew that there are Talmudic scholars and rabbis. One may define a secular Jew as one who wants nearly all aspects of Jewish life to flourish, but who does not want to be an active or regular participant in any aspect of Jewish religious life. In any case, the point that I am concerned to bring out in these observations is that there are goods that Jews want, and these goods are quite independent of a common enemy. These goods are delivered by the Jewish narrative.

Do we find a comparable set of goods among blacks? I think not. Aside from the elimination of racism, it is not clear what blacks in general can be said to want, from the standpoint of being black. But I want to bring out the significance of a group's having a narrative, and the significance of its not having one, in another way.

Consider the black church. It is widely regarded as the most influential institution in the black community. What is more, it is relatively independent of white influence. Now, there are approximately 30 million blacks in America, and let us suppose that 4 million black adults regularly go to church each Sunday. If each were to give fifty cents to the United Negro College Fund, say, that would be $2 million. Over a year that would be $104 million to UNCF. For years now, fifty cents has been barely enough to buy a cup of coffee. And I assume that anyone who attends church regularly can afford to part with fifty cents. So, the most obvious question is: Why is something like this not being done? The answer cannot possibly be racism, if only because the black church is as independent of white influence as any institution in the black community can be. And if a common enemy—racism, in this instance—were a sufficient basis for cooperative endeavors, then one would have thought that a practice analogous to the one that I have proposed would have been in place quite some time ago.

I want to say that lack of a narrative can explain the absence of cooperative practices of the sort sketched above. In order for a people in a hostile society to flourish as a people, their self-identity must be anchored by a conception of the good that is independent of the hostility that they wish to avoid. What prevents us from seeing this, I suspect, is that there are times when eliminating a harm counts as an end in its own right, and it is irrelevant what other objectives a person might have.

To view struggling against oppression as the equivalent of eliminating an imminent life-threatening harm is to make an egregious error. By its very nature, oppression is about being deprived of some options rather than others. The struggle of a people against oppression can only be properly understood in the context of what it means for them to get on with their lives as a people. And that requires a narrative which anchors their self-identity.

Thus, we must distinguish between a racist society with overt structural inequality (such as American slavery and Jim Crow practices) and a society with structural equality that is coupled with widespread racist presuppositions of inferiority on the part of the powerful toward an identifiable group of individuals who are less well-off. In either case, we have an unjust society, and the latter, of course, may owe its origins to the former. However, combating the former does not require a narrative, whereas combating the latter does. For in the first instance, there is a rigorously specifiable set of harms or wrongs the elimination of which is called for. Their elimination is called for regardless of the aims that a people might otherwise have in society. What is more, while the elimination of the harms of overt structural inequality is no doubt a precondition for flourishing, just as being alive is a precondition for flourishing, their elimination does not constitute flourishing; nor does their elimination point to what a people's flourishing might consist of, just as being alive does not.

By contrast, eliminating the coupling of structural equality with widespread presuppositions of the other's inferiority is a different matter entirely, if only because in such an instance there is no rigorously specifiable set of harms or wrongs to be eliminated and there is no socially acceptable procedure for getting the dominant group to change their pejorative beliefs. Moreover, while it is conceptually possible to have no beliefs at all about an oppressed people, in other words a null set of beliefs, what is wanted is not a case where the null set of beliefs replaces the beliefs that a people are inferior. What is wanted, rather, is for the beliefs of inferiority to be replaced by a positive set of beliefs about the people in question. But which positive set? More to the point, who determines which positive set of beliefs replaces the beliefs about inferiority? Nothing better positions an oppressed people to answer these two questions than their having a narrative. For we have equality at its very best not simply when a people must be precisely like others in order to command the respect of others, but when a people can command the respect of others for being who they are. Equality across sameness is one thing; equality across differences is quite another. And the virtue of equality is truly showcased only in the latter instance. The latter equality is a more affirming equality that is inescapably predicated upon a people having a narrative—not just a culture—of their own.

The role of a narrative in equality simply presupposes what we already know, namely that there is all the difference in the world between being moved to help someone out of pity and being moved to help someone out of respect for their conception of the good. The latter is a more affirming kind of assistance. Things are no different at the level of groups.

I have claimed that without a narrative a people cannot flourish in a hostile society. Initially, I focused on how a narrative provides a basis for cooperation among a people. As should be obvious, I want also to say that it is only in having a narrative that, in a hostile society, a people can have assistance born of respect instead of pity. It has been said that the Creator helps those who help themselves. It would be stunning if human beings were much different. And nothing enhances self-help like a goal. Things can be no different for a group; hence, the importance of a narrative. We can best understand the success of Jews in America if we see them as having a narrative in a society with structural equality coupled with widespread presuppositions of inferiority. In the face of widespread presuppositions of (moral) inferiority, Jews had a conception of their good—that is, a narrative. This narrative anchored their lives and provided a basis for affirmation that was (and continues to be) independent of the values of society at large, not readily appropriated by mainstream American society. Again, I submit that the pain of slavery can be seen in the fact that it robbed blacks of a narrative.

V.

A narrative is the cornerstone that secures group autonomy. In claiming that Jews, on the one hand, have both group autonomy and a narrative and that blacks, on the other, have neither, have I made an invidious comparison? It is true that I have drawn attention to a differential between blacks and Jews of extraordinary significance. But that does not make the comparison invidious. After all, it is generally agreed that Jews as a people have flourished in American society, whereas blacks as a people have languished. Yet, few would call that comparison invidious. Why? Because by any reasonable assessment, that differential between Jews and blacks would seem to be the truth of the matter—a truth that neither distorts the present social reality of either group nor requires distorting the historical experiences of either group. If this should be the guide to whether a comparison is invidious or not, then the differential between blacks and Jews regarding group autonomy and a narrative is not invidious.

Furthermore, there is the explanatory power of the account offered. Some insight is gained into why Jews have flourished and blacks have languished without denying the reality of the horrors that have occurred in the history of the Jews. If anything, some insight has been gained regarding the toll that American slavery and racism has taken upon the lives of blacks in the United States—an insight that is not gained by focusing upon the horrors of chains, whips, and lynchings or even upon the horror of how many blacks lost their lives due to slavery. These horrors are not to be diminished. Thus, those who would object to the account that I have offered as favoring Jews might want to think again; for the account gives us a better handle on the evil of racism without detracting from the horrendous evil that others have suffered.

Finally, the account sheds some light on the tension between blacks and Jews. I have already spoken to the negative feelings of blacks regarding Jews. I want to conclude with a word about racism on the part of Jews toward blacks.

Racism is the belief, immune to a wide range of evidence and explanatory considerations to the contrary, that blacks are inferior. Nothing better invites the suspicion of inferiority than the following line of reasoning: Although Jews and blacks have suffered equally, the Jews have flourished and the blacks have languished. What can explain this differential between Jews and blacks other than that blacks are lacking in some way?

In *Vessels of Evil,* I observed that there are two ways of

understanding the claim that X is an ultimate evil: 1) No evil can be more horrible than X; 2) All other evils are less horrible than X. Far too often, in talking about the difference between the Holocaust and American slavery, people have said the first, but in their heart of hearts have meant the second. Blacks have often supposed that understanding American slavery in the second sense of ultimate evil helps to explain the plight of blacks in the United States today. I suggest that the account of group autonomy and narrative does much better in that regard. Let me observe that when the Holocaust is understood by Jews as an ultimate evil in the second sense, then in light of the comparative success of Jews vis-à-vis blacks, the result is an interpretation of the respective sufferings of both groups that is easily carried along by the winds of racist ideology. By contrast, the account of group autonomy and narrative is not.

But why do we think of drawing the contrast between Jews and blacks instead of Jews and some other group, or blacks and some other group? The obvious answer, it might seem, is the extraordinary suffering that both groups have endured. The problem with this answer, though, is that it does not take seriously the suffering of still other groups—Native Americans, the Armenians, and so on. I should like to conclude this essay with a different answer.

As the label suggests, American slavery stands as America's most brazen, systematic, and enduring institution of oppression. It is an evil that America actively sought to sustain. This it did, even as it took itself to be a Christian nation, which brings me to Judaism. According to the Christian narrative, Christianity is flanked by the experience of the Jews: The Jewish people gave birth to Christianity, and the fulfillment of Christianity is tied to the experience of the Jewish people. For many fundamentalist Christians, Israel's winning the Six-Day War was an occasion to rejoice, as this could only mean that the Second Coming was near. Thus, for radically different reasons—reasons that have nothing whatsoever to do with the comparative success of Jews and blacks, these two peoples are—or at least have been—an extremely deep part of the very psyche of Americans. It is most unfortunate that this has turned into a race for the who-has-suffered-the-most award. With the accounts of group autonomy and narrative offered in this essay, I should like to think we have a basis for leaving behind that useless competition and entering into a dialogue of understanding.